IN MEMORIAM
Lillian Gish
(1893–1993)

in the same series
PROJECTIONS I
PROJECTIONS 2

PROJECTIONS 3

Film-makers on Film-making

Edited by
John Boorman and
Walter Donohue

faber and faber
LONDON · BOSTON

First published in 1994
by Faber and Faber Limited
3 Queen Square London WC1N 3AU

Photoset in Ehrhardt by Parker Typesetting Service Leicester
Printed in England by Clays Ltd, St Ives plc

This collection © John Boorman and Walter Donohue, 1994
Copyright in individual chapters remains with the contributors
Flirt © Hal Hartley, 1994

A CIP record for this book is available from the British Library

ISBN 0–571–17047–1

10 9 8 7 6 5 4 3 2 1

Contents

List of Illustrations   vii
Acknowledgements   x
Introduction: Bulletins from the War Zone
  John Boorman   xi

The Journal

1   Journals 1989–1993
    Francis Ford Coppola   3

The Process

2   The Narrow Path
    Chen Kaige in conversation with Tony Rayns   47
3   Acting is Doing
    *Sydney Pollack in conversation with John
    Boorman*   59
4   Art Direction: From Wajda to Spielberg
    Allan Starski   69
5   Making Music for *Short Cuts*
    Hal Willner   81
6   My Stunning Future: The Luxuries of
    Pixelvision
    Michael Almereyda   101

The Career

7   Kasdan on Kasdan
    Edited by Graham Fuller   111

Hollywood Bound (Making it . . . or not)

8 The Struggles of a Screenwriter
  Michael Tolkin   153

9 The Perils of Producing
  Art Linson   167

10 Answers first, questions later
  Quentin Tarantino interviewed by Graham Fuller   174

11 On Tour with *Orlando*
  A Diary by Sally Potter   196

12 The Hollywood Way
  Gus Van Sant   213

Dreams

13 The Burning Question: Is there a relation between Dream and Film?   221

14 'I Wake Up, Screaming'
  A Diary by Richard Stanley   225

The Script

15 Flirt
  Hal Hartley   263

Coda: Cry from Croatia

16 In Front of the Cracked Mirror
  Zrinko Ogresta   283

Filmography   289

List of Illustrations

1 Francis Ford Coppola (photo by Ralph Nelson Jr.), *page 2*
2 Chen Kaige (photo by Steve Pyke), 46
3 *Yellow Earth*, 51
4 *King of the Children*, 51
5 *Farewell My Concubine*: the 'brothers' (Zhang Fengyi and Leslie Chung), 56
6 *Farewell My Concubine*: the prostitute who comes between them (Gong Li), 56
7 *Hard Target*: John Woo (centre) with Jean Claude Van Damme, 58
8 Sydney Pollack, 60
9 *The Way We Were*: Redford and Streisand, 67
10 *Out of Africa*: Redford and Streep, 67
11 Allan Starski, 70
12 Hal Willner (photo by Jay Blakesberg), 81
13 *Short Cuts*: Annie Ross in performance, 95
14 *Short Cuts*: Hal Willner and Robert Altman on the Low Note set, 95
15 *Short Cuts*: Robert Altman directs the Trout Quartet, 96
16 *Short Cuts*: The suicide (Lori Singer), 96
17 Michael Almereyda (photo by A. Greg Henry), 102
18 *Another Girl Another Planet*: Mary Ward and Barry Sherman, 108
19 *Another Girl Another Planet*: Niagara Falls, 108
20 Lawrence Kasdan, 110
21 *Body Heat*: what does the future hold for Matty Walker (Kathleen Turner)?, 112
22 *The Accidental Tourist*: what does the future hold for Macon Leary and Muriel Pritchett (William Hurt and Geena Davis)?, 112
23 *The Magnificent Seven*, 115
24 *Silverado*, 115
25 *Continental Divide*: the Hawksian woman (Blair Brown with John Belushi), 119
26 *Raiders of the Lost Ark*: Harrison Ford as Indiana Jones, 120
27 *The Empire Strikes Back*: Luke Skywalker (Mark Hamill) battles with Darth Vader (James Earl Jones), 122

28 *The Empire Strikes Back* (Irving Kershner, Gary Kurtz, George Lucas, and Lawrence Kasdan), 122

29 *Double Indemnity*: the lovers (Fred MacMurray and Barbara Stanwyck), 126

30 Lawrence Kasdan shooting *Body Heat*, 126

31 *Body Heat*: the lovers (William Hurt and Kathleen Turner), 127

32 *The Grapes of Wrath*, 127

33 *Seven Samurai*, 129

34 *The Big Chill*: Lawrence Kasdan with actors Tom Berenger, Jeff Goldblum, Kevin Kline and William Hurt, 132

35 *The Big Chill*: the ensemble ([standing] JoBeth Williams, Tom Berenger, Glenn Close, Kevin Kline, Mary Kay Place; [seated] William Hurt, Meg Tilly, and Jeff Goldblum), 133

36 *Silverado*: Lawrence Kasdan talking to Linda Hunt, watched by Danny Glover, Kevin Kline, Scott Glenn and Kevin Costner, 137

37 *The Accidental Tourist*: Control, 140

38 *The Accidental Tourist*: Chaos, 140

39 *I Love You to Death*: the family (Tracey Ullman, Kevin Kline, and Joan Plowright), 142

40 *I Love You to Death*: the assassins (William Hurt and Keanu Reeves), 142

41 *Grand Canyon*: Mary Louise Parker, Mary McDonnell, Kevin Kline, Steve Martin, Danny Glover and Alfre Woodard, 143

42 *Grand Canyon*: on the studio lot (Steve Martin and Kevin Kline), 146

43 *My Darling Clementine*, 147

44 *The Man Who Shot Liberty Valance*, 147

45 Michael Tolkin (photo by Scott C. Schulman), 152

46 *Patton*: George C. Scott, 154

47 *The Last Detail*: Jack Nicholson, 155

48 *Two Lane Blacktop*: Dennis Wilson, Laurie Bird, and James Taylor, 155

49 *8½*: Marcello Mastroianni, 161

50 Art Linson (photo by Deborah Feingold), 167

51 Quentin Tarantino (photo by Paul Joyce), 175

52 *Badlands*: Sissy Spacek and Martin Sheen, 176

53 *True Romance*: Patricia Arquette and Christian Slater, 177

54 *The Killing*, 178

55 *Reservoir Dogs*: Michael Madsen as Mr Blonde, 179

56 *His Girl Friday*: Cary Grant and Rosalind Russell, 181

57 *Reservoir Dogs*: Mr Orange (Tim Roth) and Mr White (Harvey Keitel), 183

58 *Reservoir Dogs*: the standoff (Steve Buscemi and Harvey Keitel), 183

59 *True Romance*: father and son (Dennis Hopper and Christian Slater), 186

60 *True Romance*: the standoff, 186

61 *Rio Bravo*: Walter Brennan, Dean Martin, and Ricky Nelson, 192

62 *The Good, the Bad and the Ugly*: the showdown, 192
63 *One-Eyed Jacks*: Marlon Brando, 193
64 Sally Potter (photo by the Douglas Brothers), 196
65 Gus Van Sant (photo by Eric Alan Edwards), 214
66 Richard Stanley (photo by Liam Longman), 226
67 *Dust Devil*: the car rig with Robert Burke and Chelsea Fields inside, 234
68 *Dust Devil*: the mortuary (Marianne Sägebrecht and Zakes Mokae), 241
69 *Dust Devil*: the showdown (Robert Burke and Chelsea Fields), 249
70 *Dust Devil*: shooting . . ., 253
71 *Dust Devil*: . . . figures in a landscape (Robert Burke and Chelsea Fields), 253
72 Hal Hartley (photo by Richard Sylvarnes), 262
73 *Flirt*: Emily (Parker Posey), 264
74 *Flirt*: Bill (Bill Sage), 265
75 *Flirt*: Walter (Martin Donovan), 266
76 *Flirt*: Man #2 (Robert Burke), 266
77 Zrinko Ogresta (photo by Mio Vesović), 282
78 *Shatters*: the protagonist (Filip Šovagović) obsessed . . ., 284
79 *Shatters*: . . . with the past (Nada Subotić and Matija Prskalo), 284
80 Vukovar, Croatia, 287
81 Sunja, Croatia (photo by R. Ibrišević), 287

Acknowledgements

The editors wish to thank Isabella Weibrecht, Tom Luddy, Anahid Nazarian, Bill Douglas, Celia Converse, Donna Ostroff, Hugh Ross, Trish Sullivan, Roanne Moore, Laura Morris, Tracy Carns, Colin Dickerman, David Watson, Ron Costley and and John Burgess for translating the Shiller quotation.

Stills appear by courtesy of BFI Stills, Posters and Designs. Copyright for stills are held by the following: Xi'an Film Studio (*Yellow Earth* and *King of the Children*), Miramax Films (*Farewell My Concubine* and *Reservoir Dogs*), Mirage Enterprises (portrait of Sydney Pollack), Columbia (*The Way We Were, The Big Chill, Silverado, The Last Detail, Badlands, His Girl Friday*), Tristar (*I Love You to Death*), Universal (*Out of Africa, Continental Divide, Two Lane Blacktop*), Sandcastle Productions (*Short Cuts*), Warner Bros (*Body Heat, True Romance*), United Artists (*The Magnificent Seven, The Killings*), Twentieth-Century Fox (*The Empire Strikes Back, The Grapes of Wrath, My Darling Clementine, Grand Canyon, Patton*), Paramount (*Raiders of the Lost Ark, Double Indemnity, The Man Who Shot Liberty Valance, One-Eyed Jacks*), Toho (*Seven Samurai*), Cineriz (*8½*), PEA (*The Good, the Bad, and the Ugly*), Polygram (*Dust Devil*), True Fiction Pictures (*Flirt*), and Jadran Film (*Shatters*).

Photo of John Woo by Tony Rayns; from *Short Cuts* by Joyce Rudolph; from *Another Girl Another Planet* by Jim Denault; from *Dust Devil* by Liam Longman; and from *Flirt* by Mara Catalan.

Introduction:
Bulletins from the War Zone
John Boorman

In these pages, hearts are opened, and secrets and sorrows are shared by practitioners of film craft. For this is the third annual edition of *Projections*, in which we invite film-makers to address each other, to write and talk about the process of making movies. Our aim is that these bulletins from the war zone make up a collective snapshot of a year, for to make a movie is to engage with the world in an intense way and every film is a portrait of the time and place in which it was made, whatever else it may be.

We start with Francis Ford Coppola's journals, in which the battle-scarred warrior contemplates his long struggle for independence from the mainstream, yet his need to have access to it; to be true to his personal vision, yet to fulfil his ambitions as the founder of a studio, American Zoetrope. Of all his many reversals none was as cruel as the death of his son, and the excerpts of his journals we print are drawn from the time that followed that tragic event.

We end with a cry of pain and rage from Croatia. Zrinko Ogresta, a young director contemplating the loss of his country, asks how he can ever purge himself of the hate that has devoured his heart, whether he will ever be able to make another film, and if so, what it can possibly be about.

Much of what we offer in between is either about great success or the bitter taste of failure.

Chen Kaige's spectacular *Farewell My Concubine* was celebrated in Cannes yet banned in his native China.

We are told that films from Down Under are done for, but Jane Campion shared the Palme d'Or with Chen Kaige for her moving and powerful *The Piano*.

The dismal British Film Industry slumped into further decline, but still managed to produce Sally Potter's highly praised *Orlando*, Mike Leigh's mordantly brilliant *Naked*, and Ken Loach's savagely funny *Raining Stones*.

Jurassic Park's monstrous success gave another jolt forward to computer-generated images. Chemical optical work is almost becoming a thing in the past. A crowd scene in *In the Line of Fire* was boosted from hundreds to several thousand by computer. Programs for three-dimensional moving storyboards are being developed whereby the whole film can be sketched out in advance rather in the way animators work.

Francis Coppola told me that he believes we will soon be 'painting' our movies with the computer, feeding in landscapes, locations and models, shooting the actors against blue or green screens, and shaping it all together on computer screens.

Robert Altman's triumphant return to success with *The Player* was happily followed by *Short Cuts*, which won the Golden Lion in Venice. The award was shared with Kieslowski's *Blue*, in which he again probes the relationship between women and music wherein, one suspects, the ultimate mystery abides.

There were other 'Blue' films, and the Telluride Film Festival had all of them. Derek Jarman's *Blue* had an imageless blue screen said to represent the blindness that he suffers as an AIDS victim. There was a programme called *Blue and Blind* which paired two films: *Double Blind* and *Kind of Blue*. In *Double Blind* an ultra-hip French art provocateur, Sophie Calle, and Canadian artist Greg Sheppard drove across America, aiming their cameras at each other, and secretly tape-recorded their thoughts. They put it all together producing something that feels like a cross between 'Candid Camera' and a Robbe-Grillet novel, but it indicates the possibilities of a personal cinema that the hi8 camera offers. Incidentally, Sophie Calle inspired the character in Paul Auster's novel *Leviathan* who hires a detective to follow her and report on her movements. The second film in this programme, *Kind of Blue*, argued that being 'blue' was not necessarily a bad thing. Melancholia, properly appreciated in the Middle Ages, now sends us screaming for the anti-depressants.

Blue we were certainly not in Telluride, a four-day binge of movies in this giddily high Colorado mountain town. Tom Luddy and Bill Pence have run the festival for twenty years, and because it is so brief, they are able to choose nothing but the best.

The great Film Noir photographer John Alton was celebrated. At 92 he was lucid and witty. We saw *Raw Deal*, *T-Men* and *Border Incident*, as well as the 3D movie *I The Jury*. 3D seemed a logical extension of his deep shadows and deep-focus lighting, the best use of it ever achieved, I believe. Watching his films, it was evident that the Film Noir style owed a lot to the German Expressionist Movement. It was Europeans like Alton who brought it to Hollywood and applied it to these thrillers which, typically, were heavy with the night scenes that Alton did so well. Some of his shots drew gasps of admiration from the audiences.

Modern colour cinematography is quite different. Instead of the characters moving in and out of narrow shafts of direct light, we use soft, reflected light. In place of deep-focus most cameramen like to shoot at 4.5 or wider, deliberately reducing the depth of field, using shallow focus to separate the actor from the background. High contrast lighting in colour looks as ugly as it was beautiful in black and white. On a wide screen, deep-focus colour offers too much information. We are swamped, awash in lurid colour. Differential focus charms the eye to where we want it to go.

Even so, I wouldn't be surprised if some young cameraman who has never heard of Greg Toland or John Alton rediscovers deep-focus photography and presents it as innovation.

Like John Alton, Lilian Gish was there when it all started. Her career spans the history and life of film from its beginnings. Some years ago, she contributed to a documentary I made for the BBC about D. W. Griffith. We asked her what she thought about modern movies. She said they were full of the scenes that the silent film-makers used to leave out – people getting in and out of cars, going into buildings, climbing stairs.

Lilian Gish has always been there. She seemed to be immortal, but now she is gone. I trust she will forgive us for colorizing her dress which adorns the cover of *Projections*. After all, a hand-tinted blush was applied to her cheeks in one famous Griffith scene and, as far as we know, she never complained.

It was a year in which death took a heavy toll. The great Production Designer Richard MacDonald died shortly after completing *The Firm* for Sydney Pollack. He was first and always a landscape painter who was lured into film by Joseph Losey as his visual stylist. He contrived the look of those elegant English movies, *The Servant, Accident*, and so on. He moved to Hollywood where he put his distinctive mark on a succession of movies, but he found he could not paint there. He complained that the California landscapes lacked scale and form. They were too big, too sprawling. They lacked definition.

I was luckily in LA for his memorial, which took the form of an exhibition of his recent paintings in an Art Gallery on La Cienega. The place was packed with his admirers, friends and colleagues. I had not seen him for several years and his paintings astonished me. They were Californian landscapes! Looking at them was like a continuation of our conversation. He had found a way of relating at last. All the paintings were defined by roads; snaking across hills, cutting through gorges. He had discovered that it is the highways that define California – dividing, connecting, wrapping the shapeless mass in concrete ribbons.

One of these paintings now hangs in my home in Ireland. The roads in his painting are empty of vehicles or people. It is a post-human California, where man has left behind only the architecture of the roadbuilder. But despite the emptiness, my painting has the dynamic of a movie, the eye is driven down the winding Pacific Coast Highway and the viewer becomes the absent vehicle. Richard's film work and his lifelong quest to define the inner structures of landscape combine in these works to represent a triumphant summation of his life.

Fellini and River Phoenix died on the same day. Easy, hasty comparisons were made in the press. The young actor cut off with so much promise ahead of him was seen as tragic, while Fellini had enjoyed a rich life. He had left a great body of work and so his death was somehow to be accepted as fitting. I rail against that. I grieve for Fellini's unmade movies, the many projects that are now lost to us because money could not be found at the time.

I wrote this account of my first meeting with Fellini for the *Guardian*'s tribute to the great man:

The first time I saw Fellini in the ample flesh was in Saks, New York. He was buying a hat. I was with my daughter, I pulled her behind a pillar where I could watch him unobserved, 'Why don't you introduce yourself? You practically worship him,' Katrine urged. I said I was content just to watch him. Suddenly Marcello Mastroianni was at my side, wagging an admonishing finger. 'Why are you hiding, John?' In truth, I was trying to muster up a speech that would do some kind of justice to his work and what it meant to me, I wanted to thank him for making his dreams carnate and for inviting us to inhabit them. It infuriated me when people accused him of self-indulgence. It was he who indulged us with those wondrous images. And his films were so kind to the audience, so welcoming, I knew Fellini as intimately as I knew anyone. Not only did I love his films, I loved him: yet how could I say that to a man buying hats?

Marcello led us to him. He was in New York to promote *City Of Women*. We agreed that this was the most irksome part of the whole process. 'All we directors should get together and insist that we will make our films for nothing – because we like doing that – but we must get paid for the interviews,' he said. 'Besides, I can never remember why I wanted to make a film when it is over. I certainly don't know what it is about. I invent. It is very exhausting, creative work, harder than writing a script.'

The hat suited him, we all agreed. It was a tweedy Irish cap and he wore it at a jaunty angle as he and his alter ego wandered off.

The memorial for River Phoenix was held at the Cecil B. De Mille Theatre in Paramount Studios. Helen Mirren and Christine Lahti, both of whom had played his mothers, spoke, as did Peter Bogdonovitch and Sidney Poitier, who read out his daughter's elegy to River, a cosmic effusion, inspired by her belief that the young star was now among the stars and planets of the firmament, an energized fragment capable of shaking the Universe. It seems many young women saw the vegan ecologist as a messianic figure.

I had not worked with River but we had planned to do a film together, *Broken Dream*, and I came to know him well. Everyone had the same tale to tell. It seemed that every life River touched was somehow made better for it. He had the ability to look past the sins and vices of others and to touch what was best in them. Legions of young people throughout the world rose up to mourn him. He had become a symbol of the possibility of a better way of life, a healthier planet. It was evidence of the way movies can connect people, focus their aspirations. In very different ways Fellini and River were standard-bearers of our dreams, of our hopes that beneath the cold, thin surface of daily life was a richer, warmer place that we might share and inhabit.

The Journal

The centrepiece of each Projections *has been the film-maker's journal. Francis Ford Coppola's passion for computers and things electronic is well known. For some years he has kept up a private conversation with his PC. We persuaded him to allow us to publish a selection spanning the years 1989–93. Never intended for publication, it is intensely personal and highly revealing of the creative processes of one of America's greatest directors.*

Francis Ford Coppola (photo by Ralph Nelson Jr.)

1   Journals 1989–1993
Francis Ford Coppola

19 October 1989

Ideas

If one second were a billion years, and this world we know, this beautiful earth and its creatures, existed for one-billionth of a second, then how privileged we are to have lived in it. It is a thing beyond legends, that in this imponderable void there existed such a place as this, and such beings as we.

After Reading Plotinus

THERE IS A NON-MATERIAL UNIVERSE

Even as a child I wondered what there was before the universe was born, realizing that there couldn't be Nothing before, that somehow the Universe always was and always will be, that the Real Universe cannot know time, just as the Soul cannot exist in time. All I can do is conclude that there is a non-material Universe. A Universe that exists without stars and comets and the other particulars of what we know as a Galaxy or what we consider as the Universe. The Universe is measurable; it exists in time and space, and is rather like our own bodies. We run into trouble when we try to imagine a limitless universe since, as we are taught, there is a curve in the boundary of the Universe. Then what exists beyond that curve, and what defines that curve? Nothingness, we are told, but that does not make sense to a child, and it doesn't make sense to me. How can the Universe, which is universal, end in a curve that sets it apart from Nothingness?

But when we think of the Universe, we think of a material Universe – and maybe, probably, that is not the only one, for there is an *immaterial universe* as well, just as there is a soul to a man's body.

AND ITS BODY IS THE MEASURABLE UNIVERSE

So what you gaze up into at night at the cosmos – within and beyond it, not perceivable with eyes or ears, but only within yourself, in your feelings – is the Universal Soul. It does not exist in *time*, but only in *emotion*. Just as there might be a Sight that can be confirmed by the eyes and not by the ears, so Emotion and Intuition, which are the organs of our soul, so to speak, are the only ways by which we can know it.

O

16 January 1990

UNITED NATIONS FORCES ATTACK IRAQ, LAYING THE FIRST BLOW ON
SADDAM HUSSEIN

This is a war being watched on Television – by the greater part of the human beings on earth, the enemy, the allied Nations – the attack happening as we watch Ted Turner's miracle: CNN – Atlanta becoming instantly the communications center of the earth.

I had decided to escape to Belize from the controversy and release of *The Godfather, Part 3*. I was continuing the research and study for my screenplay of *Megalopolis* and thought it would be interesting to read *The Shape of Things to Come* by H. G. Wells, which is really nothing like the Alexander Korda movie, *Things to Come*. Wells was an historian and the book (about 450 pages) starts as a history of WWI (around 1904) that keeps going right up through 2046; then I jumped into Alex Toffler's *Powershift* – just curious about how I'd feel after doing that.

Well, I was going through the second book when the UN Forces attacked and possibly destroyed this regime in Iraq, the attack happening – literally, simultaneously – with everyone in the world watching. I thought to myself: The world is forever changed. We have passed into the future. On this day, in this moment, the human race took another step towards Wells' *World State Convention* (Ironically, he convened it in Bagdad, in Basra.)

In *Powershift* Toffler discusses power in its three forms, *violence, wealth and knowledge*. Now that knowledge is in the hands of everyone, all people, all Nations, television and satellites have forever made it impossible for one group to manipulate the knowledge of what is happening; World television is bringing this vital knowledge to everyone without being diminished.

And it was *knowledge* – through computers and engineering and design – that was responsible for designing the modern war machine that could allow surgical strikes, massive war with only enemy casualties – a force for *world civilization*. *Knowledge*, which is infinite, is not like *wealth* or *violence* in that only one can possess it. Everyone can use it simultaneously. These things really take us out of feudal times, out of the Industrial Revolution and put us into the *future*.

I remember when I first heard of Saddam's invasion, on Public Radio in San Francisco, and wondering if Saddam was going to keep going into Saudi Arabia. And I remember responding to George Bush's and the Pentagon's lightning deployment. Yes, and make an American declaration of a *peace offensive*. Yes, deploy the stick, but offer the carrot. A Peace Offensive in which the world, and the United Nations, brings to pass, as a *world government*, a making right of the problems in the Middle East. Use our best minds to consider the *Arab nations* as an important and valued thread in the modern weaving of cultures that will determine the tapestry of human civilization in the future. We rightly worry about the extinction of the spotted owl, but what about Arab Culture, a cornerstone of fundamental proportions – we want it preserved and flourishing. We want their young people to participate. But what about the Jews? Israel – the beginning of our Western civilization; before the Greeks, they provided the basic pigment of philosophy. Yes. Along with every extant culture, no matter how small – we want all those threads, we *need* them all, in order to paint the most beautiful picture.

Let there be a *world government*, there must be. The United Nations can serve civilization well and deserves the chance to be it. THE WORLD STATE. 'ALL WE ARE SAYING IS GIVE PEACE A CHANCE.'

The Stealth missile is right out of H. G. Wells' 'Wings Over The World', the *air dictatorship* emerged as the force which designed the new *world state.*

○

29 April 1990

Thomas Aquinas says:
PUNISHMENT, WHEN DESERVED, IS LOVE.

Dante:
In proportion as a thing approaches its perfection, so it feels more pleasure. Thus with sorrow, it's the same. *(The Inferno).*

Plotinus:
Plotinus took all the ideas of Plato, but added the notion of a soul or a consciousness that is really controlled by images. Images ultimately giving rise to levels of feelings that transmute. If you take a grape, you get wine; if you take wine, you get brandy. So, find the single image that goes through the thing, a sense of the organic we all belong to. It's the Form that counts, rather than the constituent Truth; a beauty distinct from reality. Reality is what we all accept, the agreement among us about the way things work. Truth is beyond it and behind it. Look at *Jane Eyre*, *Wuthering Heights*, the works of Hawthorne. What is the essence of the universe? I'm not really talking about structure, how it's put together. No, find the form, since everything else magnetizes itself to it.

○

30 August 1990

Well, here I am in the Grassland drinking tequila and having a nice time. There is the Middle East crisis; Saddam Hussein attacking Kuwait; we don't know yet what will happen. But I have tried to sway the creative spirit, to the extent that he controls things, to make a vote for peace. Primarily, so that another generation of youth doesn't have to be wasted and lose their opportunity to take part in something magnificent. I think that all my life I have wanted to take part in something magnificent. I hope that I will. Of course, when I reread this in the future, it will be known and decided, and either a tragedy will have happened in the Middle East or there will have been a great peace offensive and the world will be the better for it.

This is pretty good tequila and it goes down smooth; I have a phone should I have a call, and I can let my mind just ooze into the keyboard. It goes down so easy, it's really a shame that others can't do this. Thank God, I took my typing class fairly seriously when I was a student. This thing writes with an ease that none of my other typewriters or computers ever wrote with. The feelings and sensations pour out of me, for better or worse.

But what if there is the ease and no ooze? What if I have the mechanics down but have nothing to say? Well, to tell the truth, that is impossible because I am brimming over with thoughts and ideas and feelings all the time without end, and with never-ending love for things in general. I guess I will squeak by if it is my destiny to do so – but, as usual, I am up against it.

○

8 September 1990

I was walking down the street, and I stopped because I saw a blind man. Although, in general, I prefer not to give money to panhandlers, I watched this man and wanted to give something to him. Perhaps because my grandfather was blind, and I always had a great fear of blindness. He had a sign hanging on his back: 'Except for the grace of God, there stand I. I am blind, please buy a pencil.' There was only one maroon pencil in his cup, and I saw that the few people who gave him money didn't take it, because they must have thought it was his last pencil. But I wanted a pencil from this man, because I thought it would be lucky for me.

I went up to him, and pressed a dollar into his hand and said, 'I want that pencil; that's a powerful pencil.'

He said 'Sure' and started to take another pencil, one that he chose for me. I took it and walked away, very satisfied with my purchase. When I looked at it, it was a good pencil. Its name was 'Integrity', the company was U.S.A. Empire, and I took it home with me.

○

8 September 1990

Good and Evil

A Darwinian concept of good and evil, based on the idea of the principle of natural selection, multiplied on the time frame that we're dealing with when we're talking about the evolution of this organization known as the material world. One given is, of course, that it exists because of a certain concept of love and harmony: 1) Love, the source of the energy which is the raw material of what we consider the Universe; 2) Harmony is the way it tends to operate and organize itself for its maximum perfection. So that elements that are not in harmony with the fundamental principles in the original energy itself, or Love, do not tend to function well in it, and fall away.

Is this why I love children so much? I see them on the street, I see their little faces and the spirit in them, so new and full of everything I consider wonderful, and I think: God, what is it about me and children? And I realize that I see in children those fundamental principles at work; nature has perfected children to be like that. Of course, so that they would survive. There are races in which the people did not feel that way, genetically, about children. And, consequently, those races died off and what remains is what was most in harmony with the basic energy. So, it's a double function of Love itself and the harmony which it generates that basically has to do with how the Universe got to be the way it is. Because it was in harmony with Love. Love is the only force – we could call it good, we could call it God, we could call it any of these things and, very definitely, it would be a force. But evil is not a force – evil is purely what is in the shadow of the good. When the harmony is not vibrating, it causes random permutations, some of which we perceive as evil or horrible because things certainly fall into positive aberrations and negative aberrations. Therefore, my theory of Good and Evil is that evil is the absence of good, evil is what is out of harmony with what is good, evil will always be dominated by good.

There is no devil and the force that we perceive as the devil is much weaker than the force we perceive as Good.

11 September 1990

On Fear While Directing

I find that I develop acute fear or anxiety when actually directing. On the set, during the actual production. It has to do with freezing up, having an actual anxiety attack right when I have to tell everyone how the scene is going to be staged. It's not that I don't have lots of ideas. I always have lots of ideas. But there is a moment when my skin goes thick and sweaty, and everyone is there expecting me to pull something good out of the air. The actors read the lines, wandering all around. It's clear that the scene doesn't work, that it has to be *made* to work. That's when the anxiety hits me and I go through a sort of mind-freeze, which precipitates more of a mind-freeze and then real anxiety sets in.

This is a pretty big problem, in that I am a professional director and should not suffer anxiety just when I need to function.

It has something to do with a lack of confidence just at the moment when I need it most. Panic sets in, and a cold sweat, and it's tough for me to go on. I need to stop; to get some space. To be alone, to calm down. It's as though I am held together by something fragile, and a challenge by a so-called cynic can put me on the defensive.

I need to tell myself: 'Stop. Calm down. Don't panic. Don't worry. A path will surely come. Just relax.'

It has partly to do with embarrassment. Is it because of all those horrible first days at school, with those strange kids watching me, perhaps judging me – as being inadequate to whatever task I am supposed to be doing? At a preview – especially one that isn't going well – I feel behind the eight ball and get an anxiety attack. These things are real; it is a phobia. It is my phobia.

How can I correct it? I need to find my path my own way, eventually. When I am writing, I have the time and the calm to find it. But when people are present, I am on the spot. That is the difference.

Well, it will be okay. I know it, but it sure makes me uncomfortable. Very uncomfortable.

I don't have it when I am cooking. Even when I am cooking in front of a lot of people. What is the difference; why do I have more confidence to cook than to direct?

I just do.

○

16 September 1990

What the fuck, it's my life to live. You make your standards regarding how you want to live with other human beings, and you live by them. Revise them if you wish, but as long as each man holds his heart true, and lives by a code of behavior that's consistent and based on sincere love and respect for others, and all of Creation, then let things fall as they will. A person is an event, not a thing.

It's more like, you love to go to the Festa. The Festa is an event in time and space, and you love it when you go there.

You are happy when you anticipate going there. You are happy when you are there. And you are happy thinking about having been there. But you can go once again, and not love it. It is no longer the same. That's because it's an occurrence, and not an object.

This gets in the way of people's thinking about the material world. All material things are actually events. A certain moment in a certain structure of atoms organized into molecules, i.e. a pattern of electrical charges, a modulation of energy, a surge or drop – but not a thing, a thing you think of as holding in your hand, like a metal cigarette lighter. I guess we perceive these events as things, as a code to live by and work with in a material world.

It's easier to understand the basis of our existence when thinking of lighting that lighter. At the moment that flame bursts into existence and prevails, an event has taken place. Because we can understand that the flame is nothing more than burning gases, it is easy to understand that it is an event. But so am I an event. A chemical event; an electrical event; a molecular event; a genetic event; a cultural event; a sexual event . . . and so on.

Why am I made of skin and bones and blood and hair, and not of molecules? The molecules are just energy in structure; blood and hair is software, a pattern or design of something that makes me. That software, or idea, is what counts.

What we call the material world is one of the many ways that energy is working itself out, dispersing itself.

Death occurs when the event is concluded. Like turning off a TV set. But the energy goes on, it can neither be created nor be destroyed. So what? Then it's just you and the trees and the birds.

○

19 October 1990

I am sitting on a park bench in Indian country in Arizona, looking at this enormous gorge, reaching down many thousands of feet. You can see the different strata of time marks in the rock. How old is the earth? Some of the rock at the base of these gorges is over two billion years old. And life didn't appear for a very long time after that. What is one to make of it? How do we fit in? Was life just an accident? The clock ticked, each tick being eleven million years. It ticked and ticked and nothing happened for well over thirty-four ticks, and then, finally, there were some simple one-celled animals, and then a long time after that some amphibians – much later, many millions of years later, there were huge reptiles. Why were they so big, and why did they dominate the earth? Then what happened? Why did they die? Was it like in Walt Disney's *Fantasia*, where the water just dried up, it got hotter, and they just crept off to their destiny? Then why did the mammals persevere? Was there some kind of great flood? The Bible has it; and also, a very old Native American legend tells of two gods, one good and one evil. The good god had a daughter, and he wanted her to bring life to the earth. But the evil one wanted nothing to do with that so he fashioned a great flood. Then the good god took a huge tree, hollowed it out, and put his daughter into it. She survived the flood in this ark, and when the flood subsided, and there was land, she took conception from the sun, and gave birth to a male child; then later, to a female child. And these two, Adam and Eve, were the parents of all the humans on earth, where they were to live in peace and plenty for ever. This is the ancient legend. There probably was a flood; that must be true. And then the mammals and humans came into being and this is their story. This is our story. This is my story.

Was the evolution of organic molecules after so many millions of years an accident, or was it waiting for conditions to make it happen? Will I ever know?

○

15 February 1991

Here we go, I'm going again and it's *Dracula*, it's going to be Bram Stoker's *Dracula*. I have to do a lot of listening to music because I want to have a truly great composer, I want the score for *Dracula* to be like a Prokofiev score for Eisenstein. I want it to be performed by symphonies. I want great music. Not just theater music, but great music.

Everyone knows that phenomenon of being under water, of trying to hold your breath: how at first it's all right and you can handle it, and as it gets closer to the time when you must breathe, panic sets in, you begin to think that you won't be able to breathe and then – finally when you do breathe – then you take in the air and the hysteria subsides. *That*'s what it's like to be a vampire and need blood.

Blood is the primary metaphor. Even if people today don't feel a sacramental relationship with God, I think they can understand how many people renounce their blood ties to the creation – to the creative spirit, or whatever it is – and become like the living dead. The vampire has lost his soul, and that can happen to anyone.

○

17 February 1991

Berlin.

Today's my first day of press interviews. They are going to be showing *The Godfather Part III* to the press and then this evening it will be presented at the Festival out of competition. I'm here with my father and Sofia, and at the end of the screening we are supposed to walk out on the stage to greet the audience.

My mind is on the future. I realize that there is what I call the artificial jelly bean philosophy. It's a capsule with a b-b in it, so that if you tilt it slightly, it flops over. Not only the public's perception of things, but also my own impression of things is such that when they are good, they are very, very good and when they are bad they are horrid (as the little fairy-tale goes), whereas, in fact, most of the time the state of events is highly interpretable. This encourages us either to overplay our case or underplay it. It's safe to say that in any circumstance things are neither as good nor as bad as they seem. It has to do with the way we perceive things. Good news and bad news, so to speak.

My problem with writing this new project really seems to be the fact that I'm not into a regulated pattern of work. It's very hard. You're in a different mode when you are in normal life, casting about in a spatial way, looking for little impressions that give you confidence that you have a concept. It's a process of thinking, of creative thinking where you're not really thinking anything concretely, but you're kind of scanning through a mechanism (probably more spatial than linear, but somewhat linear), like a hard disc scans for information. And you're picking up little sensations which are not in themselves tangible information, but which are little radar answer-backs that let you know something is there in those areas. Upon later scrutiny you can see what it was that sent that sensation and you can go back to develop it.

I think in the writing phase you have to revisit your work on a regular basis, just like you do your exercises in the morning. Each time you do that you will be getting a good segment of work which will be made into more linear or . . . how can I put it, 'acceptable' is not the right phrase . . . but it's almost as though you are operating in two universes and in the first universe you are getting back these little answer-backs, or glitches or sensations or biases that tell you that something is there, and in the second mode you actually take those answer-backs and translate them into some sort of linear data that is perceivable language or is, you know, actable work.

That's where the session concept comes up. A session is an actual work session in which you translate the non-useful format of intuitive answer-back into non-intuitive, analytical work. The session proceeds by 'getting yourself into the mood'. This is nothing more than allowing your whole organism a comfortable dedication to a particular area and then once you are there, you can proceed to work, you can make the honey, so to speak.

Question: What are the conditions necessary for a work session? Well, a work session requires, above all, 1) a reduction of anxiety [You cannot enter a work session if you are worried, or distressed, or emotionally engaged in any way other than in the particular realm of that session]; 2) time; 3) privacy. Privacy can mean either being alone or with collaboratory participants – the actors, the writer, whoever may be your collaborators.

○

9 March 1991

(dictated)
Riding in the Citroën from San Francisco to Napa, via the Golden Gate Bridge. I am proceeding up towards Sausalito Pass – the collection of houseboats, helicopters, driftwood sculpture, that make up the coast of the San Francisco Bay, as you move along the Golden Gate Freeway. I am very much

in control now of my environment due to a number of legal and other business manoeuvres. It's interesting to see that the only effective way to control a company is through managers who can translate your desires into action. This is very, very essential. This environment here in the car is a very good one in which to work, because I'm able to be totally private, to listen to music, to do any of this type of thing.

It might be a good idea to consider the following: two or three screenings a week in which we invite any of the key actors or personnel [of *Dracula*] to come to the screenings. These screenings could happen at the Yoakum house, or they could happen in the CAA screening room, or they could happen any number of ways. I'll be making list of classic films just to look at, and one of the ways we will prepare the key personnel in these next five weeks is by having showings to which they're invited. It could even be coupled with discussions, and snacks or spaghetti.

○

10 March 1991

Sunday afternoon in Rutherford, Napa Valley

The sun shines on the green of my place,
The lawn slopes,
and the trees blow with blossoms . . .

This is my home,
and yet it is so perfect.
How can I have something like this?
Without worry
Without fear of loss.

It surprises me
that my life is so lovely.

○

11 March 1991

Watching *Citizen Kane*.
Floors and ceilings. What about the floors, what ways can you give the illusion of floors?
Int. to Ext. with actual snow and snow falling works good.
Extreme subjectivity, using low angles for point of view of the little kid.
Response cutting into new scene, sort of what *Tucker* had when the end line of one scene becomes the first line of the new scene.
Newspaper headlines leading you to the next scene.
Handwritten script as with the journal entries, with Mina's journal entries.

Extreme depth of field between two characters involved in a scene, way upstage, and totally unfocused.

Books and documents on big tables, as in the library scene in *Kane*.

Ceiling pieces, ceilings, etc.

Camera moves, dollying down or up, revealing new levels, then floating down.

Good shop window in London street, like apothecary or something with a very entertaining window.

Giant map, giant walk-in fireplace.

Painted cathedral windows in *Kane*.

12 March 1991

Watching *Ivan The Terrible* (Eisenstein)

Front projection matte of sea by battle.

False perspectives and painted light-beams; light pouring in through things is painted into false perspectives of arches.

Low ceilings, low arches, a few steps up, to another chamber room with a throne on a platform.

The hair and wigs have to be individually created, the degree of dishevelment, how the hair is cut and worn: page-boys, and other – what we would consider bizarre – haircuts.

Scene where Dracula is sitting and rises up, and comes to his full height, and just seems to go higher as though he's elongated.

All these Byzantine goblets and oil lamps and other burnished and golden pieces.

Furs – would there be all kinds of exotic furs in this region?

Beard-cuts and haircuts, providing a tremendous visual stimulation on the characters, also use of candles and tapers, and other light sources.

New element: Eastern Orthodox icons and other religious icons as well as all Eastern Orthodox symbols, candles, etc.

When you cut to one image, let it make a statement that the next statement is in response to.

Ceiling pieces, a lot of ceiling pieces, torches.

The fur really takes up a lot of space in the frame; half a set can be the fur.

Courtiers bowing.

Grotesque painted faces on the jesters.

The incredible shawls and embroidered tapestries on the women's faces.

Image coming down into frame or rising up into frame, effective.

Big close-ups making striking compositions with the hair and beards and fur.

The gold costumes, sumptuous costumes in *Ivan The Terrible* are just like mountains of gold taking up a large part of the frame.

Men's voices in dirge-like section of *Ivan The Terrible* when they are following the idiot czar.

Shadow figures with candles, dark-shrouded figures with candles look good in the background.

Dragging person or body away by the long train sliding across the floor is pretty effective.

○

13 March 1991

Chimes At Midnight (Welles)
BATTLE SCENE:
 Low angles
 21mm lens
 Ceilings
 Dolly shots; side dolly shots
 Spears as element
 Process: warriors on horseback holding spears, banners or flags.
 Process: time-lapse of clouds, shadows falling, etc.
 Great trees
 Horses' breath
 Mist, fog
 Left-right movement, against right-left
 Close foreground action: fighting, spears and swords
 Right-left, left-right and clash
 Close-ups on battle stuff
 Pan: arrows, right to left
 Horse left riderless
 Hand to hand on ground, slugging it out. Some falling dead.
 New element: infantry
 Arrows
 Dead and dying and being killed on ground: high angle
 Big CU's of faces
 Arrow in body coming out of frame
 Horses on ground
 Archers, right to left
 Close, fast cutting: Horse falling; arrow in it
 Extreme CU guy in chain mail falling into mud
 Guy being killed; screaming
 Armor coming off, slow death in mud; boots in mud
 Horses left to right
 Up angle on horse bolting
 Dying in armor, like a mechanical man

21 April 1991

Notes for art director:

1. Use of skies, *low angle skies*, clouds, clouds moving fast as in *Rumble Fish*, storm sky, *dramatic sky*, etc.
2. A piece of detail, here and there – rather than detail everywhere.
3. More austere setting, not so baroque. Light and shadow sets also. Very simple and stark.
4. Sets should feature *awesome space*.
5. The use of texture, *Victorian wallpaper* juxtaposed with the texture of the fabric, and the fabric of the *costumes*.
6. The clothes, the beautiful fabrics – put them on a couple of main characters, and that is the set. All you need is a big empty space behind them. Let the costumes be the set and the set be the lighting.
7. Movie should have the sensibility of *first photographs*, that first silver-plate era of photography. Shoot some *second unit* with the actual Pathe 3mm camera to give the impression of the beginning of the photographic age, the beginning of cinema.
8. Battle in empty space, ridge in cardboard. Possible piece of lake with ice. Maybe fifteen warriors, five horses that can lie on back and flail legs.
9. *Hillingham*. River, grounds, cemetery, mansion.
10. Journey: picture-book, map.
11. Caravans of gypsies. Puppet show telling story of Turks v. Christians.
12. Castle Dracula: partially destroyed, and rebuilt with steel with sections in a Bauhaus style. Like D'Annunzio's Vitorine palace near Fiume.
13. Mirror room with girls (Venetian room with mirrors). Pasolini's *Arabian Nights*.
14. The boxes of earth: patent leather, like D'Annunzio's boxes; Harker begins his descent over the river like Indiana Jones.
15. *On shipboard*: blood sweeps through the ship.
16. Each set for the storm is linked by *storm movement*: the *ship*, the *zoo*, the lunatic *asylum*.
17. Flying over the model/painting.
18. Add paragraphs so that Harker is trying to get back to save Lucy. Try to make Harker's quest to get back more heroic: as though he truly loves Mina and is trying to get back to her.
19. Marriage: two scenes in one, with Dracula and Lucy, standing, separating Mina and Harker as *they* are getting married.
20. No London docks to redress.
21. *White snow limbo for ending battle.*
22. Back at Castle Dracula set for crypt ending.

○

14 April 1991

The film's flaws are my flaws – too many ideas and ambitions, but not the patience or ability to bring them off. The talent and the imagination to bring them off, but not a clear, simple mode of thinking to bring them off. If this was someone else's movie, I would say:

1. Build Mina's character.
2. Make all transitions very smooth.
3. Continue to refine and use narration.
4. Shorten chase or make the elements so much more clear that it is suspenseful – that you root for them to catch the gypsies. Maybe a problem is the split loyalty – you're not really for them against Dracula, or for Dracula against them. Somehow they must be racing toward the end of the prophecy – where Elisabeta gives grace to Dracula. It should all be inevitable ... something that has to happen ... *he who must die* ...
5. Continue thinning it out and clarifying it.

28 July 1991

Writing is therapy. If I would do it every day, I would feel much better. I am losing respect for my own ability to work. I feel lazy, and yet I work very hard. I need to modify my work habits. I need to write each morning. Only then will I feel OK.

I think I could be a dramatist. I think I could express emotion about how human beings are. I need to do that kind of work. Now I am a movie producer and director. That is somehow secondary. Big mistake.

So much seems to be affected by mood. If I am in a creative mood, then the ideas flow and I am very satisfied.

These things are common to all artists: the self-doubt, the panic attacks. Go easy on yourself, Francis – it is not necessary to suffer in order to be an artist.

8 August 1991

Family vacation in Mexico, very nice. My wife Ellie, my grand-daughter Gia, and my children Roman and Sofia. I am fairly well done with the shooting script for *Dracula*, and so this is one time when I really don't have to do anything but rest.

One lesson of life for me seems to be *not* to think in terms of the future, of acquisition and dreams of things to build. To begin living as though I had built, or achieved the dream. I probably don't have more than twenty years, one way or the other, from the date of this entry. These are the twenty years to live fully in the present. Live in the present and the future will take care of itself. Anyway, between the Napa estate, American Zoetrope and the Blancaneaux Lodge in Belize, there are plenty of dream projects to work on.

My son Gio is gone, but his memory is not. And his laughter lives on in his daughter Gia. It is amazing how much she is like him when she laughs.

DRACULA. The main thing is to remember how much I loved going to horror films with my brother. My favourites were *Frankenstein*, *Dracula*, and *The Wolfman*. I loved *Dracula Meets Frankenstein*, *Frankenstein Meets the Wolfman*, and Abbott and Costello meet them all. This film ought to be called *Francis Coppola Meets Dracula*.

The Gothic Horror genre; do it as a classic horror film – but really scary. Also, I would like our film-making to give Dracula his due in terms of his place in history – that he was considered an extremely modern Renaissance prince and very brilliant. He was an extraordinary figure. Use this to ground our fantasy, as Bram Stoker did.

I remember as a kid going to the *Encyclopedia Britannica* to look up Dracula – and there he was, Vlad the Impaler. I read about this fierce guy, how he literally stopped the Turks by impaling his own people on stakes, and I was just thrilled to think that he really existed. It was a brilliant innovation of Jim Hart's to use that history of Prince Vlad to set the frame for the whole story. Also, I felt immediately that he had written it as a story of passion and eroticism – the Brides weren't just standing around looking dead as in the Bela Lugosi version; in Jim's version they actually rape Harker – and that filled my child's heart with enthusiasm.

I'm amazed, watching all the other Dracula films, how much they held back from what was written or implied in Stoker's novel, how they played havoc with the characters and their relationships. In our movie, the characters resemble Stoker's in their personalities and function, including many characters that are often cut out. And then the whole last section of the book – when Van Helsing is uncovering Dracula's weaknesses, and the Vampire Killers pursue him back to his castle in Transylvania, and the whole thing climaxes in an enormous John Ford shootout – no one has ever portrayed that.

The movie should tell itself like the novel: with all the journals and letters leading up to some dreadful thing. It's very suspenseful and it helps the audience to know where they are. Stoker composed his novel in an innovative way: as though it were a compilation of notes and journals and fragments of diaries he had pieced together. So as you read the book, it's like he's saying, 'Look, we have these fragments, judge for yourself whether this is true.' The journey into Transylvania should be unveiled in layers, in multiple dreamlike images and writings, snippets of documentation. Finally, the letter from Dracula takes us across to the other side . . .

Stylistically, I want to create an image that flows like a tapestry, undulating like a dream. I like what Cocteau said about poetry not being fuzzy, but being very precise. That was the basis of surrealism, he said. I understand it is a very *selected hard reality* that becomes surreal. Also, the Symbolist idea; really think about certain objects that have become symbols: the key, the lock, the clock, the cloak, the dagger, the spade, the diamond, the coffin, the angel, the gorgon, the eye, the heart, the cup, the coin, the candle, the skull. It will be fun to make a complete list: anything that is interpreted as having a meaning and an emotional response.

Tai Chi for Gary Oldman; a choreographer who specializes in backwards motion, someone who has made this a skill and can do complicated things backwards. Perhaps shooting something backwards, and then using it to train someone to do it backwards.

REHEARSAL. This one can be the best. I have more time to plan it. The first thing is to make a Rehearsal Script – a fat dialogue script with no camera directions, just things that actors can do. Tai Chi and dance should play a part in it. Improvisation sessions with improvs, sense memory and other theater games. See if someone who specializes in theater games can help, or assist me. We are looking for very *deep* emotional connections and resonances in these characters. Where it's not in the dialogue or behavior, I have to put it in. Make Gary, Winona and Keanu make very personal connections with these themes.

Start out with a professional, quality reading of the entire book by the cast. Let each take turns reading the descriptions, just to open them up and lay it all out together. Just by reading together, they will be able to emerge and experiment.

Discussion of the themes and history of Dracula – and what these myths and themes have to do with modern life. Maybe even be able to make a scary environment – a haunted stage – to pretend in. We need props – all symbols – and a real coffin. Triangles, measuring instruments.

Then read the screenplay of *Dracula*, with Steve narrating.

Scenes from plays, etc.: Oscar Wilde: *Earnest, Salome, Dorian Gray. Faust, The Doll's House, The Master Builder. Dark of the Moon.*

○

9 August 1991

And now, my children, I will tell you the story of Dracula. The *real* story of Dracula – if you can take it.

The dramatic, emotional line between the characters, especially Dracula and Mina, is the prime task to establish. *Dracula* is a dark, passionate, erotic drama. Above all, it is a love story between Dracula and Mina – souls reaching out through a universe of horror and pathos. The counter-force to all this is Harker, the husband. And the subordinate characters – Van Helsing, Quincey, Seward, Holmwood, Lucy – all interact as lovers and partners in the story. Van

Helsing is in love with Lucy first, then with Mina. Renfield has a crush on Mina who has a crush on Dracula who has a crush on Lucy who has a crush on Quincey has a crush on Seward has a crush on Lucy has a crush on Dracula has a crush on Mina . . . sort of like *La Ronde.*

Blood is also the symbol of human passion. I think that is the main subtext of our story. We've got to depict feelings so strong that they can survive across the centuries – like Dracula's love for Mina/Elizabeth. The idea that love can conquer death, or worse than death – that she can actually give back to the vampire his lost soul.

We've got to convey the sense of a very specific reality.

We need to create *the poetry.*
EXPRESSIVE AND FRONTAL LIKE *The Exorcist.*
SYMBOLIST AND SURREAL.
VAMPIRE'S MOUTH LIKE A BAT'S MOUTH.
EIKO AND FANGS – WHAT FANGS SHOULD LOOK LIKE.
BLOOD IS MAINLINING, THE MOST EFFICIENT, PURE WAY TO GAIN NUTRIENTS. VAMPIRE PUMPS THE WASTE BACK INTO THE VICTIM.
ALL ABOUT DISEASES OF THE BLOOD – SYPHILIS.

10 August 1991

My grandmother used to ask me if I wanted to 'gna gna'. I think it meant 'to eat'. I'm not sure, but I remember 'gna gna' – maybe it was because she was Tunisian.

At any rate, I liked my grandmother and thought she was very interesting. She always wanted to make something for me to eat.

I am here with my family in a tropical paradise in Mexico. Very, very nice beach, warm breeze, everything perfect. My children are here. My wife is here. My little grand-daughter is here.

This is the full realization of all the potentialities currently operating in my life.

13 August 1991

Taking it easy; but seem to be comfortable always with some sort of emotional stress. Worked on Agenda* for a while; got the idea, it could be very useful to me. Everything systematized, I am a one-man module working in a design that I created. Keep the ideas flowing, and keep them being acted on.

Why not? Anyway, I get closer as I get further.

*The Lotus Agenda is a software spreadsheet of ideas, rather than numbers.

I could zip through the *Dracula* screenplay one more time. Why do I find the storyboard so boring?

Use shadow-puppets for the battle, and then recurring during the rape scene. Interesting.

In fact, do much of the battle with real extras and horses in combo with puppets . . . so that it can be used later in the cinematograph scene. Can a vampire be photographed? The theme of early photography is a good one. It can run through the entire movie.

The idea of the rape is a good one: keeps the focus on Mina and Dracula, against all the nonsense.

Van Helsing is the important key; must seem almost as evil as Dracula to be effective.

○

18 August 1991

Most of what I have to do is to set the design, the final images of the storyboard and all of the styling. I need to sit comfortably, maybe in the screening room of the Sentinel Building and watch the storyboard, making good notes on what to change. I need to let my creative ideas get going about how to tell this story in pictures and sensations and emotions. Right now, I feel removed from the center of things; dependent on others to get to what I really want.

This is the dress rehearsal stage, where I really give it my own touch, and hopefully have lots of fun with it. Make it my own: my own fantasy, my own horror. Then, if I make it very specific, it will become poetry.

POWER IS A PERCEPTION, BASED ON SOME REALITIES.
The *coup* in the Soviet Union is apparently over. It shows how the perception of power by others is the source of it. That is why the Establishment always has an edge, or the incumbent, or those with the best PR, the most believable PR. In the past my problem is that I haven't been aligned with the Establishment. Always keep in bed with the Establishment without letting them think they have you completely.

○

5 September 1991

Last night, staged reading of the Dracula script at Morty's theater. Preview cards from the audience. Then down to LA to rehearse and stage each scene. Last several days' dress rehearsal with video shot as per storyboard. Mad rush to post production, editing the video, readying for me to screen ASAP.

Set up someone who is really going to handle the preview cards throughout all this until the actual Seattle preview.

Post-Production should be really humming once they have rehearsal storyboard VHS. All Post Production – music, fx, etc – must be on the same standard.

The whole process should be production managed – squeezing out as much of conventional costs as possible. The next point is to turn the other way, and have Chuck take out as much $$$ from each department as he can.

Rethink the whole Post-Production set-up: With Glenn and Nick as co-editors, and the whole process pulled up, so that as the material is received, the Post-Production process is under way.

Notes from Dracula reading at Morty's:

1. Audience liked historical aspects. Also liked erotic emphasis.
2. Felt some of dialogue was clichéd and old-fashioned.
3. Some felt it was borderline with campy, funny intention.
4. Wanted there to be more of Dracula in second act: more of his actions, more dynamic, interesting action from him.
5. They wanted Mina and Dracula's love to go beyond the merely erotic, into more intellectual, exalted areas.
6. Dr. Van Helsing a bit too familiar to them; wanted something more from him. More knowledgeable beyond the obvious vampire lore that everyone knows.
7. Second act slow.
8. More from Mina. In general, more character development from Mina and Dracula in second act. My impression is that they would like more of historical references from Dracula, more of what he is really about.
9. Disappointment over ending: too much as expected. Some saw it as Hollywood 'happy' ending; seemed to want more twist of the screw at end.
10. *Main negative* seemed to be: why do this old chestnut *unless* there are new and exciting takes on it – new imagery, less predictable; more surprises in interpretation and realization.

◯

14 September 1991

These are my opinions on scenes/matters coming up in the next sequences:

SCRIMS AND PROJECTIONS:
There is no question that this is a valuable tool and one I want to use in these scenes whenever possible. The limitation: the effect is as good as the projection sources. Slides, architectural elements, and sharp images; stars, comets, etc. are better than stage effects. Scenes through patterns, foliage, icicles, branches, etc. seem best.

Double scrim works very well; shadows etc., strong images, realistic storm, weather all seem that they could be useful. If we get too close to the scrim, then it all hazes out and looks like a problem in the lab.

THE BATTLE AT THE END:

The sub-theme of this sequence might be called 'A Race Against the Sun'. At each phase of the battle it is important to know which phase of the sun we are in. The color and mood of each shot is according to three main divisions moving to sunset: *light sunset, medium sunset,* and *deep full sunset.*

The entire battle should be filmed as thought it were a *horse race* – mostly in motion but with certain reference shots, wolves, other stationary or watching elements (Mina and Van Helsing).

There should be some element of surprise in some of the stunts: something happening as you expect and then it doesn't – something else happens. The stunts should be exciting, but eccentric.

THE BRIDES:

We will need less nudity, so that we can be more powerful when we have nudity. There's the jewels, ankle-bells, and other slave-concubine-mistress things. They should have their own personalities; Michael Smuin will be arriving soon to begin working with them as far as movement is concerned. The Romanian improvisation is important, they should work on that. There will be more ideas as they come.

○

18 September 1991

FEAR

I think that fear is the antithesis of creativity.

Fear has a chemical impact on a person, preventing him from feeling or behaving normally. One becomes paralyzed, can't think, breaks out into a sweat. All this is the sign of fear. One cannot have an erection when one is afraid.

ONE CAN BE FROZEN IN TIME.
ONE CAN BE BEYOND TIME.
ONE CAN BE AHEAD OF TIME.
ONE CAN BE BEHIND TIME.
BUT, ONE CANNOT BE WITHOUT TIME.
ONE CAN BE IN TIME.
ONE CAN BE OUT OF TIME.
LANGUAGE ITSELF DOES NOT POSSESS THE ABILITY (RESOLU-
      TION) TO DESCRIBE THE SECRET LIFE.
PLAY WITH TIME.
TIME IS A DISTANCE.
MAKING TIME.
JUST IN TIME.

IN THE NICK OF TIME.
TIME WILL TELL.
TIME OF YOUR LIFE.
SUSPENDED IN TIME.
IT'S TIME.

TIME WAITS FOR NO MAN.

○

4 March 1992

A pleasant three-day escape to Acapulco. Ellie is here and so is Sofia. It is a luxurious few days of sitting around, reading (though not much), swimming and drinking. I am pretty relaxed, with no need to work whatsoever. I guess I feel that my movie, *Dracula*, is OK and so I am just not bothering with it. Or anything else, really. I am enjoying thinking about Max Planck and Nils Bohr and the like. It is always such a struggle to understand modern physics, but I feel I want to know.

I will go back home today. There will be the cut of the film to supervise, and maybe I might even do a little real cutting myself. Just pick a weak part of the film and dig in.

I saw the ad for the new Compaq computer and it looks like a nice one: long battery power and very light and small. I might ask to see a demo.

What else is new? I am fifty-two years old, will be fifty-three next month. I am pretty happy. Need to solidify my health regime, my work regime and all that. Will try.

Look forward to a new life in SF, in North Beach, being a Bohemian. That would be nice. Acapulco stretches out before me like some grand vista you usually see in a postcard. I like to be quiet and not worried. It's a very calming feeling. Who cares? All that matters is what you learn.

In seven years I will be a month before sixty. Sixty is a nice age for a man.

○

16 April 1992

Belize, Blancaneaux Lodge, at the end of a fine vacation and birthday. Most of my family came here to see the Lodge and enjoy the many adventures that I had arranged. Gia was here – the little pixie – and it was a pleasure to watch her cavort in the very same Maya cave that I had first explored with Gio. I watched her swim naked in the river that runs through the cave and I sensed that Gio was watching from somewhere in the mysteriousness of those depths. I seem to have responded well to the lack of pressure and strain. It makes me think that if I were just to spend six months or a year in this mental state, that I could recover pretty well.

Many things are ahead of me. Playhouse 90's 'Top of the Ninth' is a gigantic challenge; Jonathan Reynolds will create the play; then I will be able to find a way to do it.

Generally, I have no plans or dreams in the creative field right now. I would like to have *Megalopolis* ready for Fall 1996, but there will be a major writing stint before that can become a reality.

I have been tired and forlorn these last years. It is understandable. I have come a long way, and am very changed from the journey. My mood is good now, which I think is my natural state – especially when I make a little progress in getting things designed and happening according to my vision.

I will return to Napa tomorrow, and to our annual Easter party. Will see a lot of old friends. Maybe this coming year we can return again to Belize and have an authentic American Thanksgiving here.

Life is like a trail you follow in an unknown jungle. Only when you became familiar with the part you have travelled do you become secure. But then again, there is always uncharted territory ahead.

○

17 April 1992

Returning from Belize, I feel calm and good. I don't really have a lot of confidence about my film-making, however. I guess I feel that a preview mark of about 66 is pretty poor for my early version of *Dracula*, although I also know that sometimes very good films have a low score at first. It has to do with the fact that it just does not serve up their expectations. At any rate, no matter what happens, I have been a bit humbled by the experience, and so I have not been feeling confident. However, on the brighter side, I don't care so much. There are so many things for me to be interested in, so many things to do and enjoy that a poor showing for a film doesn't seem to drive me into despair as it would in the past.

Things might indicate an improvement. In Belize, I was very relaxed – I did not attempt to write, or read, or do anything except think about cooking and preparing the Lodge. It's sort of like film-making anyway: planning and dreaming about something that you bring to life. Only without the film.

I'm not so sure what awaits me. I will work very hard on *Dracula* in SF over these next three weeks. I hope I can get the audience to like it better than they did in San Diego. That was really one of the worst previews I've ever had. About the level of *Peggy Sue Got Married*. Maybe worse. So what? I sort of like the film myself, but now feel very insecure about it.

I like to cook and watch people eat. I like to read the paper, swim, smoke, flirt, sleep and make plans. That's really about it. I should run a hotel.

I'm fifty-three years old now; I don't have a lot of interest in my old stuff: directing plays and films, writing, etc. Nor do I like to watch plays or films. I need something really new in my work; maybe it truly is *live TV*.

Maybe something new is coming and that is why there is this apathy.

14 May 1992

In Paris, still at the Ritz. Very strange and very intense, I said to *Dracula*'s composer, Kilar. And he said, this music will be very different. At times avant-garde, and yet later very simple melodies. My hope is that he goes more into the avant-garde area and doesn't dwell on the sweet – although, God knows, the movie craves sunlight as badly as Dracula craves blood.

Sofia's 21st birthday!
The family has arrived; we are ready for dinner tonight. Let us celebrate Sofia's official coming to womanhood!

○

15 May 1992

This trip is proceeding fine. I did various interviews and we had a great time with Sofia. This is one of those 'sacred moments' I think about; Sofia's birthday party; having that snazzy *Dracula* trailer that leaves people impressed and wanting to see the picture. Tonight, dinner with Barry and Carol Hirsch, the kids, Roman, Katrina; it ought to be very good, and I ought to think about times like this when I get depressed.

I gave two interviews for *Hearts of Darkness* today; the first, Henri Bhar (the fellow who prepares dubbing and subtitles for pictures), wanted Ellie to call him. The second was the nice man who remembered my father and wanted photos taken with his girlfriend in Berlin. I gave him a bottle of wine and he wrote a kind thank-you note.

Here is a letter I just got on Hotel Ritz stationery: 'Dear Mr Coppola, Rubicon will be the very first American wine on the wine list of the Ritz! The order comes from Mr Klein the President himself!', signed by George Lepré, the chef sommelier and head of the Restaurant of the Ritz. Good news comes amid the bad; be grateful that you have lived.

This is an especially nice afternoon. It looks, for now, that *Dracula* will be a good film. I hope so. I would like to have done justice to the Bram Stoker book, as I always felt a personal attitude toward it. When I was a teenager, I was a drama counselor at a camp in upstate New York, and had a bunk of eight and nine-year-old boys. I would read aloud to them at night, and one summer we read *Dracula*. And when we got to that chilling moment – when Harker looks out the window and sees Dracula crawling across the face of the wall like a bug – even those little boys knew this was going to be good! Also, there's the memory of seeing all those old horror films with my brother Augie. And the thrill of presenting the real Dracula, Vlad the Impaler. For those reasons, and for love of the story, I hope I have done it justice.

17 July 1992

This is a time of desperation, I guess. I feel that old familiar feeling of inadequacy and lack of confidence. I bet if I ran a computer search in my journal for the phrase 'lack of confidence' it would come up many times. But isn't this so for everybody, really? We do the things we do – the work, the sport, the humor, whatever it is – to bolster our confidence.

The key thing for me is: To what do I apply myself? Am I a writer? If so, a novelist, a short-story writer or a dramatist? Am I a director, a mogul or a screenwriter? Am I a scientist, an entrepreneur? What am I? What am I good for? I am fifty-three years old, so whatever I am, I will not be it for a very long time. But still there's Time; there's always time to play and hope and lay the groundwork for . . . ? My flaws are very apparent: too ambitious; too much, too too too much for my patience and industriousness to answer for. I set out further than I am able to go.

There are worse flaws in people, I imagine. So why not just accept whatever it is I am, and enjoy the rest of my life? What would 'enjoy' comprise? I like to *not* be frightened; fearful of losing the things I care for, even love. The people I care for. Fear of loss is exaggerated in my case. I understand why and it makes perfect sense. I will never be able to overcome those scars or the impressions that make me this way; only be able to discount those feelings when I feel them. When things feel like a catastrophe, they may only be a semi-catastrophe. That is a comforting thought. No matter what happens, I will be all right – unless I am in pain, and until I die. But I am in pain all the time. Unnecessarily, but in pain none the less. Can I lessen it? I have tried, and have been somewhat successful. So I can be more successful, if I continue to try.

Now, what are now my greatest problems?

I have made a movie that looks like it's going to bomb both critically and at the box office. If I really total out on a big-budget picture, it's going to be difficult to get another comparably paying job for a while – maybe for ever. But then again, do I really want another one of those jobs? I hate doing them, and that's probably the main reason why they don't work out. Also, I think I do have great limitations as a director for this present-day lay audience. I don't think the way they do; or, at any rate, my thinking is bizarre compared to theirs. That's a familiar theme. Maybe it's because I didn't watch a lot of network television over the last thirty-odd years, that I've lost touch with the popular culture. But that may be a gigantic advantage.

Whatever the reason, I am what I am now – and I sincerely think there's some value to me . . . If only I could bridle my thoughts and passions and ideas.

17 July 1992

When you write a screenplay you hold the audience's consciousness in your hand like the end of a long stick. It's harder to do than it seems. You have to hold one end of that long stick, and point it always on the mark. Try it with a stick, say about eight feet long. It's very hard. That's what it's like writing a screenplay.

I do think I am a good writer. I always come up with something, even though it doesn't seem like it at the time. There's always something of value whenever I write.

My problem with directing is that I am sloppy. I don't particularly need an idea to be worked out in the same way that other people need it, so it satisfies me in an earlier, non-worked-out way. But I need it to be substantial and real and original in a way that other people do not. So that's that.

○

22 July 1992

So it all comes down to this: nothing is assured, life is how you take it, and it will change. We are on the cusp of disaster and of sublimity. Treasure the good. Don't worry that you can't really figure it out, just live it as best you can. As for the people you love, love them as well as you can. Be loyal to them and treasure them, for you shall lose them one day. But loving them, you keep them forever.

○

23 July 1992

OK, arrived in Paris – it really is Alphaville. Now, after the conference in Amsterdam, I see the truth about this AIDS epidemic. People will never make love again without prophylactics. Even if there is a cure or a vaccine, there will still be new viruses waiting to be discovered. Sex can never again be as innocent and natural as it once was. Except in monogamy. True, pure marriage as the ceremony implies. People cannot be as promiscuous as their instincts; sex with a stranger can kill you.

How sad for the future of love and romance! They never take away the tollbooth after the bridge is paid for; they never take the security check away from the airport, no matter how much peace is promoted throughout the world; there will never be that kind of exciting sex with a newly discovered mate without prophylactics. This is the world of the future. How sad. Will we make a new bargain with the idea of death? Will the people of the future be a sort of Brave New World kind of people: rated Alpha-plus, HIV positive, what is your rank? How will the young people do? How will my children, Roman and Sofia (they are at the transition age), and little Gia, so full of love and affection

and imagination. How will that little angel do? It is the function of the times
– this modern age, with its big, overwhelming population and tremendous
communication and travel. Strange microbes waiting for us: pieces of our
own life-matter; the DNA virus. I realize how different the world has
become. What will become of us?

O

15 August 1992

A little bit of bad news: my opening scene for *Dracula* didn't cut together as
well as I thought it would. Winona refusing to read her voice-over irritated
me and got me down while I was in New York. Otherwise, I was feeling good
and accomplished after the Tumor Cell* meeting in Washington. So now
I'm on a plane and I'm a bit sad. Is it chemistry? Is it me? – but then again, I
am my chemistry. I'm finding that the methods and style of work of the
professional film industry are more and more out of synch with the way I like
to work. I just don't like the tedious, do-it-as-it-was-done-before, costumes-
all-look-the-same, shots-all-look-the-same, everything-all-looks-the-same
way that we (the industry) make films. I was thinking that when I was
younger, I enjoyed Hollywood movies, but I never really wanted to make
them. Maybe musicals, a little. What I wanted to make were Art Films, like
the European art films. Weird films, more like strange novels, rather than
phoney entertainment films.

So what do I do now? Where do I go now? Once again, the same conclusion: forget the money; make the films that you have a burning desire to
make, for only in them will you find the desire to go through all the obstacles
that film-making presents.

Do films the same way Ingmar Bergman did them, with a little group of
collaborators that you know, making a script that you wrote. Otherwise, you
will finally get beaten down by the fact that you are making things that you
are not really interested in, from a script that you don't fully understand, by
means that you don't approve of.

The question is: Can you make bigger films, like *Megalopolis* or *Cure*, in
that way? Certainly, the determining factor is the cast, because with a star
cast comes the financing, but the rest of it also comes along with it. You get
the stars, you get everything else that you hate. Another thing I learned is
that if you give the new or young actor (who is not a star) the part, that
doesn't mean that they will not behave like stars.

Look at some of the frustrations I had during the making of *The Conversation* which, after all, was made in the (so-called) style that I prefer. Also *The*

---

*Francis Coppola attended Dr Robert Gallo's Tumor Cell conference as part of the research for a
forthcoming film project, *Cure*, which tells the story of the search for the cure to AIDS.

Rain People. So maybe it's not possible to avoid the unpleasant parts. I don't know for sure.

What are some of the alternatives?

Suppose I didn't have to work? I would have no obligations whatsoever. I would wake up and the day would be My Day. What things would I do? Well, I would try to exercise each day. I would have breakfast and read the paper each day. I would write two hours each day. I know how good I feel when I have written in the morning. It's as though I've earned the good feeling that lasts the rest of the day and night.

Maybe two evenings per week, I would hold an actors' workshop: Tuesdays and Thursdays. How could that work? Ideally, I wouldn't pay them and they wouldn't pay me. Is that possible? Also, of course, these would be SF actors, so you wouldn't have the spread of choices you'd have in LA. Would that be all right?

What would we do? We'd read the stuff I had written, so acting exercises – sort of like the Actor's Studio. Then there would always be the possibility of a week or even a two-week period in Napa, where we could work in Stage 22 doing either theater or film/TV. Both the small night-club theater in SF and Stage 22 would be equipped to do recording or to interconnect with the Silverfish (a motor-home equipped with video recording and editing equipment) at any time necessary.

The differences would be that in the city, you could invite small audiences, and *not lose the relationship to the audience.*

Also, the radio interface could be interesting in that it would give you the opportunity to go on the air, either live (which would be a great stimulus) or later on replay. The night-club would have the necessary emulators and midi facility to create music as well, and it would be possible to work with musicians as part of the group.

I've been thinking about this for a long time, but mainly when I'm down, such as I must have been in those last weeks in Sicily when I was finishing *The Godfather Part II.* But then, when something goes well, as *The Godfather Part II* ultimately did, then I am right back on some enormous task, such as *Apocalypse Now.* Get independent financing and own the pictures. Now this is really possible with films like *Megalopolis* – and maybe, depending on how things go, with others as well. I don't know; I really don't have an answer. I just know that I am unhappy and/or angry or frustrated most of the time. It gets in my way. I'm not sure what path to take, but financial independence is part of it, whatever it is. You cannot spend so much of your time and energy on projects for hire and expect *not* to be frustrated.

So what are the steps?

1. Do what you can to make *Dracula* work for its audience.
2. Do what you can to convert your assets into guaranteed income-producing

ones, so that you are not working for money, but for love.

3. Handle problems, such as the Sherry and Blancaneaux deficits and the family budget, so that you are not required to earn so much money.

4. Try to institutionalize certain months or periods of weeks as being family get-togethers each year with regularity.

That's about it, I guess. If I did these things, I ought then to have a better and more satisfying life.

○

22 August 1992

This is my last additional shooting day on *Dracula*. I am nervous about it, as I always am on a shooting day – and glad to get it over with. What is clear is that after I finish this, I will head right back to SF and lock this film – and try to be done with it.

Then, with only some of these development chores left, I plan to be free for a while; maybe even a year. I will live a life of sameness, of routine: coffee and papers in the morning; nap at four-thirty. Hopefully, every day the same thing for a while. No creative obligations. Think about what I would like to write about. Is it *Megalopolis*? Yes, maybe, but in a new form. A form more connected to me personally.

With *Megalopolis* it's really a question of outlining; creating an outline that I can follow in writing a new draft. Also, I need to pull in more personal elements from my life and family, so I am writing about something I know.

But that's enough for work – I don't want to work. I want to live a simple life and be happy. I want to enjoy my family; spend time with my kids in a realm that isn't connected to worrying about a specific project, or financial problems. I do think that if I lived for a little while without a schedule, I would feel much better about things.

This is 22 August: all 22nd days are blessed days because of Gio. This is a lucky day. Today as I was coming to work, a black cat crossed my path. But it had a white foot.

Whew!

The secret of the future of the movie business is scripts that are about relevant things.

Imagine how good you would feel if you had worked two or three hours in the morning on some good creative project. A script that you felt you were doing well on; expressing your feelings and having good ideas. It would buy the rest of the day, and you could enjoy just observing and listening to the ideas and dreams of other people. It is not very interesting when you are pre-occupied with your own thoughts and problems. Imagine that you could drive for an hour and a half and be in a beautiful country place; drink wine and relax and walk in the mountains. Also, be with Gia. Spend time with young people:

listen to them, observe them, teach them what you know about life – that is the ultimate pleasure.

Start here and now. Forget about what you used to think. You are who you are now, not what you were. It is interesting to think about the past, but you should not root anything there. It is over.

○

2 September 1992

Although I enjoyed the cut quite a bit at our Dolby screening, and although this cut seemed to me an improvement, it was evident from the remarks of the audience that the film failed to connect with them. They were not so sophisticated as to be intrigued by the 'artistic' slant of the film, its style or unusual aspects; yet they were turned off by the 'grossness' and 'gore' of the horror aspect. They found the setup inadequate; things in the beginning were not explained enough (why was Harker going to see the Count in Transylvania?). They did not seem to like the use of stylized elements (the miniatures etc.) and felt, as a whole, the story-telling skipped around, that transitions were bad, and often they did not know what was going on. They felt that many scenes were not too long, but rather, many *key* scenes were too short.

They did not like being confused by the so-called 'poetic' elements like the Storm. They didn't really get the attempted use of the blood as a metaphor, and even thought things like the rats were overdone.

One of the key story points that bugged them: the long time Harker was in the same situation at the castle; some thought he was dead and were surprised to come back to find him trying to escape from the same situation. They did not grasp or enjoy Quincey (what's a Texan doing there?), and found many parts of the story 'predictable'. They didn't get at all the fact that Dracula finally felt the need to 'flee' London and that the others 'pursued' him. They especially didn't like the last twenty minutes or so, feeling the chase was too long and like an old Western. They wished for a more dramatic *kill* of D. They were vexed that it wasn't clear whether Mina was a vampire or not at the end; they didn't like the sappy way she was 'cured', and they hated that she went from D to kissing Keanu at the end. The end especially let them down – which seems to be a big reason for the poor ratings. There was not enough 'thrill' in the movie for them. They wanted more character development in the beginning, especially in the area of Mina's internal feelings about her love for the Count.

These very discouraging findings make it clear that, when the film fails on these basic levels, it makes it hard to appreciate all the good that the film might have in it. Even though they acknowledged that the film was not too long, they found the experience tedious. This is what I got from reading their cards. And yet, as I watched them, it seemed that they were pretty focused and attentive and I felt, in retrospect, that much of their negative reaction had to do with what *was* good and unique about the film. Sometimes when a film is unique – and possibly potentially even great – but doesn't connect with its audience, all the *positives* become *negatives*. That is the glimmer of hope I had from their reaction. They disliked it so much that it just might be a potentially great film. Sometimes when an audience senses that, it disturbs them more than they know and for reasons they don't know. This may be the case here. I myself liked the film, and realize that some of the Columbia associates who had seen the film earlier had been very impressed. I've been here before, but frankly this was among the worst reactions I've ever had at a preview.

The whole experience encourages me perhaps to try a new structure: one that will keep the narrative *clear* and direct, not leaving the audience *ever on its own* to fend for itself. Perhaps even eliminate the multi-character narrative (diaries, journals, etc.) and try a one-character narrative: Van Helsing. Use him, one of their favorites, as the one who tells the tale. A new opening, in which – like the trailer – *he* starts with the book, and from that we lay out all the elements, the old history, Harker's background, Mina's situation. Then we might use more of the establishing scenes of character in the beginning that we lifted (Mina, Harker, Lucy, etc.), trying to root the audience *in* something and *in* some people before the adventure begins.

See what happens if we do that. We can use lots of the description of the story from the book as the basis of Van Helsing's narration. Also, take the last two reels of the film, and working backwards, take a lot of time crafting the end (Mina-Vampire-or-not; Dracula's final death etc.) and focus on those steps, backwards to the earlier point where D flies and they pursue him.

So what I would like to do is take a shot at an entirely new structure that would use Van Helsing as a device to eliminate the audience's feeling that they don't know where they are, and that the story is skipping around; thin out the less-good gore, and take more time to set up the characters. It would be interesting to see if, once done, this would allow the more artistic qualities of the film to rise up and be perceived. Also, I will see if I can come up with new final moment with Mina and Dracula, perhaps even involving his head being decapitated or even something not yet thought of that is more unusual and less predictable, before she walks out into the courtyard.

I intend to stay in our video domain for the next four to five weeks, testing some of these more unusual versions on video each week at a room like the Delancy St room.

These weeks are obviously the most challenging we have before us, so we should use fully our ability to make many radical and experimental versions in trying to *lock in* the regular type of audience that the San Diego people represented, knowing that the more we can do that, the more the artistic, sacramental and unusual aspects will emerge.

○

13 September 1992

This is the first leg of the flight back to SF. The Venice Festival was what I expected: a TV production, a lot of chaos and flying.

The press conference was a Marx Brothers production. The paparazzi shouting, one group running behind the three honorees: myself, Jeanne Moreau and the Italian comedian. Then the group of paparazzi in front shouted to the group behind. People shouted about the lack of translation, and then about too much translation. The questions, as usual, were obvious and actually dumb, and the whole thing took place in a 'Casino'. Nowadays, it would seem that these types of honors – overshadowed as they are by the press, the commercial needs of the festivals, and the enormous TV production that, I guess, pays the bills – seem to give little real gratification. The only honors really worth cultivating are from those few individuals who speak to you, such as Pontecorvo, who seem sincerely to have been moved or motivated by work that you've done.

It was not an unpleasant trip though, and the dinner in that small restaurant that Vittorio and Tonia Storaro took us to was really exceptional. It was quiet and modest and the food (all fish) was great.

A few thoughts that occurred to me during this time: perhaps there is a need for a new kind of art house exhibition set-up similar to what happened in the late fifties – small, really good seats and projection, showing really interesting movies whether from the US or the World, truly unusual art films. These theaters could cost a little more, serve decent coffee and adult snacks – creating an environment that really does not exist anywhere right now. Also, the films could change each week, so the habit of movie-going could be cultivated.

Now my focus must return to Napa and the real *composition* of my *Dracula* movie. Give it the finesse and final touches to make it as beautiful as I can. I feel that I have dealt with each of the flaws that have been observed in the various previews, and that if the new ending has power, the film will be OK. If I only achieve forty per cent of what I tried for, then that is par for the course, I guess.

The next real opportunity for me would be to advance from the adolescent writing period that I was in when I last tried to write seriously, and see if I can move to something more interesting and reflective of what I have learned from my life at this point. It seemed to me after reading some of the essays of Pirandello, that it would be helpful for me to understand and verbalize for myself what, in fact, my own philosophy of life is.

This is probably something I can do. It would have something to do with sacred moments, and the continuum of life being misleading to the real understanding of life. Something about energy's primacy over matter; and the Moment or Memory being the true experience of oneself.

I am very determined to alter the way I work, and try to have this career – which has dominated everything in my life – be turned to something more satisfying and productive in a personal sense. To do this I must stabilize the financial tornado that keeps me swept up in efforts to earn money. Two things can change this: either to be completely ruined, or completely enriched. One way or the other, I will gain the time that I need to work calmly. It is *time* now that is the precious commodity that eludes me. Time and the freedom to spend it as I choose.

○

28 October 1992

I'm flying at nine thousand feet in a little Seneca airplane, Napa to Burbank. In the back are the print masters for about four reels, including the last-minute picture changes I was able to make to *Dracula*. You never know in those last few days, when everybody is giving you their opinion, and you're not sure if you should tamper with the film or not. But I think that the alterations I made were quite worthwhile: altering the cut between Jonathan and Dracula walking down the hallway to a dissolve to the portrait of Vlad seemed to make a story point, which ought to pick things up; taking out Drac's last line in the dining scene also moved things along in a place that is probably our slowest; reversing the reverse-tear sequence also got us the transition from the etching to Dracula at Rules, which is very nice; adding more to the Brides makes it a bit more erotic, and tends to affect Dracula's scary entrance, since you are focused on the love-making. Also, the second cut of the Brides huddling around adds more punch and horror to that scene without showing the baby again. The added shot of Renfield's dish of hors d'oeuvres might get more of a laugh, and the picture of Renfield in the castle might help more people understand who Renfield is when we go to him in the asylum. The Carfax subtitle will help clarify where we are as well, and the little tweaks in the last opticals. So, by and large, I think I did gain by doing the Denver preview, and certainly by being so stubborn about getting these changes into the final picture.

Now what is in store for me? Maybe a few more thrills and spills, like last night when the sound mixer told me we might not be able to get all these reels done. Someone will *always* tell me something that will make the stress factor shoot up. Post-production is basically a period of anxiety. But it's wonderful when a film is really finished, in a beautiful answer print, all the sound perfect and in synch – and you know that whenever you show it, people enjoy it. I hope I'm lucky this time and people enjoy this film.

I'll be in LA at the Yoakum house for a few days. I'll make a few calls and maybe even drive over to my mother's house and visit her. That would be nice. Tomorrow afternoon, Ellie and I will fly MGM Grand to NY and spend a few days there. Friday night will be the main press screening at the Ziegfeld theater, which has a good memory for me: my father conducted *Kismet* there, and later *Apocalypse Now* and *Koyaanisqatsi* opened here.

It would be fun to have a success. It seems so long, really as far back as *The Godfather*, since I have had a true success. That was also half my lifetime ago.

My kids look good, seem good – I should really do many more things with them. The secret to financing things is to put whatever money I get straight into an income-earning fund, so I don't have to worry so much any more.

And do more experimental work: one-act plays, experimental radio, TV – even experimental cabaret. That is where the ideas and writing may come from for the real cinema that wants to be born in the next few years. I should really enjoy these holidays: Thanksgiving and Christmas.

○

7 November 1992

An incredibly beautiful day on the porch of the Niebaum Home in Napa. I think this must be one of the few times that I can recall since I've owned this property that I have been relatively secure and that my continued residence and ownership of the property is secure as well. Usually, my emotion while sitting here – looking at the beautiful fields of grapes, the trees, the other beauties of the property – is an over-riding anxiety connected to whichever my main problems might be: lack of money to make the various bank payments, fear that someone else held title or would come and take the property away from me – all these thoughts seem to be fused and intertwined with my appreciation of the place, so that it was a form of torment having something that you really loved and desired and yet were worried that you would lose. Of course, that is a basic human problem. Life itself is beautiful and yet we know we will lose it. There are possible dangers out there that affect us, affect the people we love, affect livelihoods, but one cannot enjoy the benefits and yet at the same time worry about it. As long as the present is secure, then everything is secure. The future is by no means secure. Even at this moment, some huge asteroid or meteor or intergalactic iceberg is hurtling on its way to an appointed time in the near future which will obliterate everything in an instant. So, clearly, it's pretty silly worrying about anything in the future. Equally, the past – unless there's something you're aware of that's happened in the past which will affect the present, it's the present that's important. It's what can happen *now*, what can affect us *now*.

Later.

Drove into Calistoga in the yellow Cord with Ellie. It drove perfectly well. It's an incredible day in Calistoga: the forests, the sun going down.

16 November 1992

Guatemala

Ellie and I arrived in Antigua, where we stayed in a hotel that was hundreds of years old. Antigua was one of the first capitals of the Spanish empire in America. There was an earthquake in the late 1700s, and so the capital was moved eventually to Guatemala City. Antigua is laid out in perfectly square, flat streets with occasional ruins of the old Spanish colonial buildings and churches. It is beautiful, with cobblestone streets and remainders of the old days. There is also a curious weather, what is called 'The Eternal Spring', very moderate with wild flowers in bloom, temperate and very desirable.

Here we met one John Heaton, a Frenchman (half-American) about forty years old, who deals in art and artifacts, and is one of those pirate characters that I occasionally run into. These are the expatriates and 'export-import' figures who buy and sell, but usually have everything they own up for sale. Jerry MacDermott in Belize is one of these. I guess the first one of these characters I met was the fellow I called Auge Kessel in Hong Kong.

We are buying fabric and decorations for the Blancaneaux Lodge in Belize, and already have a bunch of them in our rental car: textiles to make bedspreads, and some jaguar masks to give our lodge a Mayan theme.

Bram Stoker's Dracula opened last Friday, and so the results of the first full weekend are in, but we don't know what they are. I have successfully avoided the ups and downs, the depression of that first week when the reviews and box-office results are in. I feel good, because I have hope that it did well, but don't really know anything yet. We are in a little house in the city of Panojial near this beautiful mountain lake in Guatemala. It was lent to us by another of these 'pirates', a woman named Iliona Sotela from Costa Rica. I am listening to marimba music, and soon we will go into town to buy some more stuff for the lodge.

This is a beautiful day; maybe later we'll get a boatman to take us across the lake to the town of Santiago, where we'll look for more things for our lodge. Then eventually we'll drive with our horde of treasures back to Antigua, where Ellie will fly to LA, and I to Flores in Guatemala, later to drive across the border into Belize and to our little lodge there.

The relaxation and freedom from anxiety is good, and already I feel little creative stirrings in me: the desire to tell stories and describe things that I see and feel. Creativity is a wonderful thing when it is not forced.

Life should be free and carefree. If you have the few pennies for some coffee and tortillas, or occasionally for some simple fare, you allow yourself the latitude to find out what you really are. Your being is simple, and the only necessity is to be in harmony with the creation; what you see and feel.

The Eternal Spring – a good title.

One of those innocent stories with marimba music about a young girl in the town whose father wants to marry her off to a rich older man. The boy she loves does nothing, and has no money – so she cannot deny her father. But everyone in the town knows she loves the boy and he loves her. So they all buy lottery tickets for him, and tell her not to marry, that one day he'll be rich and her father will relent. Day after day, they find ingenious ways to stall the marriage, hoping luck will be with them. One day, one of the lottery tickets comes in, but the boy has already left town on the old bus in despair. The marriage with the rich man is under way, so the town sends a message through drums and music until they are able to stop the bus and tell him. A mad old inventor, who has been trying to fly in the style of Icarus, takes him on the back of the flying bird he has been trying to fly for tens of years, and flies the boy back to the town, where the people are trying to slow down the ceremony. All the boys in the town are flying their kites, and everyone looks up as the canvas 'bird' comes overhead.

Meanwhile, the brother of the girl has been practising his part in a pageant in which he plays an angel coming with a prediction. Over and over throughout the play, he practices his lines. At this point the older man has been gotten drunk by the people, and has fallen asleep. When he is awakened, the brother immediately goes into his lines of how the man will be forgiven his sins if he will repent and give his money to the poor. The old man believes it, and gives up his claim to the girl. The boy and girl are married and everyone lives happily ever after.

○

19 November 1992

Here in Guatemala I have no idea how *Dracula* has done. Anything could happen. We had some very good previews, and there was a good interest in seeing the picture. I also knew it was sort of 'out there', and that the public usually likes a film in any style – as long as it's realism. Naturalism is the order of the day. I think I can do a film in naturalism, but something in me just doesn't want to. Walter Murch once explained that to me when he told me the 'waffle' story. He said that he once sat down at a table with me and I was eating a newly served waffle. I asked him if he wanted half and he said OK. So I took the knife and cut the waffle – not in half, but in quarters like two giant bow-ties. That, he said, was an indication that I could never make a totally straight film.

I've run off here to Guatemala, so I didn't have to wonder or worry about how the film opened, how it did and all that. No phone call on Saturday morning with the news etc. because there isn't a phone in this house. So I've been happy, just relaxing here.

But yesterday – five days after the film had opened I began to wonder. So I hinted to Ellie that if she called in 'for other stuff' from the little public phone in the telephone company in town, she might get the results of the first five days.

I started to worry about it while I waited for her. When she took a long time to come back, I began to fantasize that the news was so bad, she didn't know how to tell me.

I sat there, very cool, and listened to records.

Finally, I heard her coming and my heart stopped. Her face gave away no hint of what had happened.

I said, 'Well, how did it go?' I knew that it would have to do at least seven or eight million dollars for it not to be a disgrace. Over ten would be really good.

Without a word, she dropped a few folded scraps of paper in my hand. I panicked; what does this mean? I opened one, and it had the number seventeen written on it. But was this multiple choice? What were the other little pieces folded up for? Was it seventeen, I asked . . . that would be great. She indicated that I should open the others. I did, still not understanding. It was five, then another two and a half . . . I was getting very nervous – which was it?

She looked at me as though I was a moron. 'Add them all up', she said.

I was too nervous to add them up. Kept getting it wrong. Finally, she did: thirty-one and a half million in the first weekend. It was a success and it saved my neck.

○

24 November 1992

Belize. Incredible tropical showers, very beautiful to watch. I was sitting in the alcove of the Blancaneaux Lodge with Dean, Nicolas, Sofia, Roman, Gia and Jacqui watching the rain come down. Ellie and Dana Kennedy were in the kitchen preparing the Thanksgiving dinner. It smelled very good. Eiko arrived in the storm, and thought it was very exciting. She said I was becoming like Hemingway in my jungle resort.

Now the river has turned golden-brown, and looks like a sandy pathway winding up into the jungle. Yes, this is a good place, a holy place.

○

28 November 1992

Too many things going on even to take the time to write them down. Today is Saturday, Privassion Enclave – Blancaneaux Lodge, Belize. My idea was to set down in a letter to the Prime Minister a request to set aside Privassion Enclave in the name of the Baron Bliss Foundation dedicated to artistic and cultural purposes. If this works, it could be the site of the future University of the Pine Ridge, and Bliss City – a communications and cultural center of the Creative states of America: Belize, Guatemala, Honduras, El Salvador, Nicaragua, and

Costa Rica. Among the other projects could be a theater, an outdoor amphi-theater, a museum, a hospital (Don Eleo Panti Hospital and Clinic), an observatory, a medicine research center, a music conservatory (including Steel Band and Drums), a new radio station, a television station, a newspaper, a youth apprenticeship center, a monorail, a college of fine arts (including Literature and Philosophy), a college of archeology. All programs would be bilingual: English and Spanish. Underground sound stages and recording studios. Also, caves filled with Electronic Memory. Hydro-power. Satellite uplink.

O

16 January 1993

I'm in Rome airport and have just gotten word that the airplane is delayed. The old hour-delayed airport routine. I'm especially frazzled: didn't sleep much last night, I have a terrible cold, I don't feel well, I feel oppressed by – even when I am free of all the people in my life, even on the level of just celebrityhood, there are people who want you, people who want to know you, people who want to deal with you, people who want to give you things, people who want to contact you. It's the old Gong Theory – nobody ever passes a gong without striking it.

I was awakened by an Italian assistant director who wants to work with me, then I found out I was late for the airport. It's just one of the many things connected with travelling. It's much simpler to live in a little neighborhood where you get around by walking, you have a car when you need it to go to the country or when you don't want a cab; have a lot of cash, don't have a lot of stuff in your pockets; and your mind is alive, alert, unoppressed, and free. And then there is the area of the press asking you questions, trying to get you to say things that they can then pull out for headlines, even though you didn't bring up the subject.

O

17 January 1993

At this point in my creative life, it's important for me to understand what it is I want to say. I think of that quote from John Lennon, 'Say what you mean, make it rhyme, and give it a backbeat.' I think for me it would be, 'Say what you mean, make it beautiful, and give it vitality.' That's how it would apply to me. It's very important to say what you mean. Say what you mean, or say nothing at all. Don't participate in idle talk – or idle Art. The question of what to choose to work on: it should come out of an over-riding need for that *particular* project. Many times I've wanted to paint a little water-colour, yet didn't really know what I wanted to paint. Then on certain occasions I would paint something I missed, or paint something I saw.

O

18 January 1993

I went alone tonite to the Brasserie Lipp and had dinner. It was about six, so it
was fairly empty.

A distinguished man sat down next to me, and after a while we started
talking. His name was Henry Nathan, and he said he was Danish, a mathema-
tician. We talked a little, about Nils Bohr and Einstein, quantum physics, the
top Quark, etc. He said that on this level, occasionally, there was a big 'score'.
But none of it really existed, except in mathematics. It was all really in the
realm of – well, what does it matter? Mathematics is really about beauty. He
said he had fought in Palestine, and that the Palestinians were used to living
with other peoples. They had lived that way for over seven hundred years,
under the Turks. He thought that the Palestinians should occupy Jordan, and
that would be fine. He said most of the people in Jordan were already
Palestinians. He said it didn't really matter. All of them had lived well together
for years, so that now this big fuss was about nothing. After all, the Palestinians
had rejected the partition in 1966, and now they (hopelessly) wanted it back.
He laughed. What's the difference? What does it matter? Well, I thought, it
would make a difference to the Israelis, wouldn't it? Though it seemed true,
they had all lived together; couldn't they again? I don't know if I totally
understood everything he was saying – about mathematics or Palestine. It
seemed that it didn't really matter, that it was all about music and beauty.
Maybe I do understand it.

○

4 March 1993

Blancaneaux Lodge. Drank a lot of Pina Coladas last night but, in the end, all
those stimulants – whether you smoke them or drink them – bring you down.
They are poison, and in the words of Goethe, 'A little poison in moderation
makes you feel good.' Moderation is the key when you deal with things that
you add to your body system.

This morning Mrs Chuc confided in me; she knows that the black girl,
Gloria, takes bread and lots of things when she goes home. She is disturbed by
what she sees. I told her that she need not mention it, but if Karin asks her,
then she can tell her what she's seen.

Funny, there's politics everywhere, even in Paradise. Especially in Paradise.

I had a very nice swim with Manolo, the architect. He is a fine young man,
seems to be very pleasant, and has a good feel for what I am doing here. After
we talk a little more, I had to bring up what the basis for his work will be, and
try to limit it to a given, set fee.

If you feel fine, you feel fine, and there is no need to alter that state of
being

○

21 March 1993

I plan only to work on what my heart is in – simple to say, but difficult to do.

O

31 March 1993

Another perfect morning at the Lodge. The weather these days has been sunny, yet never too hot. Always cool in the evening. I think today I will work on *Megalopolis*, plotting out the sequence of events and the roles of the different characters. Otherwise, I am just blindly writing sketches.

I liked Bunuel's description of the 'Ultraists'. Also, that quote of his about things 'coming from traditions, everything else is plagiarism'. There could also be, I suppose, the 'Omnists'. Isn't that what Catiline represents? He's a sort of Marinetti, a man who wants to push things to their furthest possible point into the future. The Ultra Future. Definition of *The Ultra Future* – the furthest point into the future from a given time. It would represent that view in which the given, present-day technology, mores and society can be extended furthest out.

So certain characters of *Megalopolis* are concerned with the Ultrafuture; whereas others, notably Cicero, are locked in the secure Past. It then would deal with that point in which future and past interact.

Catiline deals in 'prescience' – forecasting what the world will be like in a generation, and therefore being prepared with structures that can serve it. But the Cassandra story has great wisdom to it, and those who see the future are often not believed.

Catiline serves the purpose of being the first modern man, a contradiction of moral and amoral, Animal and Spirit, Pagan and Civilized, the constructive and destructive forces of nature.

He preceded Faust by a thousand years. Serge Catiline is man as Man understands himself, in all his complexity, in modern times.

The best musical approach to this type of dramatic novel is symphonic, with complex choral work to express, on the greatest scale, the importance of the themes of the piece. Symphonic and choral music, augmented with sampler, synth and modern processing.

The Orchestra of Yesterday, one hundred and twenty pieces with a conductor as soloist to perform the individual tracks, some of which are kept intact, and others to mix together forming the final five-track digital audio master track for the film. The Grandeur of the Human idea, the Pageantry – heroic, mammoth, even romantic, but considered against the symphonic style of the whole.

We attempt to see ourselves against a precise and yet always unknowable design of Nature. We exist in the surface of the front between Chaos and Order.

Contradiction and complexity on a gigantic scale (Lutoslawski/Messiaen). Symphonic Grandeur.

Vaughan Williams' *Sea Symphony*.

Choral at first. The rolling of the Sea – big, orchestral, brilliant.

I like Vaughan Williams' general use of the orchestra. It is colorful, romantic – but not too much – big and overwhelming. The clarity of orchestration. Many evocative effects – good, grand theater music. Good use of brass and horns.

This symphony, though, is a little square for my purposes – a little too *H.M.S. Pinafore*, but very good.

Descriptive music.

I like symphonic music that evokes images and emotion.

Stravinsky: Concerto for Double String Orchestra.

Very beautiful. Beautiful composition, very exciting and pleasing. Modern, but not obviously. Very nice music.

Nothing in *Melgalopolis* more Romantic than this.

○

3 April 1993

In Blancaneaux – waiting – writing some notes now as the men from Apple Latin America are in their cottages, relaxing. We'll have drinks etc. while they lay out all their tools and media aids, and put on a show for me. I'm thinking about what it is I am going to lay on Minister Musa and the Education Minister, George, about the University of the Pine Ridge.

Writing is like sitting on a nuclear-powered laser pen.

Go ahead with your plotting. Lay it out on cardboard, try to plot a clear-lined story through to the end. Chart out the most interesting way to present the story. Try to use, as a novelistic device, the time set in the distance between Real Time and True Time.

It's just a matter of doing it. You have the characters and you have the plot. You have the supporting characters and you know what some of the issues are. You know what the themes are, you know what the images and the textures are, so all you have to do is kneel down with the cardboard in front of you and chart it out, step by step. Tomorrow morning. Straight and clear-headed, and with some coffee. It will be fun. Bring one of the pillows down here and plot it out.

The truth that I have learned in this period is: You don't get anything unless you work for it. You have to plot it out. Step by step, note by note. It is a composition.

○

16 April 1993

I was just talking to one of our writers about his treatment, about the script, and scripts in general. I was trying to express that principle of essential dramaturgy that George Lucas always referred to as 'ball bearings'. The principle that is able to suck the audience forward to the outcome. It is the factor of Dramatic Curiosity, or Narrative Curiosity – what will happen when the veteran who's lost an arm returns home to his fiancée, what will happen when she sees his deformity. It's a kind of 'Bernoulli's Principle' as regards the design of an airplane wing. That the surface of the wing moving through the air creates a vacuum above it, so that the wing is sucked or lifted up. Without that, the airplane cannot fly. and without the equivalent of that in commercial narrative cinema, the film won't fly. Minimalist or artistic cinema can exist with the audience being semi-bored during much of it, and sustained by the quality of the ideas in the dialogue or images. Eric Rohmer's films are like that. But in a regular commercial film, one needs to have this curiosity so that the audience is never bored for an instant and is constantly in a rare state of involvement; an interest created by the mere sequence of the scenes and by what we know about the characters, which induces the audience to keep its attention rapt and never relenting.

○

28 April 1993

There is an element of impatience in all aspects of my feeling; even in moments of most content, impatience and distraction seem to rule me. Perhaps this impatience and this distraction are related to a 'yearning' for something that does not exist.

If, as Ortega´y Gasset has noted, the unique expression of the masculine imperative toward the feminine lure is the basis of the evolution of human civilization (as it now exists), then it would be difficult to realign our present civilization without a profound readjustment of all elements of our society.

According to Gasset, this 'sportive' collectivization of male youth preceded the home, and spawned religion, authority, the military and then, through a form of rape, gave birth to marriage, then subsequently the home and the family.

○

Coda: My Apprenticeship and a Guide to Youth

One of the stories that was often repeated in my family was about my first words. I was getting older and hadn't said a first word. Then I spoke a first sentence. That I had grown to an age and still had not said a first word. My mother says that I had been taken to an amusement park and was put on a ride – a horse – by a man, who told me to hold on. Later, supposedly while being trained to sit on the toilet, I said, 'Man say hold tight, don't fall.'

The Process

Some of the best films of recent years have come out of China. As so often happens, a surge of energy within a society is reflected in its movies. But the process of film-making for Chen Kaige and his contemporaries is complicated by the fact that their films are banned in China or only seen by a minority of that country's population. Furthermore, they have to be true to Chinese experience yet make these films accessible to foreign audiences.

Sydney Pollack's films achieve a consistently high level of performance – one thinks of his association with Robert Redford – and so we asked him to define his methods.

Allan Starski has had a long association with the great Polish director Andrzej Wajda. He recently worked for Steven Spielberg on Schindler's List. *We asked him to write about these contrasting experiences.*

Hal Willner is unique in the music business – not a composer, not even a musician, he has nevertheless produced some of the most innovative albums in recent years. Robert Altman saw in Willner a kind of musical version of himself and hired him to put the music together for Short Cuts. *Willner's piece describes this experience and raises fascinating questions about the role of music in film.*

The Pixel 2000 camera was made as a child's toy. Michael Almereyda turned to it after a number of his projects had been consistently rejected and refused by every imaginable source of film financing. Exulting in the limitations of the Pixel camera, he produced a film that is the equivalent of primitive painting. In describing the process, he investigates the relationship between the viewer and the image, and discovers some extraordinary insights.

2 Chen Kaige (photo by Steve Pyke)

2   The Narrow Path
Chen Kaige in Conversation with Tony Rayns

Introduction   Tony Rayns

Chen Kaige was born in Beijing in 1952. His father is the veteran film director Chen Huai'ai (also known as Chen Huaikai); his mother was a newspaper editor. Thanks to his parents' eminence, he had a rather privileged childhood; he attended one of the city's best middle schools, where his classmates included Liu Shaoqi's son and the sons of other Communist Party leaders. He was in his first year of high school when the Cultural Revolution (1966–76) closed down all China's schools. Like all other urban teenagers, he became a Red Guard; and like all other Red Guards, he was eventually 'tamed' by being sent to the countryside to 'learn from the people'. His posting was a remote commune in Yunnan Province, south-west China; his job was to defoliate large tracts of land to make way for a huge rubber plantation. During his later years in New York he wrote an autobiographical account of this period in his life *My Life and Times as a Red Guard*, so far published only in Chinese and Japanese.

He escaped from the rubber plantation by joining the Army, and served four years on and over the Vietnam border before he managed to return to Beijing. He found a menial job in a film-processing laboratory, and applied to enter the Beijing Film Academy (China's only film school) when it reopened in 1978. He was one of twenty-seven students accepted for the Directing Class; his classmates included Tian Zhuangzhuang, Wu Ziniu, Hu Mei, Peng Xiaolian and Li Shaohong, and their contemporaries in the Cinematography Class included Zhang Yimou and Gu Changwei. When these students graduated in 1982, they made their mark in Chinese film circles by opting to work in small, regional film studios – where they quickly won opportunities to direct features. The films they made marked them out as a group apart in Chinese film history. In Chinese critical jargon, they became known as the 'Fifth Generation' film-makers.

Chen Kaige has been one of the most commanding figures in 'Fifth Generation' cinema since he began directing. His first feature *Yellow Earth* (*Huang Tudi*, 1984) divided China's film establishment, but was the first modern Chinese film to win global acclaim. His second, *The Big Parade* (*Da*

Yuebing, 1986), about a platoon of air cadets training for places in China's National Day parade, was held up for over a year when he refused to make cuts and changes demanded by the authorities. His third feature, *King of the Children* (*Haizi Wang*, 1987), was based on a story by Zhong Acheng, who had worked alongside him on the rubber plantation in Yunnan; the film was selected for competition in Cannes in 1988.

He moved to New York at the end of 1987 and spent three years in the city, initially as a visiting scholar. The two films he has made since then have been shot in China but financed from abroad. *Life on a String* (*Bian Zou Bian Chang*, 1991) was a mysterious fable about the master–disciple relationship between two blind musicians; it was a British–Japanese–Dutch–German–Italian co-production and it too was selected for the Cannes competition. The recent *Farewell My Concubine* (*Bawang Bie Ji*, 1993) is Chen's biggest and in some ways most controversial film. Adapted from a novel by the Hong Kong writer Lilian Lee, it is essentially a gay love story, tracing the often fraught relationship between two Peking Opera actors across a span of fifty years. It was financed by the Taiwanese Tomson Group through its Hong Kong subsidiary, and was the first Chen Kaige film with *bona fide* stars: Leslie Cheung from Hong Kong, and Gong Li and Zhang Fengyi from China. The film shared the Golden Palm at the 1993 Cannes Film Festival.

Although sold for distribution in every major market, *Farewell My Concubine* was initially too much to take for the authorities in Beijing. China's President Jiang Zemin demanded a screening after hearing about the film's success in Cannes, and apparently disliked what he saw. In consequence, Ai Zhisheng (Minister for Radio, Film and TV) decided that he, too, disliked the film and ordered the postponement of its scheduled release. As usual in such cases, the rumour-mill went to work. The best story is that 'senior leader' Deng Xiaoping himself saw the film and commented that it should be released as soon as possible 'after modifications'. Nobody knew quite what to modify, but three small cuts were eventually made: one of Master Yuan (the warlord, played by Ge You) seducing Cheng Dieyi (the female impersonator, played by Leslie Cheung), and two violent incidents in the Cultural Revolution scenes. There were nevertheless further arguments about the film's 'suitability' for release and the film did not appear in Beijing and Shanghai cinemas until late August 1993. It attracted full houses, despite a substantial increase in ticket prices.

The following transcript is edited from a three-hour conversation with Chen Kaige that took place in Beijing on 27 April 1993, shortly before Chen and *Farewell to My Concubine* went to Cannes. A few minor details have been added to the text from earlier conversations in Beijing (1987) and London (1988). We deliberately avoided going into specific discussions of Chen's films (no production histories, no interpretative analysis) and concentrated instead on Chen's position as a Chinese film-maker with a large international audience but many unsolved problems at home. Chen spoke throughout in fluent, lightly American-accented English.

TONY RAYNS: *Since your father was a film director, was it inevitable that you'd go into films yourself?*
CHEN KAIGE: Not at all. When I was a kid, my father once took me to the studio, which was then very far outside the city, to watch him shoot a film. He was making *People of the Great Northern Wasteland* (*Beidahuang Ren*, 1961, co-directed by Chen Huai'ai and Cui Wei). I came away with the very strong imporession that I didn't like film-making, because it was so boring. I'd been there for a least three hours, and nothing had happened. I used to go to Saturday evening screenings of films organised by China Film Corporation in the embassy district of Beijing; I can't remember any titles, but there were American and European films and, of course, plenty of Soviet films. But the fact is, I knew next to nothing about films until I went to film school in 1978. As a kid, I was like all other kids of my generation in China: we just wanted to follow the Communist Party's call to be engineers, farmers, or whatever the Party wanted us to be. It never crossed my mind to have a career in the film industry.
TR: *But that changed during the years of the Cultural Revolution?*
CK: I was fourteen when the Cultural Revolution began, and seventeen when I was sent to work on the rubber plantation in Yunnan. I don't know what to say about that period; the whole nation was suffering. Film was even less of a possibility than it had been before: all the studios were closed down, and no feature films were being made. We had only the eight 'model revolutionary works'. My father was sick and under house arrest in Beijing. I had no idea whether I'd ever get off the rubber plantation or not. But that was when I first felt some urge to do something creative, although I had no specific idea of what to do. I'd managed to keep a book about classical poetry, and I read that a lot.

When I think back on that period, no matter what terrible things happened, no matter what tragedies we witnessed and appalling things we did, it now looks like my generation's good fortune to have lived through it. We learned so much. Of course, we had no control over anything; history was going along its own track, and we couldn't change it. But I think we can say that that period became the base of our creative lives. Certainly we came out of it with a lot of anger and frustration, and that was what fuelled us during our years in the Beijing Film Academy.

Actually, none of us learned that much at the film school. We did see a certain number of foreign and Chinese films, and we learned a little about the basics of cinematography, editing and so on. I never got to make any student exercise films, because there wasn't enough equipment. Some of my classmates, like Tian Zhuangzhuang and Zhang Yimou, collaborated on student films and videotapes; other students were sent to the studios to work as production assistants, and I was one of them. Anyhow, we didn't graduate from the Academy as 'professional film-makers'. We were just young people who wanted to create something different – with our passion, our anger and our strong feelings about China and Chinese culture.

TR: *How did you see Chinese cinema at that time?*

CK: As you know, there was a golden age of Chinese cinema in the late twenties and early thirties: the late silents and early talkies. Nothing like enough work has been put into studying that period. Some of the directors of those films were intellectuals; some had even studied abroad. They had very clear ideas about social issues, and they knew what they were doing when they made their films. But the Japanese invasion brought that period to an end.

When the film industry came back to life in Shanghai in the late forties, it was different. There were much stronger influences from Hollywood. If you compare *The Spring River Flows East* (*Yi Jiang Chunsui Xiang Dong Liu*, 1947, directed by Zheng Junli and Cai Chusheng) with a film like *The Goddess* (*Shennü*, 1934, directed by Wu Yonggang), you can see what I mean. *The Goddess* had one of Ruan Lingyu's strongest performances, and a way of seeing people's lives that still looks fresh today. *Spring River* is far more a Hollywood-style melodrama; it tries so hard to be entertaining.

And then the Communist Party took over in 1949, and intellectuals were out. Most of the directors working in the fifties came from Ya'an [the Communist base in the remote wilds of Shanxi Province during the years of the anti-Japanese war and the civil war]. My father and Xie Jin were among the few exceptions. The Yan'an people knew nothing about cinema. I'm not saying that they were bad people, but how much had they seen? How much did they know? They were sent to Moscow for six months, came back, and they were directors. What could you expect from their work?

And then everything was wiped out in the Cultural Revolution. When it was over, there was still a garden, but no flowers. The film industry was still making a few propaganda features in the late seventies, but there was no audience for them. That was the state of things when my classmates and I graduated from the Academy. We didn't trust the older generation to do anything to change and improve Chinese cinema.

TR: *But you once told me that you didn't approach your own first feature with a clear set of aims . . .*

CK: Right. The shooting of *Yellow Earth* passed like a dream. I couldn't have told you what the film was getting at. I just felt something here, in my heart, and I felt a strong need somehow to express it through the film. We didn't really know anything about the way films work in other countries, didn't know which films were popular or why. In other words, we had few points of

3 *Yellow Earth*

4 *King of the Children*

reference when we made the film. We just went at it and did what we felt was right. What I'm really saying is that I still thought of myself as a student when I directed *Yellow Earth*. I had nothing to lose, and potentially a lot to gain.

TR: *So what kind of thing did you feel was 'right' when you made* Yellow Earth?

CK: Zhang Yimou and I talked about that a lot, and we found ourselves drawn instinctively to the peasant aesthetics of the region. There's a school of painters in Shaanxi Province who use large expanses of foreground and background in their work, and to some extent we followed their lead in the way we shot the earth and the sky. I guess there were two reasons why we went in that direction. One is that we were looking for something that was distinctively Chinese; we wanted to make a new kind of Chinese cinema, and it was essential that it should have genuinely Chinese roots. The other reason is that those peasant traditions had been blocked off during the Cultural Revolution, and so we had an interest in reasserting them and taking them further.

TR: *And the same kind of feelings were at work when you made* King of the Children?

CK: By then, I think, I had a more sophisticated understanding of the whole relationship between a nation and its culture. *King of the Children* is a film expressly about Chinese language and traditional Chinese culture – about the way that language and culture end up controlling the very people who formulated and shaped them. I hope that the film captures the measured quality of Ah Cheng's original story (his writing has a kind of dream-like calm), but underneath that both the story and the film are very angry. They struggle against the prisons of language and culture; they argue that it's vital to create *new* things. I built the school-house set at the top of that hill so that it would look like a *temple* of culture, and the symbolic meaning of the time-lapse shot at the start, with the light exchanging and clouds racing by, is that everything is changing *except* the school. In the same way, the burning of the forest at the end represents my wish to burn everything down!

TR: *You often find yourself reaching for these larger, symbolic dimensions?*

CK: I like simple stories. I don't feel comfortable with melodrama, because I don't like emotional excess. I could never make a film like Xie Jin's *Hibiscus Town*, which says that there are good people and bad people and that everything will be fine if we can just get rid of the bad people! It seems to me that all of us have positive and negative sides, and the same capacities to love and hate. Simple stories ought to be enough to trigger our responses, and yes, I look for stories that seem to have more than surface meaning.

TR: *At the time, were you aware of putting autobiographical elements into your early films? In* Yellow Earth, *the soldier-intellectual coming to the remote village parallels you being sent to the rubber plantation. The Big Parade obviously reflects your own time in the Army. And* King of the Children *is directly about an urban teenager sent to Yunnan in the Cultural Revolution. How conscious was all this?*

CK: I think I was quite deliberately drawing on my own experiences, but it's impossible to make it clear to the audience which parts were from my life and which were pure fiction. It was all mixed up. When I look back on those first three films, I think of them as a first step. After making them, I knew I had to do something different. But I believe there's still an underlying continuity with my new film.

When I answered questions from Chinese journalists about *Farewell to My Concubine*, one of them was whether I was carrying anything over from my old films. I could have said 'Yes' or 'No'. I chose to say 'Yes' because I identify with the character of Cheng Dieyi [the Peking Opera actor who specialises in female roles, played in the film by Leslie Cheung]. He is the soul of the film, and I think a part of him can be related to my own life. Cheng Dieyi is part of me, or I'm part of Cheng Dieyi, I don't know which. Anyhow, he's a character who expresses some of my deepest feelings . . . like the teacher in *King of the Children*, the old musician in *Life on a String*, and the soldiers in *Yellow Earth* and *The Big Parade*. These characters are, in effect, channels for my own feelings about life, love, death and all the human passions. That's why I call them the 'souls' of the films.

TR: *Still, there are obvious differences between the first three films and* Life on a String *and* Farewell to My Concubine. *Do they have something to do with your growing sense of your audience beyond China?*

CK: After making *King of the Children*, I was sort of confused. By that time I knew something about the outside world: I'd been to Hawaii, to mainland USA and briefly to Europe. I was starting to think about what my future direction should be, and I don't have the full answer yet . . . I'm still thinking it through.

Actually, I wasn't very experienced when I took *King of the Children* to Cannes in 1988, and I didn't anticipate what happened there: I didn't expect that people wouldn't be able to relate to the film. What I said in all the interviews was that I had to make the film the way I did. It's the way it should be, and I don't regret it. But at the same time it struck me that the people I was talking to had never been to China and knew very little about Chinese culture. If a film takes too much for granted, it's bound to be hard for them to understand. And so since then I've consciously tried to provide more points of reference for the audience. But it's not my intention to try to bridge the gap between East and West; nobody can do that. But I would like to make a film that a western audience can see in the same way that they see western films.

TR: *So how do you see the possibilities?*

CK: To be very frank, I think the path is pretty narrow. The question is: How much can I tell the international audience about Chinese culture? If I go too far, no one will understand. That's not my fault, and it's not their fault. But if I limit myself to very simple things, the film is bound to be very superficial.

Sometimes you can't even find a channel of communication at all.

When I decide to make a film, I now have to ask myself: what is the basic audience for it? Is it Chinese or western? Of course, I hope that Chinese audiences can enjoy my films, but I have to face the fact that the distribution system in China hasn't worked for years, and so there's no real way for Chinese audiences to see my films. I'm certainly not giving up on the China market, but things here are beyond my control.

I think my basic motivation when I make a film is to satisfy myself, not to 'please' an audience. But I do want to go on making films. I can admire a lot of the American films I see, but usually I don't see any point to them. I want to make films that have real meanings – things that people can realise for themselves and feel at different levels. In that respect, I'm the same as I always was: I want my films to have a point. Sometimes I've been quite lonely and sad, and I haven't known what to do. If people don't come to see my films, my creative life will be over. It will be a kind of death. That's why I have to find new ways to survive. You can see me trying to do that in *Farewell My Concubine*.

TR: *How did you make sense of the mixed reactions to* Life on a String?

CK: I describe *Life on a String* as a 'theological' film – it's about our belief system, about our spiritual life in this huge country. Many Chinese people have travelled abroad in the last ten years, but most of them haven't actually lived in western cultures, and they haven't got any sense of the way that spiritual values work in other societies. As a result, very few Chinese viewers can relate to this film.

I spent three years living in New York, and I think that this question of spiritual values was the strongest impression I came away with. You don't hear too many Americans talking about religion, but it's clear that people do feel something above them, and they do have this sense that problems can be solved through the power of love. But not in China. I don't want to get into politics but these questions came to a head for me when I watched the television in 1989 – you know what I'm talking about. I wasn't surprised or even particularly shocked, but I was very, very sad. Afterwards, I couldn't stop asking myself why Chinese people lack the impulse to forgive. You don't hear people saying 'I'm sorry' or 'Maybe it's my fault, let's talk about it' in this country.

TR: *It isn't only a question of spiritual values, is it? There's also the generation gap between the old man and the young man in* Life on a String.

CK: The real point is not just the age difference. It's their different ways of thinking. The old man has no sense of an alternative to what he knows and does. Maybe at the end of his life he realizes that something is wrong, but it's too late. The boy doesn't share his view of the world, and he's brave enough to decide to go his own way. Obviously, the boy represents my hopes for China's younger generation. His decision raises all the questions that are commonplace in the West, but not in China: Who are you? What's your identity? What kind of person do you want to be? In the West, though, these questions are asked in a cultural context that *includes* spiritual values. Chinese people these days run away from the notion of responsibility. Their attitude is that they've had enough of doing things for the country, for the Party or for society. Now they want to do things purely for themselves.

TR: *From a Western point of view, the most surprising element missing from your early films was any discussion of sexual questions.*

CK: I know what you mean, but in one way I think my first three films were very sexual, especially *Yellow Earth* and *The Big Parade*. Maybe that's something very personal! The reason I came late to sexual questions is that I grew up without contact with girls and women. I went to a boys' school, and then I was sent to the countryside and lived with a lot more boys, and then I joined the army and found no women there either. I played basketball in the army, and there *was* a women's basketball team too. One woman in that team came from Beijing, like me, and I tried to find a way to talk to her, but it didn't work out. I'd become self-conscious about dealing with sexual matters by the time I made *King of the Children*, and I wanted the film to contain a love scene. But it simply wasn't possible in China at that time.

TR: *And so* Farewell My Concubine *is some kind of breakthrough for you?*

CK: There are many reasons, good and bad, why so many Chinese films of recent years have avoided dealing with sex. But I'm very well aware (and so are my friends and contemporaries) of the importance of sex in people's lives, and we all know that it's an element that's been lacking in our films. One problem is that we've been steering our film characters away from their sexual feelings; we haven't known how to *respect* the characters we've created! Characters in films should behave the way they *have to* behave, they shouldn't be twisted and distorted by the author. Let them be who they are!

In *Concubine*, the characters are strongly motivated by sexual feelings. But we see them struggling with their feelings at an age when they don't know how to deal with them. That struggle emerges in clashes between male and female, or masculinity and femininity. Some people have criticised me for playing down the homosexual elements, but I really don't think that homosexuality is the main issue in the story. It's easy to see why Duan and Cheng become so close as boys in the Peking Opera school: they eat the same food, suffer the same hardships, sleep in the same bed, and so on. And Cheng, the effeminate boy, takes Peking Opera characters like the concubine as his role models. For him, there's no difference between real life and drama. Of course he's horrified when his older 'brother' gets married, especially when the bride turns out to be a prostitute. But the fact that he feels jealousy and morally disapproves of the Gong Li character doesn't mean that he understands his own sexual feelings. Actually, he knows almost nothing about sex.

TR: *Do you still hope to make films outside China sometime?*

CK: Yes, I'd really like to make a film in the USA or Europe. I'd really like to

5 *Farewell My Concubine*: the 'brothers' (Zhang Fengyi and Leslie Chung)

6 *Farewell My Concubine*: the prostitute who comes between them (Gong Li)

know the borders of my own territory. It would certainly be something different from the films I make in China, but I wouldn't be able to make a 100 per cent foreign film. The first step will probably be to make a film about Chinese characters but in the English language. There are several 'international' subjects I'd like to tackle. For instance, I'm very interested in the Dalai Lama, and would love to make a film about him. But that's far too 'sensitive' to be done in China.

Actually, I've had approaches from some agents in the West. I've always told them that I can only do films that I love. I'd be no good with assignments. I couldn't do an action movie, for instance. Speaking of which, I hear that John Woo has just finished his first Hollywood movie. His producer Terence Chang told me that it went quite well, but that John wasn't really satisfied with the script they gave him.

TR: *What about the question of overseas investment in Made-in-China films? You've now made two features with foreign backing.*

CK: That's the immediate way forward, I think. I certainly couldn't imagine going back to work in the Chinese studio system. I've been abroad too long to speak about this with any authority, but my impression is that the studio system in China has broken down already. I've heard that no studio began any production of its own in the first three months of 1993. They have no idea what they should be doing, or whether they can recoup their investments in films or not. China Film Corporation's old monopoly in distribution has been ended, so the studios suddenly have to deal with small, regional outfits. They may need to send, say, thirty people around the country, to look after distribution of their films in the various provinces, and those agents would certainly come up against corruption and have to pay bribes. The studios cannot handle all that! It's rather like what happened when the Soviet Union collapsed: instead of one monolithic bureaucracy, you now have dozens of small, local bureaucracies.

At the same time, there's a growing amount of investment in Chinese films from wealthy individuals and companies outside China. Basically, most of it is coming from Hong Kong and Taiwan. The Beijing Film Studio, where I made *Farewell My Concubine*, has had around twenty-four 'joint ventures' like that in the last year or so. I live in hope that this foreign investment will be a turning-point for the film industry. The whole system will eventually be forced to improve.

TR: *Has foreign investment raised technical standards in China?*

CK: Not that much, because most of the overseas producers who have worked here aren't that professional to begin with. They just have money! But doing post-production abroad [often in Tokyo] has certainly given us films with higher technical standards. Working with the Tomson Company on *Farewell My Concubine* enabled us to rent a very good camera and a Steenbeck for the editing room. That's the only Steenbeck in China!

7 *Hard Target:* John Woo (centre) with Jean Claude Van Damme

TR: *Aren't there possibilities for independent production in China? Some young directors like Zhang Yuan, Wang Xiaoshuai and He Jianjun have already taken matters into their own hands by raising money privately and making low-budget independent features.*

CK: I've heard about that, and I look forward to seeing the results. The films may be very good, but of course that doesn't necessarily mean that they'll be able to recoup the money invested in them. We'll have to see. Actually, Zhang Yuan has invited me to see his film. I like the title: *Beijing Bastards*!

TR: *I asked Zhang Yuan whether the English title should be singular or plural (the Chinese title* Beijing Zazhong *could be either), and he said: 'Plural! They're all bastards!'*

CK: What I would like to see in China is a lot of private production companies. That is, privately *owned* production companies. Unlike the old studios, they would run efficiently. They would spend money carefully, work hard and pay attention to quality. And they would certainly promote and distribute their films much better than it's done now. What we have now is a half-socialist, half-capitalist country and everyone is understandably confused. As soon as the state stops owning everything, all those tired arguments about 'artistic' and 'commercial' films will stop. Everything will be tested in the market, and the market itself will change. Right now, for instance, I'm sure that my films have a huge potential audience among China's students, but I have no way of reaching them. And so I think the government is right to do away with the old system, even if it makes for great confusion in the short term. In five years' time, I hope I can invite you to my own production company office in Beijing!

3   Acting Is Doing
Sydney Pollack in conversation
with John Boorman

Sydney Pollack trained as an actor and taught acting before he became a director. I first became interested in his work when I saw *The Slender Thread*. The acting had a special intensity. We were both working at MGM in the late sixties. I sought him out and we became friends. Since then, he has gained a deserved reputation as a director of actors; his films display a range of remarkable performances. Whenever we meet, we exchange news from the battle-front. This time, I put a tape recorder between us:

JOHN BOORMAN: *I want to ask you about directing actors. I've always admired the extraordinary performances you get. How do you do it? What is your process? Let's start with preparation. Do you have a rehearsal period before principal photography?*

SYDNEY POLLACK: Well, it's changed a lot for me over the years, but it seems to me from my own experience, having started in the theatre, that the objectives of theatre directing and film directing are completely different. In theatre directing, the objective is to wean the actor away from dependency on the director, because the only time it counts, the director is absolutely useless. Totally and completely useless. Curtain goes up and the actor is on his own. And that's what you're gearing everything towards. Whereas in film, the opposite is the case. The only time it counts, there is no actor, no cameraman, there's nobody. There is you and an editor. And all the arguments in the world don't hold any water unless you can put the performance together from all those separate shots and moments. And that means you have to have gotten each one of those moments, even if you shot them out of the logical order in which they are going to play when you cut them together. So it seems to me that you want much more dependent actors in film than you do on stage. So what's happened with me over the years is I've come to rehearse less and less because I feel relatively confident about knowing what it is I want, and if I've cast the role properly, I feel fairly comfortable that I will be able to find a way to get those moments which I can eventually assemble in the cutting room.

JB: *But surely you discuss the scenes with the actor beforehand, discuss the character, how to build the character?*

SP: I don't really, not very much. I sort of do what I feel the actor needs. The less the actor needs, the less I do. I will do as little as possible. My preference would be to say absolutely nothing, not even 'hello', but instead just come in

8 Sydney Pollack

in the morning and go to work, because there is some kind of marvellous, dangerous tension when that happens. It's a very scary thing to do and you have to have confidence that, if it starts falling apart, you'll be able to find a way to put it together again.

JB: *So describe your routine.*

SP: First thing in the morning, I send everybody away – everybody. Usually I have a big fight with the script clerk, whoever that is, because they always want to stay, but I can't do this kind of rehearsal with anybody there. Not anybody. I mean, if there was a dog, I'd send the dog away. You need to have everybody feel that they can be foolish, including me.

JB: *You do this on the set? On the stage, or location?*

SP: Yes. Right there on the set.

JB: *And you use all the devices around you – the trees, or the furniture?*

SP: Yes, everything is in place. And then I try desperately to make the actors believe me when I ask them to 'do nothing'. I mean just that. We start by doing nothing so that there is no feeling of reaching for anything. We simply step through the scene.

JB: *Flat?*

SP: I don't ever say 'do this flat', because then they will concentrate on doing it flat. What I say is, 'Don't work for anything, don't try for anything. Let's get to know the scene, let's just read it like you were taking a little walk in the emotional woods of it and see what we find there.' If I've done this right, what will happen is that the actors won't be able to do nothing. They will start to do the scene. If they start to do too much, I will stop them. I might say, 'Don't work for the performance, let it sort of get itself on its feet in its own way.' And then we start moving it around. This takes sometimes as little as ten minutes, sometimes as much as an hour and a half.

JB: *Are you blocking as well now?*

SP: Yeah.

JB: *You're moving them around?*

SP: Yes, and even if I've drawn it all with stick figures, which I have sometimes, I won't ever tell them that but I'll sort of . . .

JB: . . . *Guide them into those places you want them to be?*

SP: Yeah, let them do it their way first, do anything they want but kind of nudge them into position. I think the biggest mistake that's made in film directing is talking about and working towards results instead of causes. It's a tricky thing, but I know from being an actor how tough it is to work directly towards results. And most directors direct in terms of results. Most directors will say, 'Be more angry,' or 'Be more upset.' A good actor can always do that for you. If I say to an actor, 'This is a suspicious guy that you're playing,' he will look for general ways to play suspicious. But if I say to the actor, 'Watch his left hand, watch it move towards his left pocket, because there's a gun in his left pocket.' Or whatever. Now he will have to deal with that gun in there, and that's giving him something very specific to do here which will lead him to behavior which even he can't predict.

JB: *We're talking, of course, about a scene in which there are relationships involved between two or more characters and there's some kind of conflict. But in an action scene where, let's say, the actor comes into an office and he wants to break into a filing cabinet and he's got a knife and he's afraid he's going to get caught. How do you go about rehearsing that sort of scene – an action sequence?*

SP: I always ask myself, 'How do I keep it from being a movie scene? If this were really happening and not a movie scene, what would actually happen?' Our heads are so full of movie clichés that it's very hard to avoid them. It's like trying to keep from falling asleep when you're driving. You have to keep slapping your face. I feel like I have to do that to myself, particularly when I'm directing a thriller or something where the clichés really abound. I have to keep slapping my face and saying, 'How do I keep this from being a movie?' The thing I always look for is more fear. I don't think that anybody's ever scared enough in movies. I know how scared I get in real life.

There was a show on here years ago called *Candid Camera*. It always amazed me. Is it on in Europe?

JB: *Yes.*

SP: I think it is one of the best acting schools in the world – watching real people deal with extraordinary circumstances. My favorite is: you take an engine out of a car . . .

JB: *Oh, I saw that! Then you run it down to a garage.*

SP: Yeah, and there's a woman in the car, right? The woman says, 'I don't know what's wrong; I just can't get it to start.' The mechanic says, 'Well, let me take a look.' The camera pushes into this guy's face as he opens the lid and there's nothing there. Well, the interesting thing is that the guy doesn't do anything.

JB: *Nothing on his face.*

SP: He just stares in there, because he can't believe what he's seeing. And the less he does, the better it is.

JB: *Well, that gets us back to Eisenstein, the theory of montage. If you have a close-up of a man's face, then cut to a clown, when you cut back to the man's face, you think you see amusement on his face. But if instead you cut to a child crying, you read sadness on his face. We make those associations. If you walk into your office and look at your secretary, who has just heard there has been a death in the family, you'd know from her face instantly that something terrible has happened, even though she has shown no overt emotion. The actor is, of course, always simulating that.*

SP: That's right, and you're asking an actor to do an almost impossible thing because we know from psychology and psychoanalysis that, once you make what's unconscious conscious, it tends to die. That's what Freud's theory of hysteria was based on. That these things were happening because one was unaware of what was happening in the unconscious, and we know that emotion is a product of the unconscious. So, you're asking an actor consciously to simulate something which works best when it's happening unconsciously. So, the thing I believe is the hardest to do is to tell an actor to relax. Because you can't relax by relaxing. You have to relax by doing something which will take your attention off yourself in a certain way. Quite often, the difference between a bad actor and a good actor is that a very good actor knows that there is very little they can do to get the emotion except rely on the circumstances or the other actor. That if they try to work on it themselves, it becomes self-manipulation in a way that always looks like bad acting. The really good actors are incredible listeners. They know that in a sense the root of the performance is in the attention they pay to the other actor. Particularly if the other person in the scene is the key to what they want, which is usually the case. The best actors will truly react to the slightest difference in the performance of the other person. You can always see the bad actor where the partner changes completely what he's doing and this guy goes on doing exactly the same thing. I've sometimes gone to an actor and said, 'I could take Tom right out of the room and you would continue as you are. You're not dealing with the other person.' Sometimes, if you can get them to focus on what the other actor is doing, it will relax them. I've sometimes found myself in terrible situations resorting to tricks, having to give actors physical activities to get them out of the place they're stuck in.

JB: *Have you ever found that what you need from an actor is just not there?*

SP: When I feel I've made a mistake in casting, and that's happened on rare occasions, then I feel I have to trick the performance in some way.

JB: *Or the alternative. I've sometimes found that if the actor is not capable of giving you what you need, you are obliged to modify the scene into something that he can do.*

SP: Yes, because you'd rather have a lesser scene that works than a better one that doesn't.

JB: *We talk about an actor having 'presence'. It's a term that is used rather loosely for any actor who is convincing. But it is a rare actor who is really 'present', absolutely 'there' at any given moment. Rare in adults, common in children. When I was making* Hope and Glory, *the kids were always instantly 'there' and I was ready to shoot, because the division between play and reality doesn't exist for children. The great film actors seem to have retained that child-like ability, don't they? No part of their mind or emotions is elsewhere. They are present.*

SP: Yes. And when you see it, you know in a second.

JB: *You work a lot with Robert Redford, who is a prime example of the kind of actor you describe. He is listening and his responsiveness to the scene and the other actor is total, isn't it? You can read it in his face. He is always experiencing the scene for the first time and he does not know what is coming next.*

SP: Exactly. A lot of people don't see that. They're impressed by large theatrical outbursts, drunk scenes or whatever, but to be solid in every scene, to be alive and listening and thinking and to let us see the thinking – that's real top stuff.

JB: *If, as you say, that simulating emotions is impossible, you start with the premise that acting is an impossible art. Somehow good actors manage to convince, but sometimes a great actor goes beyond that and produces moments that transcend acting, where he seems to be beyond himself, beyond acting, to have entered another realm.*

SP: When that happens, the material is somehow making a connection to the actor's unconscious in a way that is particular to that actor's instrument. Their psyche is compelling them in some mysterious way that you can't describe or comprehend, and that makes for stardom. I have no idea how it works, but what movie stars have in common is a slight sense of danger, of unpredictability.

JB: *You feel it's dangerous for the actor too. That he is not in control, that his self, his ego, is no longer governing him.*

SP: Yes, exactly. They surprise you, they surprise themselves, they surprise everybody. It's unplannable, unpredictable. I don't know how else to describe it. A mystery.

JB: *Let me ask you something else, about shooting. Do you shoot a lot of takes?*

SP: I don't like to. I'm like everybody else, I guess, sometimes I have to, but for the most part I would say no. Only rarely do I go over and over. Every once in a while I get a scene that just doesn't seem to be happening.

JB: *But do you always know when you've got a good take? Or do you feel that maybe there's something better . . .*

SP: Usually I stop when I've got it. With somebody like Redford it's never one take, it's pieces. I mean, he really tries things on each take, and sometimes a take will be very good for the beginning and then not so good from the middle or the end. Then I'll do another one and they'll be put together. Almost always I do that.

JB: *And do you ever find that you are surprised, when you see the dailies, that it looks either better or worse than you thought at the time?*

SP: Well, an odd thing happened to me a lot in the beginning. I couldn't figure out why. I would be very moved on the set and the emotion would be missing in the dailies. Or I would be very disappointed on the set and I would get into dailies and there would seem like there was more there than I saw on the set. Gradually I began experimenting, and now I get exactly where the camera is and I try to use the camera-operator's shoulder as the bottom frame and I close one eye. It seems odd, but the most important thing is the closing of one eye. I became aware that before that I was seeing too much, much more than the camera was seeing. I'd been moved by something. Maybe it's the hand of the actor that's twitching up against his trousers, but it's not in the shot. And so I try very hard now to see only what the camera is seeing and I try to kind of hide. I try not to be where the actor can see me. I use the magazine of the camera to crop the right or the left side and the shoulder of the operator to crop the bottom. Then I just stick one eye in and I get it as close to a flat, two-dimensional picture as I can and that's helped me a lot in an odd way. I found that when I just stood there like it was a stage performance, I was getting thrown. I was having a completely different emotional reaction when I saw more than the camera would see. Do you find that to be true?

JB: *Yes, but a lot of directors watch through a black-and-white TV monitor which I refuse to have on the set, because it's totally distorting.*

SP: There is something more important that directors often don't realize, and that is that the actors are doing it for you. Most actors won't admit it, but they feel bad if you don't get what you want.

JB: *And while you watch, you are sending out signals to the actor all the time, feeding him, and he's giving it back to you.*

SP: You're the first place they look at when you say 'cut', and they're like kids, I don't care if they're sixty-five years old. They're still like little kids looking at their father saying, 'Was that good, did I do good?' And to be off somewhere looking at a monitor ... Mind you, Francis Coppola does this all the time and makes some great movies, so you can't say that a general rule always applies, but I know that it's true from being an actor. And I've talked to enough actors about it, and they're terribly disappointed when you are all staring at a monitor and not watching them. Because they have nobody to do it for. On the stage there's an audience. Those monitors are a help sometimes if you want to know whether something was in the shot, but boy, you can get used to just standing there watching. I worked on a set (which shall remain nameless) as an actor not too long ago. The director was absolutely glued to his monitor and I was very disappointed. And I don't have a career as an actor, I don't give a damn about acting myself. I gave it up thirty years ago, but I was looking forward to doing this acting. I walked in and there was everybody staring at the monitor. I sort of lost my enthusiasm. Acting is such a mysterious business. You never stop learning about how you work with actors. I am amazed by how much I learn on each picture about working with actors.

JB: *The thing I find important when I'm staging a scene with actors is to get the right space between them. And if the relationship is shifting between the characters, I reflect that in the distance between them, and this determines the actors' movements. In television, they are always pushing the actors close together so that they can get them both on the small screen in close-up. You see their eyes, inches apart, and they're shouting at each other.*

SP: That's right. They even get their eyes crossed. When you get that close to somebody, your eyes are crossed. It's uncomfortable.

JB: *Ludicrous, isn't it? Do you agree about the importance of achieving the right space between actors?*

SP: Absolutely. I think that's a key element in staging, the spatial relationship. What's going on between them.

JB: *You do that instinctively, out of your knowledge of the scene. It's not a conscious thing usually.*

SP: I don't think it's conscious. A lot of times actors feel that they are not acting if they're not glaring into the eyes of the other actor. And so you sometimes have to dissuade them from that. In the beginning, when I used to teach acting, we used to give every actor in the kindergarten stage a physical activity that had real urgency. It was not enough, let's say, that you had to take all the pages of this Filofax out and put them back in their proper order. But you had to give that activity a time-limit, a reason, an urgency. And then you started to play the scene. So that the actor, instead of playing the scene and the words, really got concentrated on this Filofax and then as the other person began to play the scene with him, the scene got filtered through this activity. As the actors got more and more advanced, we just took that physical activity and moved it inside, and it became 'character'.

JB: *You no longer need the Filofax.*

SP: You don't need the Filofax any more. We always used to say when teaching that acting is doing. Acting is behaving truthfully under imaginary circumstances. But what it comes down to always is what you're doing, not what you're saying. Wondering what you're going to say next is doing something. If I'm wondering what you're going to say, that's a real active thing for me to do. I am always looking for the 'doing' in the scene. I know what you're saying, I know what the story says – but it's got nothing to do with the acting. So I always go back to this physical activity. And then move it inside. I do a lot of love stories, and what the characters often want from each other in love stories is always a palpable thing. This sense of seeing what the other person thinks about you. Which is what happens with lovers, it's an active thing. You watch somebody to see how you're doing in their eyes, and it's a very active thing to do.

JB: *That explains a lot about certain scenes in your films. For instance,* The Way We Were *and* Out Of Africa *have great love scenes in which almost nothing seems to be happening. There is no text. I look at those scenes and think, 'How did he do this?' How do you approach such scenes, how do you rehearse them, how do you act them? Because nothing is said, or what is said are banalities or just the simple clichés that are exchanged at those sort of moments. How do you prepare the actors for this kind of scene?*

SP: That's difficult to explain exactly. For one thing, I never talk to any actor in front of another actor. Never. After we've done that first rehearsal and I've brought the cameraman in and we've made marks and all that, I send the

9 *The Way We Were*: Redford and Streisand

10 *Out of Africa*: Redford and Streep

actors to make-up. But I don't consider that we've scratched the surface of the scene yet. Usually, I'll go running from one trailer to the other like a maniac and sit down with each actor separately. I don't want anybody else but that actor and me to know what that actor is trying to do. If the actor thinks anybody else knows what he or she is supposed to be doing, then it's as though somebody else is judging them. If five electricians are around and you say to the actor, 'Stronger, much stronger', the actor knows that every one of those electricians has heard the direction and every one of those electricians is waiting to see if they're going to do it better or stronger. So instead, I go to the actor privately and I say, for instance, 'I don't know what it's costing you. I don't know what this scene is costing you.' And they look at you puzzled for a while and say, 'What do you mean?' Well, what is it costing you to say goodbye? It's different from saying to the actor 'It's hard' or 'easy' to say goodbye, or whatever. Again, finding something to do so that there is always a 'doing' in the scene. Otherwise you get this thing of 'having text' together, which is absolutely boring shit. I don't care how good the words are, they're not the thing. It's like you want the words to be dipped in paint and the paint is the emotional life of the scene. And the emotional life of the scene can be prepared without the text, and then when you drop the text in, it's sort of dripping with the emotional activity of the scene. So I always sit down, right off the bat, and try to see the scene in terms of its emotional content. On one occasion I said to Tom (Cruise) and Jean (Tripplehorn) when we were making *The Firm*, 'This is a scene of two monologues. In each case you are desperately trying to push through this exterior and reach the other person. Like saying, "Wake up and listen to me!"' So sometimes, if I can't get it in any other way, I'll say to an actor, 'Say that! Just say that right now: "Wake up and listen to me. Wake up!" Then, "Where are you going?" You see, you're dipping "Where are you going?", which is the text, into "Listen to me!", because listen to me is the doing. I'm trying to get your attention. I'm trying to reach you.' I had a great acting teacher and he used to drum this into my head over and over again: acting is doing. 'What are you doing?' he would say. We would answer, 'Well, I'm asking her for money.'

He would say, 'You can't act "I'm asking her for money." You can *say* it, but you can't *act* it. What are you *doing*? Acting is *doing*.'

Doing. Doing.

4   Art Direction:
Wajda to Spielberg

Allan Starski

When I think about my work in film, I realize increasingly how much my life has been influenced by the fact that I belong to the second generation of film-makers. My father Ludwik was a scriptwriter in the 1930s. He was the only professional screenwriter during the first few years after the war, and was responsible for designing the sets of most films of that period. It was thanks to him that I saw a real film studio and a 'real' war.

I was born in Warsaw in 1943, in the middle of the war, in a place which experienced the full brutality of the Nazis. But I only started to remember it properly three years after the war, when I was taken to the film studio in Łódź. This is where they filmed the first Polish film, *Zakazane Piosenki* (*Forbidden Songs*). The film was set in Warsaw during the war, but they couldn't shoot there because the whole city was in ruins. I watched them filming people being taken prisoner, being shot on the streets. It was so real, it terrified me. I will never forget my feeling of relief and amazement when I was shown the backs of these false streets, the whole structure of the set. From that time onwards films have been part of my life. The post-war years meant for me – as for all Poles – Polish films, films which were mainly about the war. Despite all the propaganda and the strict controls under which these films were made, they were more honest and meant more to the Polish audience than the Soviet films which dominated the cinemas.

1956 came, and with it the 'Polish October', which was the beginning of the 'thaw' in Poland and of my first 'adult' experiences in film. I remember two films from that period which evoked in me all the emotions which real cinema can bring. The first was *Fanfan la Tulipe* with Gerard Philippe, the second *Ashes and Diamonds* by Andrzej Wajda. Soon after the premières of these films, you could see youngsters everywhere with Fanfan haircuts and dark glasses like Zbigniew Cybulski, the hero of *Ashes and Diamonds*. It was a visible sign of the influence of cinema and its heroes. When I finished my studies at the Academy of Fine Arts in 1969, I began work as an assistant set designer in the Warsaw Film Studio. By this time I was already a 'European'. I knew European films and I knew the more important American films too. In Polish cinemas more and more Western films were being shown, although there was always a delay. Student holidays to European capitals were really long-distance excursions to the cinema.

11 Allan Starski

As I began working in films, my role also changed. From being a fan, I became a professional. But then, of course, it is also important which league you play in! My entrance to the first division came in 1975 when Andrzej Wajda offered me the job of designing the set for the film *The Shadow Line*. Everything to do with that film was wonderful and very exotic for me. We shot in London, Bangkok and Bulgaria, the crew was international, there were lots of interesting sets to be built, and my favourite director of photography, Witold Sobociński, was on the team. But all of this was nothing compared to the tremendous pleasure of working with Andrzej Wajda. This man was for me a living legend, the idol of my generation. Working together on a film, however, is something more than the relationship between a fan and his idol. The director is the head of a whole team, demanding and sometimes even threatening.

At this point I would like to add a few words about the relationship between set designer and director. European cinema – and especially the 'Polish school' – created a marvellous basis for directors to work alongside the set designer and director of photography. During the period of preparation for the film, when you're looking for places to shoot, an atmosphere of team creativity develops, a sense of close co-operation between people who are all working together to construct the skeleton of the future film. New ideas are suggested which change the construction of the screenplay, interesting locations impose a new dramatic structure. In the case of a director like Andrzej Wajda, this phase of a film becomes a real pleasure. My fascination was deepened still further by the fact that Andrzej Wajda also studied at the Academy of Fine Arts and many of his ideas he simply sketches. When I go back to films with Wajda I always like to look at his sketches, which I have kept from various films. They contain ideas for the film, for a scene, for a shot. With such material in my possession, it is much easier for me to grasp the director's idea, the aesthetics of the film.

That first film with Wajda taught me how much I still had to learn about cinema. The feeling was all the more intense since I thought that this would probably be the only film I would make with him. That was how Wajda worked: he liked to take on new people all the time, to create a new team for each film. Looking back on all the films I have made with Wajda, I think that that feeling remained with me and gave a sense of unrepeatability to each of the projects I completed for him. In each new project the most important and decisive element for me is the director, his personality and talent, and not the screenplay or the production conditions. I realize that this is a rather luxurious attitude towards what is, in many ways, a technical profession, but perhaps I'm lucky, because so far I have been able to work according to these principles.

Going back to Wajda, I think that the strength of his films lies not just in their artistic merit but also in their political sense, and a strength which was always greater that any State propaganda. *Ashes and Diamonds* became the great event of the late fifties, because not only did it create an idol but it also showed that the idol can be a man who is the enemy of organised Communist politics. He is a man who is lost, unsure whether he is right, seemingly floundering under the weight of history – but yet, in my opinion, victorious, despite the tragic end. It is also important to remember that those were the days when cinemas were still showing films full of heroes without flaws, who accepted Communist dogma without questioning it. A lot of later films, including those on which I worked, became the next challenges to the rules set down by the system.

Man of Marble was such a challenge. It exposed the whole system of repression and false propaganda of the fifties. The making of the film itself was a very emotional experience. The whole crew knew that the film we were making went way beyond the limits imposed by the censor. The situation was made all the more bizarre by the fact that all films were entirely financed by the State and therefore, theoretically, under its complete control. On the other hand, the authorities were posing as open-minded people who were open to criticism of the mistakes of the past. This situation, and the courage of the director, created a film which shocked the authorities and broke another of the system's taboos.

Working on this film gave me the feeling, once again, that I was helping to create something important and that I was experiencing something new. Of the advice Wajda gave and the many ideas he brought to the film, I remember one particularly clearly. In one scene the hero, Maciej Tomczyk, is sent to what was in those days a growing threat, the Security Services. He is with a friend, but goes into the interrogation room alone, while his friend stays in the hall, waiting by the door. After waiting for hours, the friend gets worried and looks into the room. The investigating officer tells him that Tomczyk left ages ago. The room only has the one door, the one by which the friend has been standing the whole time . . . Knowing the atmosphere of the Security Services, I designed the room classically: apart from the officer's desk, a cupboard for documents, a little table and a chair, there were some typical props. Just before we started shooting, Wajda asked that the whole room be emptied! All that was left was a completely bare desk and the officer's chair. Now, when the friend looks into the room his gaze is met by complete emptiness. His friend's disappearance becomes absurd, shocking. Wajda's films, full of political problems, strong and expressive, were always greeted with great interest. There were long queues outside the cinemas, people would burst into spontaneous applause during the showing of a film. It wasn't just *Man of Marble*; there was also *Rough Treatment* and *Man of Iron*.

Man of Iron was a typical political film and came into being through the necessity of the moment. It was an expression of support for Solidarity, and we began to make it just after the strikes at the shipyards which had achieved so much. We all realized that this period of freedom was temporary and that something must happen, which is why the film was made so quickly. The shots showing the August strikes in the Gdańsk shipyards were shot during the winter, and I built the main gate – the centre of the strike, which people all over the world had seen in photos – in a studio. We shot many of the street scenes without permission from the authorities or the police; we designed the set as we were shooting. But we managed to make the film and to show it to the public. It also won the Palme d'Or at Cannes. But the following winter greeted us with martial law. Naturally, the film was immediately taken out of circulation, and landed on the shelves amongst other films which had overstepped the mark.

In the late seventies Wajda also made films which were far removed from politics and the problems which occupied the minds of contemporary Poles. There was *The Young Ladies from Wilko*, a film which is serious, reflective and beautifully shot. This time it was my turn to surprise the director. The story is set in a Polish manor-house between the two world wars. White, classical Polish manor-houses had become the symbol of Polish history. The set which I proposed was far from that stereotype. I created a small wooden house, rooms with dark walls full of shadows and mystery, sunlight filtering through heavy blinds. This is a good example of how important the collaboration is between set designer and director of photography. A large part of the atmosphere for which I was so highly praised is due to the lighting.

It was through my work with Wajda that I met Alan Pakula. It was in 1981, the time of Solidarity in Poland, a short period of freedom before the imposition of martial law. The crew who were making *Sophie's Choice* came to Poland looking for locations for the film, and they wanted Wajda's set designer to help them. That's how I met Pakula. He had already made *All the President's Men* and all those earlier, excellent films. Despite the fact that he was surrounded by his own people and that he had with him his set designer of many years, G. Jennkins, I was amazed how easy it was for me to get close to him, and with what attention he listened to my advice and suggestions. His interest and receptivity reminded me so much of Wajda. I think that there is something which all these great directors have in common: an extraordinary openness to the world, an inexhaustible interest and hunger for new experiences. I travelled with the *Sophie's Choice* team all over Poland, Czechoslovakia, and Hungary looking for outdoor locations. Unfortunately, Poland had the best locations – because that's where the events actually happened – but was not yet politically prepared for such a film. I will never forget our visit to the museum at Auschwitz, and Pakula's face, full of shock and pain at seeing the photographs which showed the whole extent of the crimes and bestiality carried out in that camp.

This period spent looking for locations was in addition to the shared meals, meetings and discussions we had. Often during our discussions I noticed that Pakula was noting down what I was saying. He told me that he was writing down some of my expressions, the particularities of my English, so that he could teach them to Meryl Streep, who was playing a Polish woman. He wanted her English to sound authentic.

I was really looking forward to working on this film. Unfortunately, however, fate plays tricks. Shooting was delayed for a year and they decided to use locations in Yugoslavia. When shooting began I was already in Paris, preparing Wajda's *Danton*. While we were shooting, Alan Pakula came through Paris. I remember the lunch we had together. I think then that I had a chance to go to America and work there, but my ties with Europe were too strong.

Danton turned out to be a huge success in Europe. It raised a storm in France and was much appreciated in England. The history of the French Revolution, as seen by a Pole, took on all the experiences of the system which had ruled Eastern Europe since the end of the War.

Danton upset the accepted, text-book view of revolution, and put the emphasis on the brutality and violence which the uncompromising pursuit of power brings. Hoping to reflect this atmosphere, we transformed palaces into offices, prisons, guardhouses. Interiors were stripped of furniture, tapestries, valuable objects and paintings, and instead we had makeshift partitions of unfinished planks, beds made of boards, bars in the windows. Against this background appeared people who were weary, filled with anxiety, forced into action by the system which they themselves had created. *Danton* opened doors for me all over Europe. It was a good moment for this to happen, since Poland was under martial law at the time and film production had been completely paralysed.

The first film I worked on after *Danton* was Wajda's *Love in Germany*, a Franco-German co-production. At the last moment the Polish authorities banned Polish actors living in Poland from taking part in the film, so opposite the excellent and experienced Hanna Schygulla was a young Polish actor from Canada. In this film, at Wajda's request, I used a lot of props which were the quintessence of Nazi kitsch, including lollipops with iced swastikas on them. The opening scene of the film, in which a small boy is sucking one of these lollipops, was cut out of the German version of the film. It remained in the French version and the image was even used on the cover of a French advertising brochure!

A few months after this film I received an offer to work on a film about Schubert. It was, I think, the biggest post-war production to be made in Austria. Following the director's orders, we adapted dozens of Viennese streets. We built vast sets in a factory which we turned into a studio. The sets were decorated with props and furniture from the Biedermeier period, the streets were filled with carefully restored carriages, the shops were given new windows and dozens of wonderful shop-signs were hung outside. We even managed to hold back the big waterfall outside Salzburg so that it would spring to life with added force during the take. The film was not perhaps a great commercial success, but it still has many admirers and I often meet with enthusiastic opinions about it.

After this film I had a completely different experience: working on a mini-series for CBS, *Escape from Sobibor*. During my work on this film I learnt about the laws which control professional television film-making: a precise director (Jack Gold), an excellent English technical crew and a regular daily shooting pattern. I prepared myself for this film very carefully. I gathered all the information available about the camp at Sobibor. I even managed to see documents kept by the Commission of Research into Nazi War Crimes. But a film has its own laws, and that affects the set. The Sobibor camp, which we built near Belgrade, reflected not only my historical knowledge but also the demands of the film's plot. The topography of certain barracks and workshops was dependent on concrete situations; the camera often had to show in one, clearly legible shot the heroes of the film moving between buildings relevant to the action. It affected the escape scene, and particularly the scenes in which the camp guards are disposed of. One way or another, we managed to make the camp look quite authentic. I remember the first visit to the set by people who had survived the real camp. The first impression was overwhelming, but after the initial shock there was a heated debate. Each of them remembered the camp differently, analysed different details, looked through the perspective of his own experiences. Situations like this often occur in films, which is why it is so important to me to research everything as thoroughly as I can. Most important of all are photos and things written at the time which deal with the film's subject. It is only by using this method that I can form my own opinions and start designing freely.

While we were shooting *Escape from Sobibor* I witnessed the most extraordinary scene. We were shooting the climax of the film, the escape from the camp. We had five cameras, a 150-metre travelling shot, a crowd of extras, while watching from behind the camera stood real survivors of the camp. The camera starts to roll, hundreds of extras burst through the wire and run towards the forest. All around them mines are exploding, they are being shot at. Suddenly, one of the actual camp survivors breaks into a run and follows them. He had come from California as a consultant on the film. At the end of the shot the extras come back, but he goes on running because he really is escaping! After several hours Yugoslav soldiers found him somewhere in the woods. Often when we make films about the war, we don't realize that we are creating a nightmare for those who survived it. After shooting *Escape from Sobibor* I returned to Poland and six months later was pleasantly surprised to hear that the film had been nominated for Emmy awards for, amongst other things, its set design.

Martial law in Poland gradually loosened its grip. Interesting films began to appear again. I made my two next films with Wajda: *Demons* and *Korczak*. Meanwhile, I also designed the set for an American film called *Eminent Domain*, directed by John Irving. Irving too managed to create an atmosphere of partnership and close co-operation with the crew. The main attraction of this film for me was the fact that Donald Sutherland was acting in it. He is very well-known and much-loved in Poland, particularly amongst my generation. On the set he gave the impression of an unapproachable, threatening man, a real star. His fight against smoking on the set reminded me of Don Quixote; he was up against a whole crew of hardened smokers who were unmoved even by the prospect of losing their jobs. I managed to get to know Donald better quite by chance. I was building the set for the house of the hero, a Polish party *apparatchik* – the role Donald Sutherland was playing. The house was filled with objects which testified to his high position in the Party. Amongst other things there were original paintings by the excellent Polish painter Beksiński. Dark and surreal, they fascinated Donald. He wanted to buy them, so I organized this for him and also arranged for him to meet Beksiński at his atelier. It was only here, far from the film-set, that Donald showed himself to be a charming man, full of humour, and a real connoisseur of painting.

Of the films I have made recently, in the 1990s, two made a particular impression on me: Agnieszka Holland's *Europa, Europa* and *Daens*, a Belgian historical film. *Europa, Europa* has such an odd and amazing story that it is hard to believe that it is based on something that really happened. It is about the extraordinary fate of a young Jewish boy during the Second World War. The main point in the plot is when he is taken for a German and sent to an élite SS school in Germany! Designing the set was quite a complicated undertaking. History throws the hero into different corners of Europe. The film opens in Nazi Germany, then goes to Poland, then to war in Russia, then back to Germany again. Most of the film was shot in Poland, where we tried to re-create the atmosphere of these different places. The most important part was the SS school. Its very appearance, the style of its architecture, needed to say a great deal about the doctrine and power of a totalitarian state. Only parts of the scenes could be shot in the studio. The rest, particularly the crowd scenes, had to take place in real interiors. And this is where I ran into real difficulties. I travelled around Poland, particularly in formerly German areas, looking for typical German schools. But everything I found was too far from the style of the film. Schools are quickly modernized, and I couldn't find what showed up in all the albums of Nazi buildings: that pride, that megalomania, that lack of restraint. Here again, my instinct helped me. I suddenly realized that, after all, there was a work of totalitarian architecture in Warsaw: the notorious Palace of Culture and Science, a gift from the Soviet Union, a stone colossus which people from Warsaw ironically refer to as being 'small but tasteful'. In those vast, pompous interiors I found what I was looking for. Although it was a different ideology, the aims were the same and so were the aesthetics. All those columns, all that marble, those rows of rooms, everything on an inhuman scale. All that was needed was to add Nazi emblems, flags, busts and banners in order to transform the place into a shrine to Nazism. The design which brought me particular satisfaction was the school swimming-pool. Apart from all the obvious paraphernalia of Nazi propaganda, I added a huge underwater swastika on the bottom of the pool. In the scene of the swimming-race the camera reveals, through the broken reflections of the water, this symbol of Hitler's power. The film was a great success, because it was so different from everything that people had seen about the war. It was also a great success for Agnieszka Holland, who brought to the film a biting sense of irony and humour. The film was supposed to be nominated for an Oscar but the German film commission rejected it. As a co-production between France and Germany, it was supposed to be entered under Germany's national colours. But the Germans felt that it was not a German movie, that it did not have the point of view of a German movie. Their decision sparked off a big debate in the press about the criteria affecting the decision and the subtext which influenced it.

The second film, *Daens*, was a completely different experience. It is an historical film, the work of a Flemish priest at the end of the nineteenth century, all about the social conflicts of the period. It was a difficult film, all the more so because I was completely alone amongst a Belgian crew. The fact that I now regard it as one of my successes is thanks to the excellent director, my friend Stijn Coninx. It is not often that one meets a director who is so well-prepared for a film. Thanks to his persistence I got to know, during our research, every corner of Belgium; we looked at everything that could help me in creating a real picture of the country at the turn of the century. When I look at the film now, I am delighted by the way that, from quite a crude, dull screenplay, a film was created which was enthusiastically received in Belgium. I was present at the first showings of the film, and was moved by the spontaneous reaction of the audiences. It was a very positive experience for me. It showed how even small countries can produce films of a really high professional standard which, at the same time, touch upon themes close to the hearts of its home audience. *Daens* also had links with Poland. The parts of the film which show textile factories were shot in Poland in old, abandoned factories. Working in Poland was a nice three-week break for me. Together with my Polish crew and some former factory employees, we re-created production processes which belonged to the nineteenth century. I was all the more determined to get it right because I had in my mind the memory of Andrzej

Wajda's *Promised Land*, with its scenes set in identical factories. Time had worked against me. When *Promised Land* was made, some of the factories still had the same interiors, and in the weaving-mills the old machines were still being used, but in 1991 we had to re-create everything from scratch. As is always the case in films I admire, the set design was enhanced by the excellent photography of Walther Vanden Ende. Last year *Daens* was nominated for an Oscar as Best Foreign Film.

And so I come to the most recent film I have made, and definitely one of the most important. I am thinking of *Schindler's List* directed by Steven Spielberg. We finished shooting in May, and two months later I still haven't recovered from the experience. The news that I had been chosen as set designer for this film came like a bolt from the blue. It was 1992, and I was working on a German-English co-production when I was invited to a meeting with Steven Spielberg in Cracow, which is where the action of the film takes place. I knew how important the meeting would be, but I didn't have time to prepare myself for it. On the other hand, I had been preparing myself for such a film throughout all the years I have been writing about, and the groundwork I had done for *Sophie's Choice* certainly helped. After three days of intensive research with Spielberg, I set about preparing for the film. At first I was in rather a difficult situation. Already, after a few weeks of work, I realized that what was for Spielberg a 'European' chamber piece was for me a huge undertaking, the biggest production I had ever been involved in in Poland. In addition, during that initial period I was left very much on my own. Spielberg was filming *Jurassic Park*, but I couldn't wait for him, I had to begin work. Luckily, after the first few weeks I started going to California with ideas and models of the set. Despite the fact that Spielberg was working on another film and our meetings were, of necessity, extremely short, he amazed me with his capacity for concentration and precision. Many of his observations led to more interesting and courageous ideas for the set. Already during these meetings he showed that faultless instinct for film which everyone was so impressed by later when we were shooting. I watched some of the shooting of *Jurassic Park*, and was impressed by the scale of everything, by the computers, the high-tech equipment packed into the stages under the floor. But the set itself – the kitchen where the children hide from the Velociraptors – looked familiar. And I realized that if the set isn't right, if it doesn't create the right ambience, no matter what the computer effects, the scene won't work. In spite of the new technology, you still have to build a good set.

When the shooting for *Schindler's List* finally began, the period of anxiety, doubts and artistic indecision came to an end. We moved into a really exciting period of creation, with a crazy tempo, incredible changes and new ideas. Spielberg lived up to his reputation as an incomparable leader, a perfectionist and a man possessed of amazing intuition. The whole international team performed miracles in order to meet his demands. Obviously, this kind of complete mobilization was only possible because everyone was conscious that we were working for Spielberg and that we were making a film which, for him, was one of the most important he had ever made.

The film had dozens of different sets; most of the exteriors were constructed in unusually hard winter conditions. At least three construction teams were working simultaneously. One team was building in the studio, the second was working on the camp, then another team or two were adapting streets and natural interiors. Despite the terrifying pace, I tried not to lose what was most important – the atmosphere of Cracow, the authentic details, the historical truth.

Up until about two weeks before shooting began, very delicate negotiations were going on about using the camp at Auschwitz for the film. But the camp is now a museum, and what we were allowed to use was the entrance gate, against which I then constructed a mirror-image of the camp. I built our camp on the reverse side of the entrance gate and fence of the actual camp.

Despite the fact that the film was made in Poland, it was real American discipline which ruled on the set. Everybody had precisely defined tasks and responsibilities. During shooting, the only person allowed to decide about everything was the director; his decision was final. Every day generally began with a different set. It seems to me that, during the whole film, there was no set which was more important than any other; they all had to be a distinct element of the story. The construction of the camp and the commander's villa required quite unusual methods. In addition to the construction crew, we employed a group of carpenters, 'mountaineers', who are tough, independent, old-fashioned carpenters used to working with wood in the traditional way. I had got to know them when we were working on the set of *Europa, Europa* and I had been impressed by their skills and the speed with which they worked. The set which we made is, as far as I know, the biggest of its kind. Despite the difficult conditions, the hard winter and the complicated scenes with thousands of extras, we finished shooting ahead of schedule. The film is now in post-production and I am already thinking ahead. I believe that this will be an important film, which will show the Holocaust to a wider audience than has hitherto seen its horrors. I also think that it will open up Poland more to big film productions because it shows that we have skilled technicians, plus the experience and the enthusiasm necessary to work in this crazy film world.

These recollections may give the impression of a whole string of successes and wonderful experiences. Obviously, this is only a part of the truth. I have worked altogether on around sixty films. Not all of them have brought me such marvellous experiences as those written about here, but I think I remember most of them with pleasure. I have got to know many interesting people, I have had talented and dedicated colleagues. I have worked on most of these films together with my wife, who is a costume designer and supports me in moments of uncertainty. All of this allows me to look with optimism towards the future. Despite the fact that this is not the best time for European cinema, I am hoping for large-scale, interesting films in which the set design will be an essential element of the final artistic effect.

5   Making Music for *Short Cuts*
Hal Willner

21 August 1993
Hydra, Greece

Dear Walter and John,

I've heard about Hydra from a number of people over the years – supposed to be a great place to relax. Brice Marden and Leonard Cohen have homes here (but they're not) and William Kunstler hangs around. My girlfriend Vicki and I are staying in a rented home that is nearly at the top of this mountain-like isle. I almost have a heart attack every time I venture out and have to trudge back up the 467 stone steps to the house. I'm only thirty-seven. I should be able to handle this, but I can't. I don't work out. I don't eat well, I've put enough shit in my body over the years to kill any one of these fucking donkeys that by hooves and bowels control the streets.

I'm planning to get the article that I've been writing for you on producing the music to Robert Altman's *Short Cuts* actually finished here. I had a weird fantasy of renting a typewriter, looking out over the sun-ripened landscape of the Greek islands and typing up a masterpiece . . . RIGHT. There's no IBM center here and the goddam donkeys don't schlep typewriters nohow. Being that the first deadline has long passed and my NY schedule's berserk, I'll attempt to write now what I can in this notebook, comic-book handwriting and all.

I sit here on a rock . . . like what Greek god sat on a rock? . . . reflecting on memories of the project; the first to come to mind happened about a year ago. I was sitting on the floor in Robert Altman's screening room next to the film production office. Assorted cast, crew, musicians, plus a few friends and relations, were gathered to watch the dailies of Annie Ross as Tess Trainer performing. I loved what I was seeing: the lighting, the look of Stephen Altman's night-club set, and Annie with the band . . .

At the end of each shooting day, Altman held open screenings from the previous day's shoot for all who wanted to see them. Once, while talking about Federico Fellini with Altman, he told me that they both felt the dailies WERE the film; it's where the heart of the film breathes. Seeing the various takes from

12 Hal Willner (photo by Jay Blakesberg)

all the different angles at their original length, I began to understand what he meant. I never got bored. The screening room was large, but laid out to have an intimate, relaxed feeling. The screen was full-size, and up front there was room for people to sit on the floor, followed by chairs and then some couches in the rear. Altman, editor Geraldine Peroni, and their assistants sat on the back couch. The room would fill with laughter and applause at each take. Even the bad takes were interesting. I became addicted to the dailies and went almost every day I was in California; they deepened my understanding of what the music needed to offer. Eventually, the production of *Short Cuts* would have me use almost all the resources and abilities I'd so far acquired in my career, and working with Altman and his associates, I began to understand the film process from a whole new perspective.

This 1 October, Robert Altman's *Short Cuts* will open the 1993 New York Film Festival. Although *Short Cuts* is the first big film I've worked on, it's the second film I've participated in which has opened this festival. The first was *Night of the Living Duck*, a Daffy Duck short (directed by Greg Ford) which contained a scene with Daffy as a night-club singer serenading all the super-star monsters with a song called 'Monsters Lead Interesting Lives', featuring Mel Tormé dubbing in the crooning voice. My job was to adapt the music to the cartoon by using Carl Stalling soundtracks from dozens of old Warner Bros cartoons, thus making a new score out of vintage ones. Ah, to count myself as one of many who got their start from Daffy Duck ... Who needs Roger Corman?

Between Altman and Daffy, I was fortunate enough to work on many wonderful projects, mostly in the record business, but some interesting film work came my way as well, including Robert Frank and Rudy Wurlitzer's *Candy Mountain* and Obie Benz's *Heavy Petting*. Film music has been an obsession of mine since I was a kid. It's a frustrating obsession for me now, because I believe that the days of the great film composer/director collaborations are over. It seems that most modern soundtracks are handled by a circle of about a dozen composers, whose work sounds much the same. Often these scores are secondary to sound bites from songs intended for MTV with clips from the film. I'm sure all of this has to do with corporate mentality studio stuff, but that's another article . . .

Back in Greece, I turned on the tube and got MTV and CNN. Vacations are for getting away – HELP! And is it me or does Greek music (playing on a shitty radio downstairs) sound like that Jewish music that you see on the Chabad telethon? Joyful mourning music. Maybe after all this MOUNTAIN climbing, everything sounds like Jewish music. Jews on Mount Olympus! Ladies and Gentlemen . . . Zeus Goldberg! . . . Sorry.

Basically I am a traditional music producer which, come to think of it, is not unlike a film director, except for the difference in medium. Over the years I've specialized in putting together combinations that would not normally meet (musicians, arrangers, and material) and guiding the process along. Outside of my record projects, I've provided sketch music adaptations for 'Saturday Night Live' for the past thirteen years; this involves scoring the comedy/parody sketches using pre-existing music. With NBCs 'blanket clearance' license (or whatever they call it), I can really use any music I wish, from Bernard Herrmann's Hitchcock scores to Miklos Rozsa's biblical compositions. For example, if there is a detective sketch, I can go directly to Alex North soundtracks, Korngold for swashbuckling sketches, Morricone for westerns – or perhaps Max Steiner. Unless absolutely necessary, I never repeat music from previous shows (though it's hard to beat Hans Salter's horror stings), so by now I have gone through and used thousands of film soundtracks.

With this background, I've always believed that I could approach music in film in a unique way while still serving the purpose and emotion of the movie – but it's not been easy. I'm not a composer nor a musician (though I can read music and conduct, if forced to). It's just that people tend to hire who they're used to, coming from backgrounds they easily recognize. Combining mainstream and experimental worlds, as I've tried to make a living doing, can be confusing to some people; when I started out twenty years ago, many music producers ventured between these worlds, now there are few. Some years ago I was lucky enough to meet Allan Nicholls, who brought me to Altman; and I am grateful to Altman, who was intrigued enough to hire me.

Allan Nicholls has been associated with Robert Altman since *Nashville* in the mid-seventies; first as an actor/musician and later in many other capacities, including first assistant director and music composer. Previously, he'd had a pretty successful career as a singer/musician/composer and actor. I'd seen him as Claude in *Hair* at the Biltmore Theater in New York when I was fifteen. A few years ago, Allan was working as an assistant director and editor for the video tape segments of 'Saturday Night Live.' Often, on Friday nights before a show, I would visit the editing room to see if any music were needed (actually to eat the leftovers from the Carnegie Deli). Seeing Allan's name on a script book in the room, I announced that I knew of an actor named Allan Nicholls, who had been in *Hair* and *Nashville*. Allan, amused, admitted to being that same guy.

We got to know each other pretty well. On Saturday nights he'd drop by to watch my spazz act when I cue in the music on live TV. I'd hate to watch myself in the throes of these maneuvers. I flail my arms around and clutch my stomach – it's like watching a lunatic conductor have a standing epileptic fit – for if an actor fudges a line when I've got a cue, or one of our cartridge machines gets stuck, the mistake goes out to four million people. During these frantic moments. Allan would tell me that I should really meet Bob (Altman), as I'd be perfect to work on his films. I never obsessed on Allan's words; the reality of working on an Altman film was beyond my imagination.

I'd seen *M*A*S*H* when I was fourteen. I made my father take me. The camp that I was schlepped to that summer (Camp Sun Mountain in Pennsylvania's bee-a-you-tee-ful Shawnee-On-The-Delaware) was showing the film but would not let the boys under seventeen attend, yet the fifteen-year-old girls could go. What was that about? Did they think that we would suddenly discover sex, go raid and rape the girls' camp? What kind of horrible film was this? Even if we had been allowed to go, at the time I was on 'movie suspension' for saying 'schmuck' twice. I learned the word from my father, who used it constantly. So I got him to take me to *M*A*S*H* later that summer. He only liked the football game segment, but I couldn't get the film out of my mind for days. The images and situations were intense for me; it turned my head around.

I eventually saw almost all of Altman's 'mass release' films, yet I wasn't aware of them as 'Altman' movies as I was, say, of Fellini or Herzog films. There was always a 'vibe' surrounding his work that would beckon me to each film, though often not knowing beforehand who had directed it. If I, as a record producer, could achieve such a feat, I would feel that I'd reached a personal ideal. Over the years I saw Altman's other films in situations that I would always remember: *McCabe and Mrs Miller* at the TLA Cinema on South Street in Philadelphia; *Nashville* upon first moving to New York; I saw *Three Women* with singer/composer Steve Goodman (we got a bad case of the 'giggles' and were almost kicked out); I watched *The Wedding* in an East Side theater in New York where I was the only one there. Each film provoked a lasting impression, just as *M*A*S*H* had done – the strong situations replayed in my head for days.

Last night I witnessed something that I will also not forget; an outdoor production of *Threepenny Opera* in Greek. Instead of the Kurt Weill arrangement of 'Mac the Knife,' they jazzed it up à la Louis Armstrong's version which was enough to make me sick, and the actor that played Mr Peachum interpreted the role as Alan Hale's 'Skipper' doing Oliver Hardy. The neighbors in the surrounding apartments were all watching TV. We left at intermission. What a wonderful vacation!

At the end of the 91–92 season of 'Saturday Night Live,' Allan Nicholls called me from Altman's Sandcastle office in New York, summoning me to 'meet Bob.' Just the day before, Altman had returned from the Cannes Film Festival where he had won Best Director for *The Player*. He was all over the place that day: on every news-stand, in stray conversations, in *Time* magazine on my desk. I was asked to be in his office the next morning.

I entered a Park Avenue office and found myself being greeted by Cecilia (she runs the New York operations) who immediately yelled out, 'ALLAN! HAL IS HERE!' like a 'RAID' commercial. I went through a door and into a large room filled with neatly arranged books and videotapes. Altman sat behind a big desk in front of a couple of movie posters and a red neon number 5 with DIME written across it (obviously scenery from 'Come Back to the Five & Dime, Jimmy Dean, Jimmy Dean'). I was a bit nervous and scrambling for something to say, I blurted out that I loved *The Wedding* (true). This produced a moment of silence, out of which Altman then growled. '*The Wedding*, huh?', rolling his eyes to invisible witnesses as if to say, 'What a weirdo.'

He began to tell me about the movie that he was about to start filming. At the time, the film was titled *L.A. Shortcuts*. The screenplay was written by Altman and Frank Barhydt Jr, and was based on almost a dozen short stories by Raymond Carver. One of the stories (the only non-Carver tale) would feature Annie Ross and Lori Singer as mother and daughter, both musicians. Annie plays Tess Trainer, who sings with a jazz band nightly in a club called The Low Note; Lori, as Zoë Trainer, plays cello in a classical group. Altman felt that together these musicians could provide all the music in the film. Eventually, Zoë commits suicide while playing her cello. Altman felt that it is Tess's music that drives Zoë to suicide, though the audience need not know. I asked if that meant songs like 'Gloomy Sunday', to which Altman replied, 'Hmmmm . . . more like Gloomy Wednesday.'

I took the *Shortcuts* script home with me. It was fascinating how the stories interwove, while each carried a despairing emotion of its own. Every once in a while the script returned to the Low Note where Annie, as Tess, 'is singing the blues.' I kept some short notes on the different emotions that I was picking up from each story, trying naturally to feel the type of music to choose. The moods in the script perfectly fit my tastes – which Tom Waits once described as 'usually dark and unspeakable.' The scripted scenes where Lori Singer as Zoë is performing suggested many musical possibilities as well, and my notebooks were soon full of ideas.

While reading the script, it hit me: I would be working with Annie Ross, and I had been a fan for years. Annie has to have one of the most amazing histories of anyone in the music/acting field. From a stint with 'The Little Rascals' as a child to gigs in the circus as a singing trapeze artist, she launched into the jazz world as a member of the extremely important Lambert, Hendricks & Ross and continued with her own solo albums; from associations with people like Charlie Parker and Lenny Bruce to later acting jobs in films like *The Player*, *Superman III* and *Basketcase II*, she's lived quite a résumé.

The script allows The Low Note's band to be of questionable musicianship, playing songs that aren't necessarily good. Altman pointed this out at our first meeting, and some other people involved in the film felt that this was the case – but I didn't feel that this could or should be done with Annie Ross. If Rip Taylor were playing the role in drag, maybe bad material would be appropriate. But here was an opportunity to create something really wonderful. I thought it best to stay away from too many standards. Annie's sung almost every standard there is and it would be more interesting if everyone involved had to stretch a little bit – perhaps be uncomfortable with new musicians and material – but go for being really good. The train of thought led to a plan where 'non-jazz' composers would write jazz songs for Annie, backed by a band of 'non-jazz' players. This is not as weird as it seems. Many of our best pop and rock performers and writers have a great knowledge of jazz and vice versa; and I have found that putting good artists/musicians into new situations can bring the magic out. You often get a type of music that is impossible to pigeon-hole, where different musical roots collide, bringing new twists to the familiar.

Finding the music for Lori Singer's character had to be approached as from a different planet. Classical musicians differ from jazz and pop – and often insist on having musical pieces executed perfectly – so I thought, in general, Lori's material should come from pieces she already knew; and I would occasionally 'throw' a few selections at her to spice up the pot. Lori has been playing cello for most of her life and I was told that she had a large repertoire of material. Her scripted music scenes alternated between group performances and rehearsals, solo practicing scenes, and one solo performed during her suicide. The music for the suicide would be tricky: too dramatic, and it would come across predictable and pretentious; too sweet, and it would be Bugs Bunny ('ya got me Doc . . . I'm goin', I'm gonna kick the bucket . . .').

At no point in the script do mother and daughter speak about their music.

And yet, I remembered Altman's words that the music is their connection, defining their individuality and tying them tragically together, I felt that there had to be an invisible dialog between the blues and classical selections; and that this musical dialog had to carry the weight of their relationship.

I called Altman. He liked my ideas and told me to go ahead, meet with Lori and Annie; if they were in synch with me, we should get the ball rolling. During this conversation he let me know that Annie's band in the film should be all-white, as the club audience would be mostly black, a reversal on the Cotton Club films. The number of people who might pick up on this would be minimal at most, but I was knocked out by his thought process and the attention to this kind of detail, which I would witness over and again.

I met with Lori at Café Un Deux Trois on 44th St, which had been an unlucky place for me. Years ago I was up for a gig on an Irwin Winkler movie and during our meeting at this very restaurant, I ordered the steak tartare. When it arrived, Winkler turned colors. His eyes were glued to the stuff. He was so disgusted, we could never get a conversation going. Eventually I had the waiter take it away, but the damage was irrevocable . . . oh well. Lori's and my lunch went significantly better. Her mind runs at two thousand miles an hour and the amount of information that she gave me was enormous. She wrote out a list of her favorite pieces featuring cello, including Dvořák's Cello Concerto in B minor, Op 104, Tchaikovsky's 'Variations on a Rococo Theme,' Fauré's *Elegie* Op. 24, and Bloch's *Schelomo.*' My classical music knowledge is spotty – I know a lot about specific composers and pieces, but Lori's flood of ideas and composers sent me off to Colony Records to start a new phase in my education.

I met with Annie next. From her bright red hair to the way she holds herself, Annie Ross is beautiful, the richness of her career and life showing through. For a while in the 1950s she stayed at Charlie Parker's apartment near Tenth Street on Avenue B, coincidentally next door to where I live now. At our dinner, her youthful energy was contagious; as she talked about Altman, whom she's known for a very long time, I began to feel that we would have the necessary freedom to do what we felt was right within the strong framework set by Altman for Tess and Zoë in the film. I told Annie my music plans, which she guardedly, at first, agreed to. I felt confident that she would be able to make whatever material chosen her own, and have it work beautifully for her character as well. By the end of our meeting, my enthusiasm had rubbed off on her and I was relieved. But I felt I had to see Annie in action. I made plans that evening to attend a gig she was doing a month later at a jazz club in Toronto.

Annie performed in a large jazz club located a few blocks away from Massey Hall, where the 'Greatest Jazz Concert' featuring Max Roach, Charlie Parker, Bud Powell, and Charles Mingus was held. The club was thin and long, with the stage set up behind two glass doors near the entrance. They also served food; I have always been impressed by musicians who could play well with someone eating cannelloni in their face. I brought a DAT machine and taped four of Annie's performances. Her sets included much of her best known work from the Lambert, Hendricks and Ross days, like 'Twisted' and 'One O'Clock Jump.' She also did a number of standards, including 'Bye Bye Blackbird'. I really loved her interpretation – and some interesting 'finds' like the old Depression-era composition 'One Meatball.' Annie was in fine form and commanded a great stage presence. Her voice, lower and rougher than the last time I heard her, was still strong. During the shows, four songs hit me as ones that fit Tess's character. The first was a song from the thirties called 'Marijuana,' once covered by Bette Midler. A little known parody of 'The Girl From Ipanema' written by Steven Sondheim for an obscure sixties off-Broadway show called *The Mad Show* was another. I surprised Annie with my knowledge of *The Mad Show*, which was based on MAD Magazine (the original cast included Jo Anne Worley, Dick Libertini, and Linda Lavin). Two more songs, old standards, from her sets were wonderful: a medley of 'A Nightingale Sang In Berkeley Square'/'A Foggy Day in London Town' and a version of 'Can't Get Started With You' brought a rousing ovation from the audience.

When I got back to New York, I made a tape starting with the Toronto songs, plus Lambert, Hendricks and Ross highlights, as well as some more recent recorded material; also included were her Zoot Sims and Gerry Mulligan collaborations from three classic albums made for World Pacific Jazz records in the fifties, as well as a collaboration with King Pleasure. I sent the 'Annie Ross Present and Past' tape with a rundown of the script to various songwriters I'd previously worked with and who would understand the project. They included Elvis Costello, Donald Fagen, Gavin Friday, and Tom Waits (who was later cast in the film).

My ideas kept getting larger, and in order properly to finance them, a good soundtrack deal with an enthusiastic record label was necessary. A friend of mine, Kate Hyman, had been recently hired to run the east coast Artist and Repertoire department at Imago Records, and immediately wanted to be involved. Imago Records, started by Terry Ellis, was opening a soundtrack division; after hearing about this project, there was no hesitation. They were proud to have a Robert Altman soundtrack be their first film album. Dealing with Imago was direct and no bullshit. Other labels we talked to had to check with eighteen thousand people and if one got nervous, it became a problem. Imago made this usually tedious process painless.

Shooting was about to start, so I went out to Santa Monica early to set myself up in a situation that allowed me to concentrate without too many distractions, and to get the personnel for the two groups organized. On the day I arrived, a marital fight scene featuring Tom Waits and Lily Tomlin was being shot in a trailer-park in the afternoon. It was the first time I'd been in a trailer-park and it took me a while to find the actual filming spot. The park was filled with old folk puttering about in the sunshine. I followed the distant sound of what could only be Tom Waits yelling, and through the aluminum-sided maze, came upon a few people with walkie-talkies. I found Altman behind a monitor in the rear of the trailer where the scene was being shot. When he saw me, he jumped up, grabbed Waits and announced, 'Okay, you guys, start composing.' Around the set, Executive Producer Scott Bushnell was keeping an eye on everything, looking for possible delays. Allan Nicholls, back as First Assistant Director, was busy keeping the crew alive and moving.

Waits and Tomlin as Earl and Dorren Pichot were tremendous. They had just met, but the chemistry was as if they had been working together for years. I felt Altman's genius for casting at work here, creating situations where the actors had a lot of freedom, yet it was unquestionably his world. It was inspiring to witness a film director with an approach to film that's similar to what I strive for in records. Luckily, I got to see this often over the next few months. Another memorable moment was watching Peter Gallagher as 'Stormy' Weathers destroy a house with a chain-saw. It reminded me of the Laurel and Hardy movie where, after demolishing James Finnlayson's house, it was discovered that they screwed up the address and wasted the wrong house. I rather enjoyed, in a childish way, Altman and Peter discussing the order in which to destroy everything in one take.

A side note on destruction: having read Bertrand Tavernier's diary in *Projections II,* I can't get his friend Milo's 'cure' for his friend's brother's drug-dealing out of my head. I quote: 'He dragged him to a car park, bought everything he had and shot up in front of him. Potentially fatal. To put him off. I did it a few times. I wanted him to see what it did to me. He's stopped dealing now.' WHAT?? WHAT??

Throughout that whole first day in the trailer-park, watching, wandering about, meeting everyone, I felt a real sense of family which energized me. I learned that many on the crew had been working off and on with Altman for as long as twenty years. Sad as it seems, this was one of the first projects I've worked on where most personnel weren't walking around bad-mouthing the top guy behind his or her back. The environment that Altman creates brings out everyone's desire freely to give their best. I wanted to do a good job for this guy, for these people.

Each day I would spend a few hours in the production office researching, assigning, snooping for material and trying out different combinations of musicians that would be right for the film. In the late afternoon, I would visit the set where filming was taking place.

Lori came out to Santa Monica early, and we fortunately got to spend a lot of time together, talking about the music she would do in the film. Lori is a hard worker and puts concentration and passion into everything she's involved with, whether it's her family or her acting, playing cello or sports. For a person like myself, who has a hard time putting his pants on in the morning, I knew it would be hard to keep up with her, yet together we came up with some solid ideas for the music to be performed. It was crucial that the music should come naturally from her, so time and preparation were needed. We spent many hours listening to material, and decided to do something a bit different here and adapt compositions usually played by large orchestras for her group, a quintet. The character of Zoë had to have a beautiful, eerie presence and adapting the music in that way would make it slightly strange, but not too much so. Usually shoeless, over-sized socks dangling on the ground, when Lori plays the cello she pulls you into the same hypnotic place she seems to be. Altman told me a number of times how he loves to watch her play, and she would often stop by the production office to play for whoever was there.

By this time, I was ready to make a tape for Annie with all the potential material. Two songs were submitted by Elvis Costello: 'Punishing Kiss,' written with Cait O'Riordan specifically for the film, dealt with a woman watching soap operas; and 'Upon a Veil of Midnight Blue,' a song Elvis had written for Charles Brown, whose version turned out a bit funny. A song that I knew by Bono and the Edge called 'Conversation on a Barstool' came to mind. They wrote it for Marianne Faithfull, and though Marianne has occasionally sung it live, it had never been recorded. I thought that it would be great as the main performance piece; the lyrics fit Tess perfectly (I'm tired, so tired/I can hardly stand/I can't breathe in the air in this city tonight'). There were two Gavin Friday contributions, 'The Last Song I'll Ever Sing' and 'A Thousand Years.' Some beautiful songs by Brian Cullman, Mary Margaret O'Hara, Maria McKee/Bruce Broady, and Joe Henry (a composition called 'Ben Turpin in the Army') were sent in. Kate Hyman from Imago gave us an unissued song sung by Marilyn Monroe called 'How Wrong Can it Be?' I also included some obscure songs from Annie's past.

Following a whim, the film got a gift from a close, departed friend. I am speaking of the late Doc Pomus. Up to this time, the assorted songs submitted were wonderful, but seemed to circle around the main body without a unifying force. A tape of Doc's work arrived, providing the necessary cohesion, 'gluing' the pieces together to form what was now becoming a striking musical sculpture. I was lucky to have been a friend of Doc for fifteen years. Besides being one of the greatest lyricists of all time ('Lonely Avenue,' 'Save the Last Dance For Me,' 'Little Sister,' and hundreds more), he was one of the most caring, open, generous, and spiritual people to be put on this earth. One of his closest collaborators during the last decade of this life was Mac Rebennack (Dr John). At my request, Will Braton and Sharon Felder, who take care of Doc's catalogue, sent a tape of a dozen Pomus/Rebennack compositions. Most of the tape had Mac playing the songs in Doc's 72nd Street apartment on the 'old faithful' Wurlitzer electric piano. Mac hated that piano but continued to use it for these demos, supervised by Doc. Mac complained regularly about that 'pain in the ass' keyboard; Doc later willed it to him.

Lyrically and musically, the feeling of the script was in every song. Lori and I drove out to Altman's home and I casually put the tape on. We sat on the floor, next to the stereo. As Mac sang 'To Hell With Love' ('I've been in love so bad, I thought that I would die; I could have built a waterbed with all the tears I've cried') and 'Prisoner of Life' ('If you're looking for a rainbow, you know there's gonna be some rain'), Altman started laughing, flipping through the lyric sheet. We both knew what we had our hands on and were equally knocked-out. He remarked that we could get all the music we needed from this tape alone. The direct, earthy lyrics in the blues medium were exactly what Altman had been looking for in the script. From this tape, we chose six songs.

Feeling great, Lori and I headed back. After taking turns at the wheel on the way there, Lori insisted on driving home. She had injured her leg playing basketball and so drove with one leg up and out the side window, which isn't exactly legal, especially when passing a cop. But she gave one top-rate performance to an admiring LAPD critic, and we were on our way again, Lori continuing to drive.

Though Altman gave us a go-ahead to pick whatever songs we wanted, I kept giving him tapes of where we were at. Altman's sense of music and lyrics is right on the money, and his direct impressions were really important. Between his and Annie's first reactions to the tape, the song list was narrowed down to thirteen. There were two songs that I was very disappointed Annie didn't respond to favorably (Elvis' 'Upon a Veil of Midnight Blue' and Mary Margaret O'Hara's 'Keeping You in Mind'), but Annie knows her instrument and it was important that she be able to relate to a song, or it would seem false later.

At this point, Sue Jacobs, my partner in Deep Creek Productions and reality check, came in from New York to put this together with me. Sue and I have been working together since the 'Stay Awake (Disney)' album in 1988, and she is indispensable at bringing these projects to life while keeping me on budget. She also understands my process and can deal with the curveballs. With her arrival, it was time to create the bands.

For Annie's band, I based the sound on the recording that Miles Davis made with Thelonious Monk and Milt Jackson, substituting trombone for trumpet. Terry Adams the genius/wild man of NRBQ filled the Monk role, and luckily, all my first choices for the rest of the band were available. Greg Cohen, who has been my favourite bass player of late (and an amazing arranger), composer/drummer Bobby Previte, and trombonist/orchestrator Bruce Fowler were hired. They sounded like an expert jazz band who'd escaped from 'King of Hearts.' Together on screen, they looked like the Bowery Boys grown up.

Bruce took on the additional role of arranging for Lori's quintet, and played a major role in putting the quintet together. Bruce brought pictures of available string players that he thought would be right for the job, most of whom are active in playing music movie dates. For a few nights in a row we placed the photos in different arrangements to get a good idea of how they would look. The pictures were spread out all over the table: new combinations were tried, shuffled, discarded and pondered over like a casino game. I'd never picked musicians like this before. Altman walked in the room, looked at the spread, turned to Lori and said, 'How do you like your band?' Along with Armen Guzelimian on piano, whom Lori had once played with on the Merv Griffin show, we had our quintet: Stuart Kanin (violin), Anatoly Rosinsy (violin), and Roland Kato (viola).

Over the next few weeks, Annie rehearsed the material with pianists Bill Ginn and Richard Ruttenberg, and skeleton arrangements were worked out. The band arrived on Labor Day. With the shoot only eight days away, there was a good deal of pressure on the group to learn a lot of material quickly. At a production meeting, half-joking to Altman, I suggested that we might as well have a gig, as we had a band. He pointed towards the set of the Low Note and said, 'Well, we have a club.'

The Low Note opened that Friday. Jim McLindon, Bob's assistant, sent out invitations. The bar was stocked, food was catered in, along with Jay from Chez Jay's (the local hangout for the crew) and a few waiters. Stephen Altman had designed the Low Note club, which was the only sound-stage built for the film. It looked and had the feel of an LA fifties-era jazz club. I loved watching its construction, from the model set to the aging of the fake brick on the walls. Altman felt that the performance would officially 'break in' the club. The turnout for 'the opening' was good, with mostly the movie personnel and friends. From the cast I remember Buck Henry and Jennifer Jason Leigh and perhaps Fred Ward being there. I put on a Bill Evans CD for background beforehand.

A few members of the band arrived late from dinner. Perhaps they hadn't understood what was happening, or maybe they were cranky after days of overwork. That night was the closest Annie and I ever got to having a real conflict, when she objected to everyone having to be in costume. I understood the pressure that she was under; with limited rehearsal, she had to perform in front of a pretty heavy audience. The band had barely played through the songs by that evening and Annie hadn't yet memorized all the words, but all in all they did great. It WAS a night-club for one night. The combination of Annie, the band and the material all mixed beautifully and was everything I'd hoped for. Of course, I wouldn't let myself enjoy any of it and spent the show in a self-destructive mode, pacing outside the set in the dark, cringing at every mistake.

At the same time that the Low Note performance was going on, Lori was rehearsing her group, the Trout Quartet (named after Schubert's Quintet for Piano & Strings in A Major, D 667, 'The Trout') across the way, concentrating on the two pieces that they would perform together in the film, Victor Herbert's Cello Concerto No 2 and Dvořák's Concerto in B minor. Both pieces were picked from Lori's list, and the Victor Herbert was an important discovery for me. I had known his more popular work, but was not aware of the piece, nor that he was a cello player himself. During our research, we discovered a bizarre recording of Herbert playing his own 'Petite Valse' in 1912. The Trout Quartet's music rose up and out to the hallways for the Low Note audience as they came and went.

For the film, we planned for Annie's segments to be recorded live, without lip-synching. It happened that the sound on the Low Note set was really good. I brought in Eric Lilistrand from New York to record everything. He's a sound designer at Lincoln Center and the Brooklyn Academy of Music as well as having recorded Diamanda Galás and Laurie Anderson. Eric and Sue hired the Le Mobile Remote Recording truck, which is a first-rate recording facility. After much discussion with John (the man in charge of sound), it was decided that, for safety reasons, we would pre-record all thirteen songs ahead of time, requiring the building of an isolation booth for Annie to sing in on the set. The pre-records were done in the next few days and the natural sound on the Low Note set sounded just right on tape.

With Lori, live recording was not possible. The external noise at the concert hall where they were to be filmed was too much. We were prepared to record live during filming, but it was almost certain that the quintet would have to play to a pre-recorded track. So the Dvořák and Herbert pieces were recorded at Devonshire Studios one afternoon.

All through this period, both Annie and Lori were also working on their acting parts in the film. In scenes with Tess and Zoë together, solo cello was often needed. At times, the sound of the cello mixed in with the conversation as almost a third voice, an eerie, beautiful voice. While working with Lori on finding the cues, Steven M. Martin, who is working on a documentary about Leon Theremin and the story of his invention, the Theremin (the first electronic instrument), gave me a copy of Theremin virtuoso Clara Rockmore's album. This featured an amazing version of Stravinsky's 'Berceuse' from *The Firebird* and Tchaikovsky's 'Serenade Melancolique.' They were among the most haunting and beautiful recordings that I have ever heard. Lori learned both selections. Along with Bloch's *Schelomo*, the second movement of the Herbert Cello Concerto No 2, and Bach's Cello Suite No 5, we finally felt prepared.

When a cello scene was scheduled for filming, Lori and I would sit with Altman while she played the choices. One night this meeting took place on a front lawn, with us hanging out on the ground while the crew near us was busy setting up a shot. The crew moved slowly, naturally picking up on the rhythms of the music. So, at cinematographer Walt Lloyd's request, Lori continued to play a bit of Dvořák's 'American' Quartet to accompany the speed of the camera panning down the street. It was a big street, and Altman remarked that at that moment he felt like John Ford.

All the solo pieces Lori prepared were used, except the Tchaikovsky. In one scene, Lori played Stravinsky's 'Berceuse' as Annie told the story of Chick Trainer's overdose. The scene played at dawn, with Annie as Tess drifting off to sleep. Later, during the much thought-about suicide scene, the second movement of Victor Herbert's Cello Concerto No 2 was played as automobile exhaust fumes filled the room. I stood near Altman through both these scenes, as he directed Walt Lloyd's camera to explore each room to the timing of the cello. Lori, who has a classical musician's need for perfection, worked incredibly hard on learning these new pieces. Having not had time to memorize the Herbert concerto, she cleverly found a place to hide the sheet music. It could be a treasure hunt for viewers to find it on screen, a contest for people reading this article: find the music . . . write me . . . and I'll send you an ear of corn.

The filming of both the Low Note and classical concert scenes went as well as could be. Scott Bushnell and Sue Jacobs worked really well together co-ordinating these complicated shoots. Fake smoke was pumped into the Low Note club which made working difficult for many, and caused Gene Estes to faint once. Ten songs were filmed in three days. The club would fill up with extras right before shooting and simply come alive. By this time, the songs had really come together; and combined with Stephen Altman's set, Lloyd's photography, and Altman's orchestration of actors and crew, the dailies blew everybody away. Annie and the band really held up through the whole thing, which was not easy at all.

All musicians had to be on the set by 7.30 a.m. each day. This was definitely not usual rising time for almost all concerned, but I cannot recall one complaint from anyone (not true). As each song was filmed (two cameras were used during these scenes, as opposed to the usual one, so more could be captured from the band), I stood next to Altman listening intensely, for at this point I knew a lot more than just the band's performance would be considered when deciding what take to use. During the scene, which was supposed to be at three or four a.m., the club was almost empty. In the middle of the song, 'I Don't Know You,' Terry Adams let loose with a wild Sun Ra-esque solo from Saturn. Everyone present was just left speechless.

The classical Trout Quintet scenes were filmed in two days. One day was used to shoot the main concert which, appearing at the top of the film, is where two talkative couples meet, eyeing Alex Trebec enjoying the music from the rear. The other day was set aside to film the group's rehearsals where Lori's character, Zoë, is edging towards suicide. In the wardrobe trailer that day,

13 *Short Cuts*: Annie Ross in performance

14 *Short Cuts*: Hal Willner and Robert Altman on the Low Note set

15 *Short Cuts:* Robert Altman directs the Trout Quartet

16 *Short Cuts*: The suicide (Lori Singer)

costume designer John Hay was fitting Lyle Lovett with his character's costume, a baker's uniform, while the quintet musicians were climbing into their tuxes. In one scene, Zoë breaks down, unable to play; the musicians had to become actors, and improvise concern. For music we chose the same piece that she would eventually play perfectly during her suicide scene. In between takes, Lori would go to a room behind the filming spot with a book which I believe she used to trigger the necessary emotions. I got to hold the book during takes. I slipped it in my pocket and felt a bit strange – something private about seeing what it was and so I didn't look (also not true). Unfortunately, this scene was dropped from the film.

With the on-screen music completed, I returned to New York for the next 'Saturday Night Live' season after recording one last session with Annie and the band. We spent our time here recording a handful of songs submitted too late to be considered for the filming. I thought that Altman could use the music for transitions source music to come from radios/TVs, or perhaps a closing theme. The excitement of being in the middle of a movie had passed and everyone was tired and irritable. It took an hour just to get started; someone was always missing, hiding in the bathroom or maybe under a car. Six complete tracks were managed that day, including a composition by the great jazz composer Horace Silver. I wanted to record more but when it seemed like lynching time was here, I called an end to the session. I would later kick myself for not pushing on. Every song except one was used.

The editing process took place in New York. Altman had two floors set up on West 17th St. The tenth floor held the editing equipment, kitchen, and offices for Altman and Scott Bushnell. A really nice screening room, big enough to accommodate about seventy-five people, was on the ninth floor. Photographs and movie posters used in the Low Note and the studio scenes from 'The Player' were hung up all over. Geraldine Peroni, who had edited 'The Player', was again on board to edit this film. Geraldine, who was present throughout the filming in Los Angeles, and I often had conversations about the music which were helpful.

Atlman informed me that there would have to be more music than originally thought. I arranged to have a small home studio with a few hundred background music records from my personal collection set up there; it was going to be a long process. This film was like a jigsaw puzzle; there were thousands of ways that it could be cut together. Almost each week, a screening was held of a rough cut for a small audience. Altman and Geraldine sat in the back and watched the guests' reactions in order to gauge the pacing and its effect.

Finding the incidental music was laborious. For one, the dialogue was fuller than most films. Also, I didn't feel that conventional scoring would be suitable. For a few days I sat at a tape machine running every type of music with the film. Nothing was working except some contrasting muzak like 'Ain't We Got Fun' against Tim Robbins as a cop on his motorcycle and various domestic arguments. Unfortunately, the contrast attracted too much attention to the music, and it was back to the drawing-board again.

Out of frustration, I put on a tape of the Low Note band's backing tracks of 'To Hell with Love' (minus Annie's vocals) against the first part of the film. To my surprise, the music matched the rhythm of the characters, and without vocals, the dialogue had room to come through. I couldn't believe it was working. I ran the track three times through to see if I was crazy. I was crazy, but it still worked. I got Altman and showed it to him. He felt that it worked too and in fact, had been thinking about using these tracks earlier.

Over the next few months, almost all of the backing tracks were used to underscore scenes. One night, I hired Greg Cohen, Steve Bernstein, and David Tronzo to record various versions of the songs to give Altman some different instrumentations to play with.

The screenings continued and I attended all I could. The audiences themselves were amazing. I saw people from Harry Belafonte, Adolph Green, Penn and Teller, and Lee Remick, to Robert Benton, and Jonathan Demme at these screenings. Lauren Bacall came to one screening, which threw me back to an evening in the late seventies at the opening party for *Evita*. I was somehow at this event, at the old discotheque Xenon. Back then, I had thick curly hair with a big beard, and looked a great deal like Mandy Patinkin who played Che Guevara in the play. Bacall was there with David Frost and thought I was Patinkin. Having had a few drinks and in the mood, I played along with them for about ten minutes, never admitting that I wasn't him, to amuse the friend I was with. About an hour later I was on the dance floor and looked up to see Bacall glaring at me. Obviously she met Che. She came over to me yelling, and I nervously started laughing. She actually slugged me, and I went reeling backwards.

Back on 17th Street, there was one wonderful evening when Elvis Costello and Cait O'Riordan came to town for Elvis' Town Hall appearance with the Brodsky String Quartet. Altman enthusiastically offered to show them the dailies of Annie performing 'Punishing Kiss.' This was exciting, as they were the first songwriters to see their composition on screen. I had previously played them a tape of the performance in Ireland at Christmas, sitting outside a party in a freezing car; they had been ecstatic about Annie's interpretation. Altman gave them the royal treatment. He set up the viewing in the screening room and engaged in a long conversation with Elvis about film music. He talked about 'McCabe and Mrs Miller', about having heard Leonard Cohen's first album during the editing and discovering that, with that album's songs, he'd found the whole soundtrack. Elvis and Cait watched a take of 'Punishing Kiss' and went away very happy. They said that Annie looked like they imagined she would.

Being involved with music in a film is difficult. You must be emotionally involved or how good can it be? Yet personal involvement has to be kept at a distance during the editing process, or chances for serious heartbreak are large. As the editing on *Short Cuts* continued, I witnessed the featured songs get chopped up. I understood that this was necessary to keep the various stories flowing, but whenever an odd music edit appeared, I would hear it and squirm. I'm sure that I occasionally whined, but tried to keep perspective; I was aware that the music was going over really well with the screening audiences, and this was encouraging. Nevertheless, it was still very hard for me. When I see a movie, the music is magnified in its importance. I'm drawn to it over dialogue, which is why I need to see movies I like over and over again. On first viewing, I look at a film like a painting and let my mind wander, soaking in the overall emotion. And often, for me, the film IS the music. In that way, *Psycho* IS the Bernard Herrmann music, *La Dolce Vita* IS the Nino Rota theme, etc. If a film has bad or inappropriate music or sound effects, I can't watch it; it ruins the film so much so that I actually don't go to films scored by composers or producers whose work I can't stand.

As the picture came close to being locked, our backing tracks were probably used for over half of the scoring. At some West Coast screenings there was a consensus that some other music would be needed, and Mark Isham was hired to score about a half-hour of the film. At first I was hurt; I'd mentally completed the music with my cast of outsiders, but hadn't yet recorded this material before the film went to LA. As Altman and I were still progressing with the original music and its variations, we had not yet discussed the last part of the film score. I presumed that decisions about any additional material would be made later. But all that aside, the end result of a project is the most important thing, and it was probably felt that another voice was needed. Sitting with Isham and Altman at the editing deck, figuring out where new scoring would be added, Isham told me that he does around seven films a year, usually composing on electronic equipment and replacing some of it with real instruments, including his own excellent trumpet-playing. I have heard a number of these scores and enjoyed quite a few. His taste is a bit different than mine, and this difference allowed for an interesting contrast to fill out the music in the film.

Bono and The Edge, Lenny Pickett, Terry Adams, Horace Silver, Dr John, Annie Ross, Michael Stipe, Victor Herbert, Iggy Pup, Elvis Costello and Cait O'Riordan, Lori Singer, Bobby Previte, Igor Stravinsky, Jon Hendricks, Mark Isham, Antonín Dvořák, Peggy Lee, Doc Pomus, Duke Ellington; on film or soundtrack album, these people directly contributed to the music in *Short Cuts*. If death were non-existent, we could have them all in a supermarket scene; Peggy Lee talking film and vegetables with Victor Herbert, Iggy and Ellington out buying eggs. At the beginning of this article, I could barely recall first sitting down at the dailies. Now, I can't seem to focus on any one event alone:

Michael Stipe's (from R.E.M.) and Iggy Pop's dueting with Annie for the album, lunches with the crew, Geraldine's inspired editing, my messy hotel room, Annie's Dietrich impression on 'Imitation of a Kiss', the great Horace Silver sending in material, recognizing Bruce Davidson (Howard Finnigan in *Short Cuts*) as 'Willard,' Altman at the helm . . .

My vacation has come and gone. Greece . . . a lovely place that I will not return to. I'm now back in my NY apartment, listening to the final edit of the soundtrack album, the collaborative result of artists with divergent musical roots. It flows much like the albums that turned my head in the late sixties and early seventies, where within a forty-minute span, every type of music could exist, some including sound effects and 'noise,' all with theatrical drive.

I wonder how much could be done with other collaborative efforts in film music. Imagine Chuck D. working with Ornette Coleman, Todd Rundgren writing for the strings; all watched over by a 'curator' steering the production, keeping an eye on the director's vision, but leaving the artists free to perfect their part without worrying about whether the track will play on MTV. Why does modern film music sound so much the same? Why must the industry rely on formula? While working on *Short Cuts*, I felt the potential greatness available to anyone willing to explore. There are so many great composers/ musicians out there. I'd love to see them matched in an interesting way. I know that, if given the chance, we could hear them take film music to a new, brilliant plateau.

I'll be seeing you.
Hal Willner

6

My Stunning Future:
           The Luxuries of Pixelvision
           Michael Almereyda

This is a testimonial for a technically defunct medium, an endorsement for a product you can't buy, and incidental proof that sometimes you can only be taken seriously when you choose to act like a child.

I'm talking about the Fisher-Price PXL 2000, a plastic video camera manufactured in 1987, marketed as a kid's toy, and discontinued three years later. Folklore has it that images produced by this camera – black-and-white, framed by a boxy internal border – are composed of a grid of two thousand square 'pixels'. This accounts for the camera's tacky, sci-fi name. The pixels shift and shimmer and seem to shed light as you watch, endowing everything the camera records with a distinct physicality, a lush trembling texture, a feel of floating weight and depth. In other words, the pixel image is alive – completely unlike the flat, cold quality of ordinary video.

In its customary use, the pixel camera records picture and sound on a standard *audio* cassette. You get about five minutes of imagery on one ninety-minute tape. Flip the cassette and you can record on the other side. This is swell, but the tape is crude and unstable and you have to contend with the cassette's considerable whirring noise which, intercepted by the camera's built-in mike, can resemble one of those machines used for polishing rocks.

Side-stepping the camera's clumsier habits, I made an hour-long pixelvision film. This involved a series of simple but apparently unprecedented technical adjustments,* but it hardly qualifies me as an expert. My introduction to the medium came through Sadie Benning, the one accredited pixelvision whiz-kid, fifteen when her father (James Benning, a terrific, under-rated film maker) gave her the camera for Christmas. Late in 1991 (three Christmases later) a friend showed me about forty minutes' worth of Sadie's work up to that time.

These justly famous tapes are basically video diaries, raw, urgent and funny. The camera (occasionally whirring demoniacally) crawls over tabloid headlines or a TV screen, or ribbons of Sadie's sharp, block-lettered writing accompanied by bursts of deftly chosen music. The main spectacle is Sadie's

---

* We channeled the pixelvision output onto a Beta SP deck; offlined on ¾" tape, then onlined the Beta to a one-inch master; transferred that to 16mm film.

17 Michael Almereyda (photo by A. Greg Henry)

tow-headed face, intently outstaring the camera while her dry, low voice says stuff like: 'My arm is made of ham.'

She also says: 'I've been waiting for the day to come when I could walk down the streets and people would look at me and say, "That's a dyke!" And if they didn't like it, they would fall into the center of the earth and deal with themselves.'

I remember thinking of Linda Manz, wistful and tough in *Days of Heaven*. And of the megawatt space embryo in *2001*. Sadie Benning seemed as vulnerable and all-knowing and, under the scrutiny of this particular camera, she seemed to radiate light. But mainly I didn't think of other movies because Sadie Benning was addressing the world on her own terms, and those terms – the honesty and grit and intimacy of her voice – seemed inseparable from the effects achieved through this strange cheap camera.

I mean, there's no mistaking Sadie's out-of-the-gate brilliance, but I also got the impression that anything shot in pixelvision might be riveting, even though (or because) the image appears in danger of disintegrating as you watch. Or rather, it *is* disintegrating, and continuously reconstituting itself, each picture sifted through a fine but distinctly perceptible sieve of white/gray/black pixels. It's as if the camera is prospecting for light. You have the sense that you're watching something intensely fragile and secret, on the threshold of visibility. You think of all sorts of images from lost or low-grade mediums: black-and-white polaroids, third-generation photocopies, pulpy newspaper photos. Given a dose of art history, you might also think of Degas monotypes and Seurat drawings and coarsely beautiful photographs made by Bill Brandt and Robert Frank. If you happen to love movies, you can't help thinking of silent films, the Lumière brothers, incunabular nitrate. For that matter, you think of dreams, cave paintings in candle light, the Shroud of Turin, breath on glass.

I was smitten, raving like this to a friend on the street, when a young woman, hovering near, pulled a pixel camera out of her purse. She said Fisher-Price was selling them, used and repaired, for $45 apiece, and she provided an 800 number linked to operators in Ohio.

'Fisher-Price is a division of the Quaker-Oats Company.' This information is embossed on the flank of the camera, which is made of dull, dark gray plastic, lightweight, not much bigger than a book or a video cassette. On the door to the tape compartment a white tab reads: 'Press *firmly* here to close door.' There are four easy-to-figure buttons: record, play, rewind, and stop/eject. You plug the camera into a wall outlet or power it through six double-A batteries stashed in the clunky wrap-around handle. A separate, spaghetti-thin cord links it your TV or VCR, allowing you to see exact frames as you shoot.

My pixel cameras – I ordered four; three actually worked – arrived in a single box, nestled among styrofoam peanuts, coiled power cords, xeroxed instruction booklets. Director of photography Jim Denault, dissecting one camera to see how it worked, discovered that there's no lens to speak of, just a plastic disk shielding a 'photo receptor' attached to a small circuit board. 'The business end of the camera,' Jim explained, 'is no bigger than the button on your shirt.'

I shot whatever was at hand, every day for the next few weeks. Clouds out the window, pictures in books, anyone who strayed into my apartment. You can kill a lot of time in this way.

I should give this some context by confessing that in the spring of 1988 I had directed a feature film called *Twister*. It was my first feature, brought in on budget ($3 million) and on time, but it was hardly a happy experience. Arguments between me and the producer, a former friend, escalated through-out post-production. By the time editing was completed, the film seemed tainted; I was furious and heartsick and couldn't bear to look at it. But the film, of course, had a life of its own – a decidedly peculiar life, as time rolled on. Vestron, the company that financed the picture, declared bankruptcy before releasing it, and all prints (only three were struck, I later learned) were pre-emptively withdrawn from circulation. But there had been two press screenings, and *Rolling Stone* magazine printed a premature review in which Peter Travers, the appointed critic, breezily summarized the film's plot before concluding on a feverish, upbeat note: 'Almereyda's debut augurs a stunning future . . . *Twister* emerges as outrageous, original entertainment.'

On a good day I might read such stuff with perfect scorn, but the whole year had been bleak and I found myself clinging to each word like wreckage in a storm. Other approving reviews trickled in – notably from the *New York Times*, *Village Voice*, *LA Times* – but these arrived about nine months later, because Vestron sold *Twister* to video before allowing an intrepid independent dis-tributor to book the film in art houses, where it reliably generated business as an off-beat oddity, a cursed cult film.

Needless to say, such a film and such a history did not impress anyone in Hollywood. My stunning future! While awaiting its arrival I proceeded to write one or two new scripts per year, attaching actors, drawing up budgets – and getting routinely dangled, rejected and refused by every imaginable source of film financing.

So by Christmas of 1991, watching Sadie's vividly brave and simple tapes, I was primed for a change. By mid-January I had written a script, about forty pages, specifically for the pixel camera. The story of two messed-up young men and their involvement with perhaps too many young women. The action was confined to two apartments, a stairwell, a roof. You wouldn't be overly literal-minded to call it a home movie. It's possible that an element of giddy desperation, specific to downtown New York and to my life at the time, found its way into the story. My downstairs neighbor Nic Ratner consented to play a version of himself, heroically supplying his apartment, his music collection and the better part of his own dialogue ('Michael,' he will tell you, 'has the humanity of a tape recorder'). Otherwise, professional actors were recruited. (In this I was aided by the unerring eye of Billy Hopkins, who took time out from casting the latest Oliver Stone movie.) I also enlisted a few obliging friends and a fourteen-year-old Indian elephant named Daisy. Everyone (except the elephant) worked without pay.

The actors, confronted with what one of them called a 'pixie camera', were all exceptional and selfless and the merest thanks I can offer is to name and commend them here in one quick gush: Isabel Gillies, Bob Gosse, Elina Löwensohn, Paula Malcomson, Liza Pariseau, Tom Roma, Maggie Rush, Barry Sherman, Mary Ward.

Tom Roma (a great photographer) also crafted aluminum brackets that allowed us to mount the camera on a tripod and dolly. There was a minimal lighting package (the guy at the rental house actually laughed when he took the order) and a crew of five. Everything was storyboarded and scripted, but I like to think we went at it with a kind of inspired amateurism, the same spirit you'd apply to something made with poster paint, pipe cleaners, glitter and glue.

The pixel camera practically forces you to be reckless and original. If you're shooting something at a distance, with a crowded background, detail goes out of the window; you might as well be using a bank camera. So it's necessary to compose shots with an eye towards compressed space, to stage action with an awareness of how silhouettes register and relate to one another, and to favor close-ups, which the camera delivers with startling detail. (The crude little photo receptor homes in on the exact grain of any surface, a face, an eye down to individual lashes, reflected glints in the pupil.)

Correspondingly, since everything the camera takes in is slightly, shimmeringly out of focus, near and far objects seem to share the same focal plane; you have an illusion of infinite focus and you can stage moving shots that'd give a camera assistant (focus puller) a nervous breakdown. Add to this the fact that the camera records with a slight delay, an internalized step-printing effect, which heightens even the most casual movement or look.

All of which makes pixelvision inherently ghostly and graphic and fun to watch, but also qualifies it as a medium particularly sensitive to actors and to their essential business: the transmission of moments of true feeling.

We shot for one week. Two newly written bar scenes, inserts and roof-top scenes were picked up over another weekend. There was an effort to create the moment-to-moment impression that the story was being cooked up from scratch, life caught with a hidden camera, a notebook in which things are pasted in, scribbled over, ripped out. But nearly all the jump cuts and discontinuous sound cues were specified in the script, and editor David Leonard and I, holed up at Gloria's Place in a back room full of video monitors, worked hard to keep the rhythm rough, open and alive.

(As a stranger to video editing, I took a while to get used to the Mission Control aspect of monitors and buttons and unaccountable electronic mayhem. Occasionally David would make an edit, hit playback and be rewarded with a blizzard of red, gray and green squiggles streaking through the image like a new kind of language. We are routinely thrilled, however, when we moved to the Calaway room to conjure up slow-motion shots, reversals, dissolves.)

The resulting film, *Another Girl Another Planet*, with its conspicuously odd look and sub-feature length, has found a life at festivals, where I'm always asked how we fit an elephant into the apartment. It's the first thing that comes up. Over time, the answers vary. I once insisted, 'That wasn't an elephant. That was a guy in an elephant *suit*.' Jim Denault, eschewing difficult technical talk, provided the best explication to a woman writing an article for *American Cinematographer*. 'It was challenging to shoot the elephant,' Jim said, 'because the elephant was very big, and the camera is very small.' This article, for some reason, has yet to appear.

But reviewers have been more than generous, their enthusiasm matched, it seems, by an underlying amazement that anyone would be foolhardy enough to make a movie with a $45 toy. All the same, the most flattering adjectives thrown at the film – 'haunting', 'romantic', 'dreamlike', 'hypnotic' – are simply direct descriptions of the innate properties of the pixel image. I have two new pixel shorts in the works, and a script for a future feature-length project, part 35mm, part pixel: a contemporary version of stories by Edgar Allan Poe, set in Poe's native Richmond, Virginia. Pixelvision, after all, seems to me the perfect medium for a world in which deep and twitchy emotions infect the surfaces of daily life, characters obsess about eyes and teeth, the walls are forever closing in, and there's no escaping the shadow of doomed lost love. Image a contemporary Poe character, looking something like Merle Haggard, at large in a Goya etching. Imagine an ethereal, raven-haired woman discoursing in a bar-b-que joint about Poe's theory of unparticled matter. Neurosis! Pathology! Fear and love! I dream of a descent into a maelstrom of pixelated images: Richmond's haunted skies, Civil War statues, candlepin bowling, a juke box glowing like an enchanted palace and, behind the basement wall, a corpse with a black cat on its head –

But I seem to be getting over-excited. Allow me to locate a glass of water, and to conclude, regretfully, with the dim news that Fisher-Price discontinued their used camera service shortly after I got wind of it. Pixel cameras are floating around but remain scarce. A hopeful rumor: the camera's inventor, James Wickstead, is alive and well in New Jersey. I hear the camera's patent has reverted to him, and he intends to retool and market the device – as a toy for teenagers! He's also working on a color version.

A final confession. I still harbor vast hopes to direct big-budget films. Films with lavish sets, spectacular action sequences, actors everybody knows. Films that feed and reflect the immensity of pop culture. Basically, I want Tim Burton's job. But what is cinema, anyway? 'Love. Hate. Action. Death. In one word: emotion.' Sam Fuller's blunt inventory makes sense to me, and pixel-vision can cover those bases as well as the usual high-priced machinery. So there are days when I'm content. Days when I can pick up a pixel camera and leave my stunning future behind. Film makers, after all, are born free, but are everywhere in chains. The PXL 2000, if you can get your hands on one, remains liberating, spell-binding and inexhaustible.

18 *Another Girl Another Planet*: Mary Ward and Barry Sherman

19 *Another Girl Another Planet*: Niagara Falls

The Career

In each edition of Projections *we feature a study of a director's work and career rendered in his own words. Lawrence Kasdan has a special place in American film. He has scripted some of the most commercial films of all time –* Raiders of the Lost Ark, The Empire Strikes Back *– yet the films he has written and directed are the most personal of any mainstream director other than Woody Allen. He must be alone among screenwriters in that all of his scripts have been produced.*

I (JB) got to know him some ten years back when I thought about directing his script, The Bodyguard. *We had the most delightful and stimulating collaboration. Finally, it foundered on casting difficulties; however, it was also due to the fact that we could never solve the inherent problem that the story was predictable – the guardian and the guarded would inevitably fall in love and into bed. I suspect that is why Larry decided not to direct it himself (he produced it). Its massive success world-wide in the Kevin Costner/Whitney Houston/Mick Jackson version merely reminds us that audiences like plots to be familiar, don't like surprise, and are interested in variations on themes they know and love.*

20 Lawrence Kasdan

7

Kasdan on Kasdan
edited by Graham Fuller

Introduction: Graham Fuller

'There's so much rage going around, we're damned lucky we have the movies to help us vent a little of it' – Davis (Steve Martin) in *Grand Canyon*.

Lawrence Kasdan has engineered himself an unusual place in the Hollywood machinery. As the writer or co-writer of *The Empire Strikes Back* (1980), *Raiders of the Lost Ark* (1981), *Return of the Jedi* (1983), and *The Bodyguard* (1992), Kasdan is, commercially speaking, the most successful scenarist of his time. This facility with hugely popular escapist material jars, however, with his vocation as the writer-director of such thoughtful, modernist, and literate films as *Body Heat* (1981), *The Big Chill* (1983), *The Accidental Tourist* (1988), and *Grand Canyon* (1991). It's significant that the above quotation is spoken by *Grand Canyon*'s slipperiest character – a Hollywood producer of schlock films who claims to have seen the light – for it's an epigram that Kasdan surely believes, yet doesn't entirely trust.

Unlike his collaborations with George Lucas and Steven Spielberg, each of the six films Kasdan has directed is, in its own way, a problem picture, the work of an A-list director who commands big stars and big budgets but who doesn't make movies that sit comfortably within that notion of 'the movies'. Even when they occupy specific genres – *film noir* in *Body Heat*, the Western in *Silverado* (1985), marital comedy in *I Love You To Death* (1990) – they come across as earnest, philosophical meditations groping toward an understanding of the complexities of love and communality, the relationships between cause and effect, and in search of a system of values. Unsurprisingly, they are movies that often leave the viewer a little troubled, fraught as they are with ambiguities and ultimate irresolution. They beg questions: what will *Body Heat*'s Matty Walker contrive next? Can *The Accidental Tourist*'s Macon Leary and Muriel Pritchett possibly stay together? Kasdan's endings aren't necessarily happy – and in this sense his films are truly adult, patently at odds with the fake panaceas offered in most American pictures.

Kasdan was born in Miami Beach, Florida, in 1949, and raised in West Virginia, the son of thwarted writers: his mother, Sylvia, had been accepted

21 *Body Heat:* what does the future hold for Matty Walker (Kathleen Turner)?

22 *The Accidental Tourist:* what does the future hold for Macon Leary and Muriel Pritchett (William Hurt and Geena Davis)?

into Sinclair Lewis's writing program at the University of Wisconsin but gave up her studies; his father, Clarence, sold television antennas in his brother-in-law's electronics store and died, an embittered man, when Kasdan was fourteen. A brilliant student, Kasdan majored in English at the University of Michigan in Ann Arbor and thrice won the Avery Larwood literary prize. He then worked for seven years in advertising in Los Angeles (winning a CLIO for the first TV commercial he wrote) and tried to force his way into the film industry as a writer. He submitted *The Bodyguard* sixty-seven times before finally selling it in 1975. *Continental Divide* (1981), written, as the story goes, in two hours on the grass in front of the Los Angeles County Museum of Art, started a studio bidding war and brought Kasdan to the attention of Spielberg and Lucas, as he explains below. Kasdan is a devotee of Howard Hawks and his hiring on *The Empire Strikes Back* placed him immediately in Hawksian mode, since he replaced Leigh Brackett, a seminal Hawks writer, on her death in 1978.

When we met at his family home in Los Angeles in March 1993, Kasdan had just delivered his screenplay for *Wyatt Earp* to Warner Bros. Starring Kevin Costner as the legendary US marshal (1849–1929) and Dennis Quaid as Doc Holliday (1852–1887), it would be beaten to the draw by George Cosmatos's *Tombstone*, released by Disney last Christmas. But as a meticulous study of a mythic figure, Kasdan's epic Western showed every sign of consigning its rival to Boot Hill.

GRAHAM FULLER: *Looking back, what aspects of your early life led you to become a film-maker?*

LAWRENCE KASDAN: I had a normal childhood, playing sports and so on. I think there was writing in the air in the house. My father had written in college; my mother had also started writing fiction and stopped. I had this feeling that it was something I could do. Then, from an early age, going to the movies was simply the best thing, although at that time I was only seeing Hollywood movies.

GF: *When did you become aware of different directorial personalities?*

LK: Two of my favourite movies were *The Magnificent Seven* and *The Great Escape* – the images of heroism and masculinity and camaraderie in those films were very powerful to me. It took my brother Mark to point out that one man, John Sturges, had made those movies, as well as *The Gunfight at the O.K. Corral*. Mark had gotten heavily into films at Harvard and started talking to me about it in a way that no one else had before. He was very enthusiastic about certain directors – a concept that was foreign to me – and came home with reports of Kurosawa, Satyajit Ray, Resnais, Truffaut. Those were just names to me while I lived in West Virginia, but as soon as I went to school at Ann Arbor in Michigan, I started seeing their films and recognizing the style of

American directors like Ford and Hawks, too. Ann Arbor was a wonderful place to see films and I saw everything that was coming out in the sixties and caught up on everything I'd missed.

GF: *Leaping forward in time, when you and Mark wrote* Silverado, *was that an attempt to redo* The Magnificent Seven *as a kind of 'Magnificent Four'?*

LK: I wanted to capture something of that. *Silverado* is a bit of a compendium of different moments from Westerns – perhaps more than it should have been. It didn't matter, because I was filled with energy and was able to make a big Western at a time when Westerns weren't that popular. I'd just come off a success with *The Big Chill*, and that's the only reason I was allowed to do it.

GF: *Did you study film at Ann Arbor?*

LK: I was interested in writing, and when I got to Ann Arbor, I started writing theater and fiction and was able to see my plays get produced. I didn't get into the film program for a while. I was never formally part of it – I was an English literature major – but I eventually started taking film courses. Very quickly I began writing feature-length screenplays. Then, in one of the film classes, I made a short. Technically, it was very crude.

GF: *What was it about?*

LK: It was a wry look at a professor I knew who was very interested in all the young female students – sort of a rough, humorous film about his fascination with one particular girl. It was shot on 16mm. I cut it and did the sound, but I was never a technically proficient student film-maker.

GF: *You marched on Washington a couple of times when you were a student. Were you protesting the Vietnam War?*

LK: Yes.

GF: *Were you a student radical?*

LK: No. In fact, the first script I wrote was about someone like me who was a passive witness to all that. It was a projection of all my feelings about that as an observer. Now, all my work as a film-maker has in some way been about my experiences of things, not the generalities of a situation. Of course, that means you're limited to a certain extent by your experience, and you only hope there is something universal about it.

GF: *After college, you went into advertising.*

LK: It was a way of making a living while I wrote screenplays – and I wrote screenplays as a way to get into production. I wrote six or seven before I sold one; that was *The Bodyguard*. I thought if I started selling these screenplays, I'd get a chance to direct. I thought that was the way in.

GF: *How different was your original version of* The Bodyguard *from the one that was finally produced?*

LK: It was very different, but the words are almost all identical right back to the original screenplay. When I was making *Silverado*, Kevin Costner, who was then an unknown actor really, got a hold of *The Bodyguard* and became very

23　*The Magnificent Seven*

24　*Silverado*

excited about it. This was nine years ago, and he never let go of the idea of starring in it. As Costner's star rose, it became possible for him to get it done. There had been constant interest in it, and it had been rewritten a lot of times with variations on the female character and her profession and so on. About three years ago Costner asked me if it was all right with me if he could revive it. I considered directing it and decided to do *Grand Canyon* instead, so Kevin chose Mick Jackson, who'd just done *L.A. Story*, but I was very involved in the production. Just before they started, they pretty much went back to the original draft, and the basic thing is as it was written when I was twenty-five, with some remnants of the other versions.

When I began to sell screenplays, and they were directed by other people, the resulting movies were never very satisfying to me, and sometimes it created some bad feelings. *The Bodyguard*, coming at a more recent moment in my career, was a reminder of that. It's not a question of blame. It's just that they can never be what you want them to be if someone else directs them. They may be better; they may be worse. But it's happened to me a few times, and it's very painful. I didn't think after all this time that I would see another one of my scripts done by someone else, though; in fact, when *The Bodyguard* was done, it meant everything I've ever sold had been produced. I just don't want anyone else to do my stuff any more.

GF: *What things tend to change?*

LK: It's always in the direction. One of the things I knew, and yet had to learn again when I started making films, was the extent of the director's responsibility. It was kind of liberating in a way. On *Body Heat*, my first film, I thought that I had to do everything, dictate every decision. I placed the camera very specifically for every shot. Every one of the ten thousand decisions I took upon myself – I didn't know any better. And what I had underestimated, and what I learned very quickly on later films, was that the director's power is so complete and comprehensive that there are many things he can delegate; nothing can change the fact that it's your baby if you're any good. There's nothing at risk. The more you invite people into the process, the more chance there is something vital will come out of it. This is a long way around to explaining how *The Bodygaurd* had ten thousand decisions made by Mick Jackson – ten thousand decisions that I would have made differently. Having said that, *The Bodyguard* is, in a way, a perfect film because the idea's a strong one, and Costner's portrayal is exactly right. His performance has been wildly underestimated because acting in America is largely misunderstood, yet it's exactly the character I wrote. Beyond that, everything in *The Bodyguard* is different – and it's painful.

GF: *If you directed somebody else's script, would you want to rewrite it first?*

LK: No – I did direct someone else's script, *I Love You to Death*, and it was a fascinating experience. I had the writer, John Kostmayer, there every day, which I had never experienced myself when I was a writer; I had never been included. Directing someone else's script, I felt what it must feel like to be an actor, where every day you are struggling to find out what it is you are trying to achieve. When you write and direct a movie, that particular thing doesn't obsess you. You believe that you know exactly what you want, though you have many moments of doubt. Hopefully, you'll be able to answer the various questions that emerge without resorting to your own preconceptions. When you take someone else's script, you try to project yourself into it like an actor has to. I'm often shocked when an actor has entered a project with a gung ho attitude and you find in rehearsals that they misunderstand the script. That's not a bad thing – it's often useful to find out how someone's ideas are different from yours. That's how I felt directing *I Love You To Death*. Every day I was struggling, and it was a particularly difficult piece, too. Even the writer, I think, did not know exactly how it should be handled. It was a problem of how to get the tone right. I used to say, and I guess I still believe it, that the difference between what I'd written and what other directors would make of it is taste. Would you like a certain face or costume, would you cover a scene that way, would you cut those two images together? It's hard to find anyone whose tastes coincide exactly with yours. I found it difficult as a young man to just let a script go. When I saw *Raiders of the Lost Ark*, I was obsessed with things that had changed much more than I appreciated what was great about it. And five years later I felt differently.

GF: *So you look back on it –*

LK: With affection and respect. I recently saw an interview with Mike Nichols. He said at one point he'd turned down a chance to direct *The Exorcist* and the chance to make a fortune. But someone told him if he'd directed it, it probably wouldn't have made any money. Me, too – I've turned down so many pictures that have gone on to be big hits, but I'm sure they wouldn't have made so much money if I'd directed them. It's a mystery what makes something a big hit anyway, but I think that my taste is not necessarily accessible to a mass audience. Take a picture like *Raiders*. I'm certain that Steven [Spielberg] directed that film better than I would have, which is what I didn't appreciate when I first saw it.

GF: *But you do have a sensibility that has enabled you to write two or three of the biggest grossing movies of all time.*

LK: Yes, I seem to be able to do that, but that's mysterious to me. *Raiders* is an unusual circumstance in that Steven and George [Lucas] were both in tune with some kind of popular feeling. Their own interests are very much in line with what makes something popular. With the *Star Wars* sequels, you were going to do well with them no matter what. I did a good job on them, but they were always going to be hits. Then *The Bodyguard* became a huge hit, and there was something mystifying about that. It's going to be like the third biggest

American movie ever released overseas, and I haven't a clue why. I could look at it in retrospect and say maybe people respond to this or that, Kevin's very popular, and the music took off, but that's the way all movies are evaluated after the fact. That's not what carried it to such astonishing success – there was something in the core idea that was very attractive to people, particularly women, despite universal critical denigration. It had no critical impact what-soever – none. It was just a huge hit. I couldn't tell you why now. I could give you a lot of hypotheses. And I think the Mike Nichols rule-of-thumb works – if I'd directed *The Bodyguard* it probably wouldn't have been such a huge hit, though Costner doesn't agree.

GF: *Is it possible to analyse what makes your style of direction less blatantly commercial?*

LK: I don't know, and I don't mean to denigrate anyone else. I think that popular movies work on a very simple premise and that I've been drawn to movies that work on a very complex level. But then maybe a lot of that is in my head. Sometimes when I go back and look at a Hawks film or a Ford film, or any film that I really love, I'm struck by the simplicity. What is confusing is that when I saw *The Bodyguard* for the first time, it evoked so many complicated feelings in me that I attributed them all to the film. But maybe really good art is simple in a way that evokes that set of responses in people and yet is very simple in its own right.

GF: *Hawks, in particular, is very simple and yet very effective.*

LK: Sometimes the artist is not aware of what he's doing. When you look at different parts of a Ford film, you can't believe that they are made by the same man. Some of them are squirmingly sentimental – the humor is phoney and silly – but there'll be moments of contemplation about heroism, or the way lives run in unexpected ways, and you're just knocked back by the subtlety and immensity of his vision. I don't think that Ford would make that distinction between those two facets of himself; he was just making a picture, you know? I think that, with good art, we just don't know. The struggle is to let go of thinking we know.

GF: *I know that Steven Spielberg and George Lucas had been fans of forties and fifties adventure serials, but how did Indiana Jones evolve as a character when you wrote* Raiders of the Lost Ark?

LK: Steven had purchased my script, *Continental Divide*, which was very different from the film which resulted. The script had a kind of Hawksian speed, momentum, hopefully wit, about it. I don't think the film turned out that way, which was one of those painful experiences I had early on. But Steven's enthusiasm for it was what got me involved with him and George. I think that what they were looking for was someone who could write *Raiders* in the same way that Hawks would have someone write a movie for him – a strong woman character, a certain kind of hero. So that's what got me the job. George

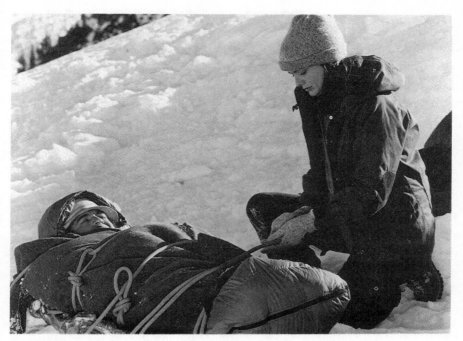

25 *Continental Divide:* the Hawksian woman (Blair Brown with John Belushi)

had already had the idea of the way the guy dressed, and Phil Kaufman had provided the MacGuffin of the Lost Ark of the Covenant, which his orthodontist had told him about when he was eleven years old. At one time Phil was going to direct it but had gone on to different things. George had told the idea to Steven, and Steven had said, 'Oh, that excites me.' When I was brought in, it became a Lucas-Spielberg-Kasdan movie. We sat down and decided on the kind of hero Indiana Jones would be, his name, his whip, and talked about the MacGuffin and serial films. After that we created the film by jumping through favorite moments from those kinds of films – the sort of thing we would like to see.

Raiders was produced on a scale, with a kind of modern technological ability, that went way beyond any of those serials, but the spirit of onrushing events and constant crises – that's from the serial. I think what they brought me in for, and what I tried to do, was to give it a Hawksian spine. I'm interested in character, whereas a lot of people approach a script from plot or story or the production angle – you know, 'What can we do here?' I think that what happened in that three-way conversation was that each of us was able to bring in something of our own.

GF: *Was the warehouse scene in* Raiders *a quotation from* Citizen Kane?

LK: I think so. That was the ending that George always had, although the fact the matte shot ended up looking like that scene from *Citizen Kane* came from

26 *Raiders of the Lost Ark:* Harrison Ford as Indiana Jones

Steven. George was interested in the fact that all these secrets were hidden away in a big government warehouse somewhere – not just the Lost Ark but all the things we don't know about.

GF: *Do you see* Raiders *as a Grail Quest?*

LK: I don't, because the search for the Grail has never been a powerful story to me. It's hugely powerful to Steven, and he sees most of his movies that way. My background is in literature, and the things that excite me are details of character – the way someone picks up something or a mood across the room. I don't look at *The Seven Samurai* in the large sense. I look at it moment to moment, at the essentials of life, the details, the direction of the story, the unexpected turns of character. I never approach a story and say, 'Oh, this is typical of life in downtown Detroit.'

John Patrick Shanley is a friend of mine, and he called me up after he'd seen *The Bodyguard* and said it was one of the best things that he'd seen recently. I was mystified by it, but I could see that as he talked about it, it went right to the heart of his own concerns, and that there was something so achingly sad for him about a man who is willing to give his life for this woman he is so much in love with but can never have. I think that's a very romantic idea, but some of that I'm aware of, some not. I approached *The Bodyguard* from a point of view of two characters I was interested in. I don't think I ever looked for a broad perspective in it, personally.

I'm having a slightly different experience with *Wyatt Earp* because I approached it from Earp's character and his life. Yet it's very clear to me that his story is the American story. So this is one of those rare occasions where it's clear to me that I'm aware of larger resonances.

GF: *When you came to write* The Empire Strikes Back, *had the decision already been made to make it darker than* Star Wars, *or was that your influence?*

LK: I think I influenced that, and George was open to it and ready to have it happen. Over the three *Star Wars* films, he saw a trajectory. *The Empire Strikes Back* was the second act, and traditionally, the second act is when things start to go bad. George had made his biggest decision when he hired Irvin Kershner to direct, even though Kershner and I were acting as his tools. When it came to the third act, *The Return of the Jedi*, which functions as the relief, he chose a different kind of director, Richard Marquand, whose world view was much sunnier than Kershner's.

GF: *Did you have an affinity for science fiction?*

LK: My brother had been a science-fiction *aficionado*, but it had never interested me. There was a wall of science-fiction books across the hall, but I'd never read them. I only became involved with *Stars Wars* because I'd written *Raiders* for George, and that was directly in line with all the things that excited me about the movies. He then hired me immediately to do *The Empire Strikes Back*. I was just a writer he liked who was immediately available.

27 *The Empire Strikes Back:* Luke Skywalker (Mark Hamill) battles with Darth Vader (James Earl Jones)

28 *The Empire Strikes Back* (Irvin Kershner, Gary Kurtz, George Lucas, and Lawrence Kasdan)

GF: *Was it like writing a Western, or perhaps a morality play?*

LK: Well, once involved in the saga, I related to it strongly because it's elemental stuff. But I sometimes kid around and say it's about Hollywood. It's about imposing your fantasies upon others. A Jedi knight has the ability to take a weaker mind and control it, and that's what Hollywood's about. If the studio says to you, 'We're not going to make this movie,' you, as a Jedi knight, say, 'We *are* going to make it.' And then the studio agrees. That's what the *Star Wars* saga is about – it's about following those things which are strongest in you and imposing them on the world. Making a career in Hollywood is like that if you want to do your own work. If you want to do what they want you to do, it's easy. You just say yes. But if you want to do what you want to do, you're constantly manipulating the chaos of the system.

GF: *Does that require immense force of will?*

LK: It's been very clear to me since the very beginning what is necessary for me. It seems like it's my job to oppose what is going on and use it for my own purposes. I've seen very talented people who will not oppose it. Their work is fine, too. I don't think they're less forceful than me; I don't think they even see a conflict. But I think there's something natural in me that saw the studios and their apparatus as the enemy. I think that a lot of people share the same agenda as the studios. So does it require a large force of will? I think that you inherently have a feeling about it. There are film-makers who are much more radical than me who would look at me and say, 'Well, he's part of a system, and he does Hollywood movies.' I don't see it that way. I think that character is destiny, and you do the things you have to do.

GF: *You've had quite an unusual career in that you operate within the parameters of Hollywood, but you function as a writer/director making personal films. You don't do contract jobs or go off to make a film for the sake of making one.*

LK: No. Oftentimes I want to, but when it comes to signing on the dotted line, I can't bring myself to do it. I don't think that reluctance comes from a pretentious place; I think that I'm not capable of doing it. I can't bring myself to do even those movies that turn out to be hits. I can't get my head around them. So my career and my work have evolved very naturally. I always do the things that are right for me – not necessarily feeling that everything else is wrong. This relates back to what I was saying about the director's power and influence over a film being so complete that, no matter what other people try to make it, it becomes a personal film. You see it in a movie like *The Untouchables*. It was a questionable script in my mind, and when I read it, I said I didn't know what to do with it, but Brian De Palma knew how to turn it into a Brian De Palma film, to take the moments he related to and blow them up so that they became the most important things in the movie, while the other stuff was thrown away.

GF: *In talking about your writing process, you've used the word 'density' – how you pack a great deal into each scene.*

LK: Anything I say about this now is influenced by the changes in my process over the years. Looking again at some of my favorite films, and seeing that they're simpler than I thought they were, has influenced my approach to the writing and directing of films. My initial response to them was that they were infinitely complex, that one image from *Lawrence of Arabia*, say, conveys so many ideas. So when I started writing, I was trying to pack all those ideas in to convey them to other people, because I wasn't going to direct those films at that time. I've been writing screenplays now for twenty-five years, and it's taken me all this time to see even a glint of where I should be heading, which is to aim for a certain simplicity and stop trying to pack the screenplay with as much as I can. On the other hand, that early approach served me very well in that the people who read the screenplays were able to see the mood very specifically and didn't have to imagine that much. Sometimes, though, I think I've been too specific in the writing, and now I'm trying to fight that urge and be more open to possibilities and experiences.

GF: *Do you write fast?*

LK: Very. I wrote *Wyatt Earp* in three months, and it's a huge story – more than three hours. It seemed fast to me. I used to outline what I was going to do. I don't do that so much any more. It's part of trying to loosen up the process and not know what's happening. But I think I'm a linear person, and when I write I don't write a quick draft and then go back. I don't like to leave anything behind me because I'm uncomfortable with it. I tend to write a scene many times over before going on. The last time I was really doing drafts was when I was working for George Lucas. Now, I will sometimes revise and make little changes, but the essentials don't change. I take a lot of time and effort with the first draft, and I'd rather shoot that.

On *Wyatt Earp* I'm doing a revision in response to certain ideas that people have come up with. That to some people might be a draft; to me it's details. The first draft is what we're really shooting. That may not be a good thing necessarily, but I believe in it. I believe in initial responses to people and things.

GF: *Do you write in a three-act structure, with each scene triggering the next?*

LK: I think I do. And now it's become so completely ingrained in me that I don't have to think about it, but when I go back and look at the work, I can see that it's there. *Grand Canyon* is as loose a film as I've ever written, and when I was done with it, I saw that I was following exactly the same kind of structure I had been using since I'd learned it in college. I hadn't thought about it once during the writing – which is what you're hoping for.

GF: *By the time you'd finished* Return of the Jedi, *did you feel the need to address more obviously adult themes?*

LK: From the very beginning, that's where my interests lay. All the time I spent with George over three pictures, there was a tension about what kind of movie we were making – between George's concerns, which are archetypal, and mine, which are very specific and human. I see myself as a humanist. All my interests are humanist ones. Anyway, I actually made *Body Heat* before *Jedi*, but George asked me as a favor to come and do *Jedi* with him. He had been very helpful to me in getting *Body Heat* made, and I felt that I owed him. So after having had the experience of directing and loving it, to go back and write for another director was a difficult thing for me to do. But we sort of turned it into a lark. George is good company, and we had fun, and I liked Richard Marquand – he was a lovely guy. We did the work very fast under enormous time pressure, but a lot of the production design, effects, and so on had already been prepared, so it was real easy.

GF: *With* Body Heat, *were you consciously setting out to reinhabit the world of* film noir?

LK: Yes, very consciously, because I didn't know if I'd get to direct again. This might be my only shot and I wanted to do something very extravagant. I was searching in myself, knowing that I needed a framework in which to do an extravagant thing – basically because I'm a shy person. Actually, *The Accidental Tourist* is really representative of a lot of my tastes and interests in that it's about the tiniest things, whereas using *film noir* on *Body Heat* gave me the license to have very extravagant dialogue and camerawork. For me it was always about projecting what interested me within that genre. In a way, *Body Heat* is just like *The Big Chill*. It's about someone of my generation who just happens to find himself in the *film noir* world, but, like a lot of my characters, is really a sixties character.

GF: *Did you look at other* films noirs *or think about them?*

LK: I had seen a great many of them in college and was very struck by them. It was a world that I found very sensual and exciting, and I was drawn to that. For me, that dark side speaks to my own hidden obsessions. I think we all have a hidden life. What's great about *noir* is the blending of the life we present to other people and our secret life. It's all about desire.

GF: *Did you read deeply in hard-boiled fiction?*

LK: Chandler, Hammett, and Cain – not beyond that. I think I got on to Hammett through *The Maltese Falcon* movie, not the other way around. That movie electrified me and I still think it's the best possible model for a first film ever made. *Body Heat* is a child of *The Maltese Falcon* and *Double Indemnity* and *Out of the Past*, but used for my own purposes. When people did not want to embrace *Body Heat*, they'd say it was a pastiche. I don't think that covers it, but when you make a film like that you know you're going to hear that kind of criticism.

GF: *I've heard you say that* Body Heat *and* The Big Chill *are films about what one wants and the price one has to pay to get it.*

LK: I don't think this was preconceived, but it's something that is so insistent in

29 *Double Indemnity*: the lovers (Fred MacMurray and Barbara Stanwyck)

30 Lawrence Kasdan shooting *Body Heat*

31 *Body Heat*: the lovers (William Hurt and Kathleen Turner)

my work that I can barely recognize it. Very often my films are about the conflict between our ideals and our desires, and that's where the drama is for me. We know how we're supposed to act, but we're constantly in rebellion against the things we've been taught, and our hearts and bodies are telling us other things. That's true from *Body Heat* right through to *Wyatt Earp* – you have an idea of how you should live your life, but it's very difficult to live up to that. That's the material that interests me.

GF: *Did you storyboard* Body Heat?

LK: What little directing I'd seen had been by George Lucas and Steven Spielberg, and they were great storyboarders. So I started storyboarding *Body Heat*, and after a while I stopped, because it made no sense to me. I was just struggling to get some artist to put on paper what was already in my head. I thought, well, I'll just do it on the set. When the picture was done, I went back and looked at the little bit of storyboarding I'd done, and I'd shot the film exactly that way without looking at the storyboards once, though obviously some things changed. I think this is why it's so much easier for me to direct something I've written. I'm the authority now on *Wyatt Earp* – not the historical authority but on this movie. No one will ever know more about this than I do, although they may see the faults. This way, I feel total confidence.

GF: *Do you think about style?*

LK: I think about style in terms of the themes. I think it has to do with every painting, photograph, and film you've ever liked – every book. When I go to make a movie, I'm influenced by Joseph Conrad as much as I am by John Ford. Since I've accepted the fact that everything on a film will go through my filter anyway, then all I want is more and more information. When you look at a film by Ford or Kurosawa, you get so much useful information, but you couldn't ever hope to achieve what they achieved if you wanted to. You've seen people try, and it's impossible. But the interesting director that you hope that you are will hopefully create something unique each time.

GF: *The style of your films is clearly yours, but that's something which is less easy to describe than, say, Spielberg's or Scorsese's.*

LK: As I say, I think that my personality is shy, reticent, in some ways. I'm conservative – I don't wear flashy clothes. I think that's true of my style, too, not that I don't like things that are startlingly innovative. If you look at *The Grapes of Wrath*, you can't believe this movie was made in 1939 – it's avant-garde for today. You never see a film like this today, and you say, how can I begin to move in that direction? It's so daring. So I've nothing against innovation and extravagance, but I also like the fact that *The Searchers* is not extravagant; it's just perfect. *Seven Samurai*, too. For me, the idea is, is the camera where you want it to be, not are you showing it off? I look sometimes at films that are wildly received, and it seems their camera movements are clearly there for movement's sake; they have no purpose in the film. What I admire

32 *The Grapes of Wrath*

33 *Seven Samurai*

about Kurosawa is the Zen perfection of his camera placement, the rightness of it. That's the idea I'm striving for – but style is not something that drives my pictures.

GF: *Your films have often been described as slick or glossy. What's your reaction to that?*

LK: This sounds unrelated, but I am left-handed as a writer – I do everything else right-handed. At the point at which I could have developed ambidextrously, my parents were told, oh no, leave him alone. It meant that I have never been able to write in a classical style – I've always smudged what I've written and I hate my handwriting. In my mind, a beautiful hand always represented slickness to me. So when people started describing my films as slick, it didn't bother me. There are slick things in Kurosawa that people would never call slick. I think I make a good-looking movie and that's what I want to do. I also try as much as possible to use a dissolve when a dissolve is right and cut when I'm supposed to cut. You're never right all the time. Sometimes you feel you're completely out of tune with the critical mode. You look around and you see lots of people being praised and then you don't *want* to be praised. It becomes bothersome after a while if you think your work is being underrated because it doesn't have a certain kind of flashiness, but that's momentary compared to your conviction that your own work is better on a second or third viewing. We live in a first-viewing world, but I don't make these movies for one viewing. I can look at *Lawrence of Arabia* or *High and Low* or *Ikiru* and be thrilled every time. That's the ideal I'm working toward.

GF: Film noir *has also stood the test of time, partly because it's a school of film-making rooted in an older school, namely Expressionism, and partly because its shadows have never quite gone away. It continues to be influential.*

LK: It also touches something deep about the way men and women relate to each other that is independent of the surface intrigues and mysteries of the stories. Sometimes they make manifest what is in us all the time. You don't have to be involved in an insurance scam, as in *Double Indemnity*, to feel the suspicion and experience the fears we have about the opposite sex – you can be on a date with someone! That, I think, is what *noir* is about.

GF: *When Mary-Ann Simpson [Kathleen Turner] is seen on the beach at the end of* Body Heat, *do you feel that she has regrets about the way she has manipulated Ned Racine [William Hurt]?*

LK: Yes, but not that she would do anything differently if she was given another chance. *Wyatt Earp* is a little bit like that – and everything else in between. Again, it comes from your ideas about what you should do with your life versus the reality of doing them. Mary-Ann was so single-minded about achieving her goal – an infantile goal – that anything that got in the way of that was irrelevant. That's what all great tragedies are about for me – that in this adherence to a single idea, we sometimes sacrifice everything. *Double Indemnity* is about that, and there's a real ambiguity when Barbara Stanwyck says 'I love you' to Fred MacMurray just before he shoots her. He doesn't know whether to believe it – and maybe *she* doesn't know. I love that, because I feel that every day in every way.

GF: *Was* The Big Chill *based on actual people you knew, or are the characters amalgams?*

LK: They're amalgams. Paul Schrader once said, 'There's a little bit of yourself in every character.' That's very true of *The Big Chill*. It was about all my friends, my feelings about them, and about me projecting myself on to them. It was also filtered through the sensibility and humour of Barbara Benedek, who wrote it with me and has a very different personality to me.

I always thought of the film as a comedy of manners. A lot of people projected that it was an incomplete summing-up of a generation, but it was meant to be specific, not a summing-up at all. One of the difficulties you face when you write and direct films is how they are received – not by the public, which goes into the theater innocently every time, but by critics, who have this terrible job where they see one bad movie after another and have to make a judgement about them. They often forget that there's a difference between a writer/director and the characters he creates. They think that you have a one-to-one relationship with your characters, but that's not the way it is for me. As much as they are part of you, you always have a distance from them. You might think that they are foolish, which I do most of the time. Certainly the ones that interest me are foolish. Sometimes you laugh at your characters, but you laugh at them empathetically. You hope that you are sympathetic to people's faults.

Everybody in *The Big Chill* is self-absorbed, struggling to deal with the realities of life in the world as opposed to the cloistered, comfortable existence of college, which they remember inaccurately anyway. They're struggling with this disjunction between what they thought the world would be and what it is like, and they're finding that it's a difficult terrain to navigate. It's hard for them to keep their feet. One of the characters says, 'No one thinks they're an asshole.' Clearly people are assholes, but never to themselves. That's the heart of the movie, because most of the characters act foolishly, selfishly, single-mindedly, and they don't see that they're acting like that – and that's where the humour is. They weren't what they thought they were before, and they're not what they think they are now, and yet they see their present day as a clear difference from their past. I think that people don't change like that. The struggle goes on.

GF: *Was* The Big Chill *about a loss of idealism?*

LK: It's about the loss of the *idea* of idealism. Whether or not they were actually idealistic back then, I don't know. Initially, I included a flashback to their college days but I took it out because it didn't work. But what it was trying to

34 *The Big Chill*: Lawrence Kasdan with actors Tom Berenger, Jeff Goldblum, Kevin Kline and William Hurt

35 *The Big Chill*: the ensemble ([standing] Jo Beth Williams, Tom Berenger, Glenn Close, Kevin Kline, Mary Kay Place; [seated] William Hurt, Meg Tilly, and Jeff Goldblum)

show was that they weren't all that different from now; you could see the seeds of everything they'd become. There was never a pristine time; there was only a pristine image of themselves.

GF: The Big Chill *has wonderful ensemble acting. Tell me how you worked with the actors on this piece. Did you rehearse them extensively?*

LK: On *The Big Chill* we rehearsed for longer than I ever have since – four weeks, which is really unheard-of in movies. I haven't done it again because I'm no longer convinced it's the right thing to do. On that occasion, when these actors who were strangers were going to have to play friends and know each other well, I felt it was the perfect situation. We actually went on location for the last two weeks and lived in the house we shot in.

I had written *The Big Chill* not just from my view of the issues in the film, but also in reaction to *Body Heat*, where I'd been cloistered with two actors in a terribly claustrophobic movie. I'd determined that my next film would have a lot of actors and that I wouldn't be stuck in an airless world. I love actors and I'm always frustrated that there aren't enough parts for them. On *Wyatt Earp* there are a hundred parts but I'll still have to say no to a lot of people I want to work with. So Barbara and I wrote a lot of parts for *The Big Chill* and I loved being in rehearsal with all those people; I'm amazed by what actors can do that I can't do. Rehearsals are an investigation enabling them to bring to a script what isn't there and exploring what is there – and seeing how that interaction takes place and changes things. At the end of a rehearsal, all that I'll hope for is that there's some understanding of the basic intent of the film.

GF: *When it comes to shooting, do you remind people what you want, or just let them go?*

LK: I tend to let them go until I'm not getting what I want. Sometimes they'll give me something new that I hadn't thought of and that I love; sometimes they'll go off what I think is right. Directing is exhausting to me because all day long you're sorting out the good ideas from the bad – plus the good ideas that are inappropriate and which can throw off the balance of the piece, which might be better stored for later on, or which will never be right. You have to sort all that and guard the actors' contributions. You never want to shut that down or discourage them for the next day. You want them to come back with the same openness toward you. It requires a certain kind of handling.

GF: *Do you manipulate actors to get what you want?*

LK: I probably do, though I never think of it as manipulation. I think about it as being very straight with them about what my needs are. Sometimes their resistance is great, and I find that a good actor is usually right if they resist strongly – and that the only mistake I've made is in the casting. If you cast correctly, it gives you enormous freedom because the actor is never going to go that far wrong. They may not even have any understanding of the part, but they are so intrinsically interesting that it blows away all your reservations.

GF: *Are you economical with takes?*

LK: I'm trying to be more so. I've never done an enormous number. A lot of it depends on the actors. You can actually impose a rhythm on most actors. It took me a long time to realize that, because I was initially indulgent of actors' desires to do more takes; and since I had some idea in my head that I was trying to relinquish by getting the take right, I was always ready to do another one, too. I began to feel that doing too many was counter-productive to everything that I was doing. Momentum is enormously important. You have two hours, say, to do a scene you've been thinking about for years. The actors may have been thinking about it for six months; they've been aiming for this day and will invariably be dissatisfied because they've built up that moment in their heads. As a director, you know that every moment in a film can't have such weight; sometimes you want much less than the actors aim to give you. The excitement is in your having just one chance to get it right. I'm not drawn to reshooting scenes, let alone whole movies, although I know some directors are. I think that's cheating. I don't see it as a perfectible form. I see it like athletics: how did you play the game that night in front of that crowd in that stadium? That's all that counts.

GF: *The way you describe it sounds close to theater.*

LK: The difference being that in theater you get to try again the next night. Film has that cutting edge; it's going to be preserved for ever and that's what's terrifying to actors. Getting them to relax is the hardest thing, because if they're dissatisfied with what they've done today, they'll be confused about the next three days, so you try to make them feel confident that they've done well.

GF: *If you do three takes, will you print just one?*

LK: I'll print all three. I try not to do more than five; after that, it tends to be a drag. A movie like *Silverado* or *Wyatt Earp* has so many other things going on – gunshots, horses – which also determine how many takes you do. But in a pure acting film like *Grand Canyon*, where your camera crew is top-notch, you're basically getting what you want each time. Then I might go again just to see if the actors will surprise me. I'll say, 'Just do anything.'

GF: *Do the actors then lobby you to use that extra one?*

LK: All the time. I've always had open dailies; anyone who wants to come can come. Sometimes you're depressed because it's bad. It's like a drug, really, but I've found that dailies don't tell you much about the way the movie is going.

GF: Silverado *is a genuinely post-modern Western in that you brought in lots of generic tropes and drew attention to them: the wagon train, Kevin Costner as a fringe-jacketed Range Rider character, Scott Glenn as the lean, laconic loner archetype, Jeff Goldblum as the card shark, the gunfight in the street at the end. The Kevin Kline character talks very consciously about the specific atmosphere of saloons. There's also the full panoply of six-guns, holsters, spurs, saddles, and hats. It's a Western suffused with Western movie imagery.*

LK: No one has ever used that word 'panoply' before, but I think that's the right way to approach it. *Silverado* caused enormous confusion in people who wrote about it, because of that quality, which they took to be a confusion on our part about what kind of movie we had wanted to make. And there may be some truth to that. It is post-modern in the sense that it is aware of its images and it does have a sensibility that is informed. I think that was an organic expression of the enthusiasm that my brother and I had for the genre.

Eight years later, I'm about to do another Western, *Wyatt Earp*, in the same kind of location, Santa Fé, and it's fascinating. I'm going to be walking the same ground, using the same kinds of horses, holsters, guns, and hats, but doing a very different kind of story at a different time in my life; sometimes that's what happens if you're lucky enough to make movies. *Wyatt Earp* will be nothing like *Silverado*, I think – I may be wrong. This movie's very much a character study, and the character represents a great many things. *Silverado* was not like that. Above all, it was about the spirit of *The Magnificent Seven* and all the movies that spawned. It was that idea, which is so powerful to young American audiences, of a group of strangers coming together and using their skills to achieve a cause. I've always thought that was a good metaphor for film-making, because when you make a film you hire people you don't know but who are enormously skilled at specific things. Cameramen, editors, actors . . . it always feels like assembling an all-star team. Film-making is that kind of journey. You meet people on the road, they become intensely intimate with

you, you rely on them in desperate situations. That's what *Silverado* is about –
relishing all those elements in a kind of jaunty, ebullient way. But it's not a
classical Western. Most Westerns have been spare in story and character; it's a
very austere form, and there's a real strength in that, as in any good, simple
story. *Silverado*, though, is a terribly complicated story with too many characters in it. But for me, there couldn't be enough moments, enough characters,
enough horses, enough ways of dressing the film.

GF: *Why were there no Indians in it?*

LK: There were Indians, but we cut 'em out because we couldn't afford the
sequence. The cavalry sequence was cut, too.

GF: *The women characters are particularly interesting: Linda Hunt as the saloon boss;
Rosanna Arquette as the frontierswoman in the wagon train. Was the Arquette
character cut down?*

LK: Yes. It was my biggest regret about the movie that it didn't work out with
Rosanna. Her scenes probably weren't written that well. I cut three or four of
them out and made it tighter. It was already a long movie and you go with what
you like best – not even necessarily what's right, but what you want to look at
for the rest of your life.

GF: *The romantic triangle involving her, Scott Glenn, and Kevin Kline was developing interestingly, I thought, and then it stops.*

LK: Yeah. It's not good. I'm not proud of it.

GF: *Where did the Linda Hunt character come from?*

LK: It came from seeing Linda Hunt in *The Year of Living Dangerously* and just
wanting to work with her. I met her and fell in love with her and we wrote the
part for her. If she didn't exist, there wouldn't have been that character. She
was fabulous.

GF: *Was the climactic gunfight between Kline and Brian Dennehy a homage to the one
in* High Noon?

LK: It's a homage to a lot of gunfights. I love the way these men end up walking
down a deserted street like that.

GF: *I mention it because Kline is dressed almost identically to Gary Cooper.*

LK: Yes, and I like that look, too! Wyatt Earp will probably look something like
that.

GF: *Now that you are doing Wyatt Earp, does that mean you won't do the mooted*
Silverado II?

LK: I actually had a script written for it by John Kostmayer, who wrote *I Love
You to Death*, and he did a good job. But I was worried that there was no reason
to do it. *Silverado* under-performed terribly and it was botched by Columbia –
and they knew it. The new regime there knew they should have made twice as
much money from it as they did, because it was a huge hit on video and cable.
Now everyone in it has become a star – Costner, of course, is huge – and I was
attracted to the idea of getting together with these guys again because they're

36 *Silverado*: Lawrence Kasdan talking to Linda Hunt, watched by Danny Glover, Kevin Kline, Scott Glenn and Kevin Costner

all in my circle of friends. But I began to think that there's nothing in this story that warrants making the film, although I could change my mind. There's enormous pressure for me to do *Bodyguard II* and you can imagine what kind of ambivalent feelings I have about that! It was never intended to be a series and nor was *Silverado*, though we left the door open for that. It's just that there are so many movies to make and so little time. Each one you do is a huge commitment.

As much as anyone, I'm sure, I am affected by the popularity or acceptance of a film I make, but that's minor compared to the actual process of making it. I wanted to direct movies because I thought it was the best work for me to do; being able to write and direct is beyond my dreams. I love being on the set; I love working with the actors; I love cutting and mixing. That's ninety-five per cent of my work life. The other five per cent is the reaction – and it can cut you like a knife. But the first ninety-five per cent is your job. That's why, when I choose my crew – and I tend to work with the same people – and actors, I always choose who I want to be with. People say, 'Well, so and so is an asshole, but he's worth it.' I never approach it that way – nothing is worth it. I am interested in the quality of my life and there are too many good actors around to make you want to put up with an asshole; there are so many people who desperately want to be in your movie. Why would you want to put up with a horrible person who is going to make your life miserable every day? It's hard work. When you go to the set at five-thirty in the morning – which is the hardest part for me – you want to see a face that makes you happy. That was my feeling going into each of the six films I've directed. Most of those days I was happy to be there. I've had terrible days, of course, but when I arrived I was usually feeling good about the people in the film. You miss a shot when you tense up. That's why I try to create a feeling of relaxation for the actors and the crew. I don't like screaming, I don't like fights. Some people thrive on it; I don't. I essentially want people to be comfortable. They don't have to be having a good time – I gave up trying to keep everybody happy a long time ago – but they should know that their work is respected and understood. I never want them to feel that the sword is hanging over their head.

GF: *Can you get tough with people?*

LK: I think so. When I was searching for a way to make a living while I wrote movies, I went back to school and got a Masters degree in education. The lesson I learned from student teaching was that you can control an unruly class at almost any level, but the more you yell, the less effective yelling becomes. That has influenced my approach to directing; for me, being hard is giving someone a look where another director might scream at them.

GF: *Let's move on to* The Accidental Tourist. *What attracted you to Anne Tyler's novel?*

LK: I was going to do *Man Trouble*, which had been around for ten years, with Robert De Niro and Jessica Lange, and I worked on it for a while before it fell apart. I didn't want to read *The Accidental Tourist* while I was working on *Man Trouble*, because *Man Trouble* is about an upper-class woman who gets involved with a crazy lower-class dog-trainer, whereas *The Accidental Tourist* is about an uptight, upper-class man who gets involved with an eccentric lower-class woman. Thematically, they are totally different. What appealed to me enormously about *The Accidental Tourist* was that it's about control. What the accidental tourist tries to do is control his environment so that he always feels at home even in the most exotic places on earth.

That idea spoke directly to me, because I, like a lot of people, am fearful of all the chaos in the world. I try, in my own way, to control it. Everybody works out a system of control: either they exercise, or they eat too much, or they do drugs or drink, or they work very hard. In *The Accidental Tourist*, you have a man, Macon Leary, whose world has been shattered by the unexpected tragedy of the death of his son before the movie starts. The world *cannot* be controlled, and he sinks deeper and deeper into this hole. His wife rejects him for his lack of responsiveness to the tragedy and he takes refuge in the tightness of his world as a travel writer. Then he meets someone who accepts chaos in the world and saves his life. Control and fear – those are very strong themes.

Anne Tyler is an unbelievable writer. What I have just described to you is the *story* – but she's a consummate stylist. When I read the book I felt not only that it should be a movie but also that it should be a movie that doesn't violate the book. A lot of people in Hollywood thought it was a crazy movie to make. There's not a lot of action in it, hardly anything, in fact, that Hollywood looks for. And I've got to tell you that I thought that all along, though it was only on looking back at the movie later that I was surprised that I had done it. It's not really what people go to the movies to see and I'm surprised at the size of the audience we got. It's very slow. It's about tiny things. It's grim. The hero has a stick up his ass; he's a horribly difficult guy to get on with.

GF: *When you wrote the script, was it difficult to bring a sympathetic quality to a protagonist who's so self-pitying?*

LK: No. In my mind, Anne Tyler didn't see him that way. I have two sons of my own, and so the thought of Macon Leary's loss was so enormous to me that I understood his behavior completely. To me, it's not self-pity; it's devastation and he's been incapacitated by it. Frankly, I don't know that I would react as *well* as he did. Making the film, I knew he was a difficult hero. That's why I love William Hurt's performance, because he doesn't pander for a second; he doesn't ask you to like him, and he is a hard guy to like.

GF: *The tension in the last part of the movie comes from the dilemma he faces: will he accept this life-force, the Geena Davis character, into his life, or is he going to relinquish it and be doomed?*

LK: Every day we're faced with those kinds of choices. You don't have to experience enormous change to be faced with the choice between letting your life expand or staying in your room where you know certain things can happen and you control some of them.

GF: *It's about fear.*

LK: That's what everything's about.

GF: *Was Anne Tyler involved in the film?*

LK: When I went to Baltimore to scout locations, she drove me around, showed me the places she was thinking of. It was one of the high points of my life. I think she liked the movie and I think she was taken aback a little by what she'd written and seeing it embodied in that way. She may have been a little shocked by how grim it was. But in person she's very funny – and there is a lot of humor in the movie.

GF: *The look of the movie is very autumnal.*

LK: Yes. Macon's world is very closed-in. It's burnished, in a way. You know, he hasn't 'left the house' and there's something comforting about that, except there's no air in it. Everything stays the same. I have an aunt whom I've been going to visit for thirty years and nothing's moved in her house. A magazine will be in the same place it was five years before. That's her way of controlling her environment and that was the mood I was trying to achieve. It's a melancholy mood justified by the tragedy. But I don't think I realized how melancholy it would be for people coming to the movie fresh. A lot of them said, 'Why is it so depressing? Why is he so depressed?' But to me it was obvious.

37 *The Accidental Tourist*: Control

38 *The Accidental Tourist*: Chaos

What saves you, when you make a movie, is that you become a true believer in it. That's what gets you through it, not the thought that you're going to make the greatest movie ever. The only chance that you're going to do anything good is by being fanatical about the ideas as you see them. Sometimes other people will not see those ideas the way you do and it doesn't work for them. But a movie has a different relationship to everyone who sees it, and you hear enough people say to you, 'Yes, I got it,' to make you feel glad that you're doing this work, even though it may not be that popular. Sometimes you do work that is enormously popular and you say, 'I don't know if I should be doing this.'

GF: *Did you face resistance from Warner Bros. when you said you wanted to do* The Accidental Tourist?

LK: It was an odd thing. They wanted to do it and I don't know why. It was probably the easiest job I had to get a movie green-lighted. When it was done and the studio started sneak-previewing it, they didn't like it that much, but then we won the New York Film Critics' prize and they liked it better. We did well at the box-office, considering the kind of movie it is. I have sometimes been frustrated by the size of my audience, but not on that movie. I'm amazed we got as many people in to see it as we did. It was one of the most satisfying experiences I've ever had. I'm as proud of *The Accidental Tourist* as anything I've done.

GF: I Love You to Death *came from a true 1984 case about a woman [played by Tracey Ullman in the film] who tried to murder her husband [Kevin Kline] for his philanderings. It didn't do very well. Do you regard it as a missed opportunity?*

LK: I have more regrets about *I Love You to Death* than anything I've done, because Kostmayer had written an odd and interesting script. It was very funny to me, but there were things in it that were ugly. In post-production we started sneaking it, and most of the sneak audiences hated the movie – *despised* it. They hated certain things and I started taking those things out. We reshot the ending, added new scenes, and took out scenes that were difficult. I wanted to make the movie more popular and that was weak, because it got worse and worse. As a result, I've never used those sneak preview cards since. It wasn't as if the studio was making me change things.

GF: *What do you think went wrong?*

LK: I ruined the movie, I think. I don't think it would have ever done better than it did, but it would have been a better movie had I not taken out those things that were ugly and odd and unexpected. Those were very real things that Kostmayer had conceived and he was all for taking them out, too. But he was a novice and I had the responsibility. There are things in the film that are funny, that I'm proud of. Tracey Ullman did the opposite of what we expect from her; she held everything in. Other people did great work. But I think audiences didn't like the film because they want to go and see good-looking people achieving things. That's what American movies are about.

39 *I Love You to Death*: the family (Tracey Ullman, Kevin Kline, and Joan Plowright)

40 *I Love You to Death*: the assassins (William Hurt and Keanu Reeves)

GF: *The scenes involving William Hurt and Keanu Reeves as the zonked-out assassins hired by Rosalie [Ullman] to kill Joey [Kline] push the movie toward surrealism.*

LK: But it's not funny to a general audience to see a couple of drug addicts as Laurel and Hardy. That's what they were like – Mutt and Jeff.

GF: *Were you attempting to address the archetype of the sleazy, macho Latin lover in the character of Joey?*

LK: Yes. The film touches on a lot of archetypes in ways that are tasteless, which is another reason it's difficult. For me, Joey is the absolute clearest embodiment of a man who wants to be a good husband, gets married, and then wants to fuck every girl he sees. That's what leads to disaster.

GF: *The film's tacky-seedy flavor partly comes from its setting, Tacoma, an industrial town in a beautiful rural region of Washington.*

LK: I love that town, despite the terrible smell from the pulp mills. The actual story took place in Scranton, Pennsylvania, another ugly town in a beautiful setting. That was something familiar to me because I grew up in Wheeling and Morgantown, West Virginia, oppressively ugly towns with steelmills and coalmines in one of the most beautiful places in the country. Tacoma is part of the overall ugliness of the movie, which was intentional, but, again, I don't think that's what American audiences want to see.

GF: *Some of your images of Americana – such as the coffee-pot restaurant – are redolent of the way the country has been casually despoiled by commercialism.*

LK: And describing this is painful. People want to succeed, they want to be good people – all of them – and they're not making it. And there's Joey blithely enjoying his life, which is about to go out of control . . .

GF: Grand Canyon, *which you wrote with your wife Meg, was an altogether more spiritual work. It depicts a cross-section of people in Los Angeles, the haves and have-nots, some of whom come together during the course of the film. It was a prophetic picture in that it showed the social distress in Los Angeles, made all too apparent by the riots that followed the Rodney King verdict. It also struck me as a personal film with an element of wish-fulfilment about it. I wondered if it was prompted by your feeling guilty, to some extent, about living and working in Hollywood, on the edge of one of the most depressed areas in the country?*

LK: I think you can feel guilty *anywhere* in the country, any day, because the disparity among different social groups is so great. I know that some people said, 'This is a Hollywood film-maker feeling guilty,' but I think that if you were a lawyer in Cincinnati you'd feel the same way. It's not about my guilt; it's about the fact that the system doesn't work. The ideas we have for the country are in conflict with what's happened. People are not treated fairly. The world isn't fair.

That is accepted in most societies, but Americans are taught at an early age that everyone is equal and everyone has an equal right to happiness and security, but society hasn't delivered on that promise. To me, Los Angeles is a perfect example of that because of its physical layout. If you walk outside in

41 *Grand Canyon*: Mary Louise Parker, Mary McDonnell, Kevin Kline, Steve Martin, Danny Glover and Alfre Woodard

Manhattan, you never have a fantasy that you can separate yourself from poverty because when you cross the street you'll find yourself in the middle of it. Los Angeles has always had a fantasy of separation because of the distances between communities, but it's become clear that it *is* a fantasy – because if any of us are going down, we'll all go down. *Grand Canyon* was about the fact that, even within this lovely setting, there is enormous despair.

GF: *Did you set out, then, to make a social picture?*

LK: Yes, but again it started with the characters. I think that everybody in the movie is struggling to make a life and to control their fears and to make some kind of connection. There is enormous loneliness in the movie. The Mary-Louise Parker character [the secretary who has slept with her married boss Mack, played by Kevin Kline] embodies a lot of things that I see every day. She's someone struggling to make an investment in a relationship, to be happy.

GF: *It's the same with the Sarah Trigger character, who bursts into tears in the limo because she believes that her boyfriend [Steve Martin], the Hollywood producer, won't commit to her.*

LK: She can see that the world does not work that well, that it's a frightening place. Yet she's ready to demonstrate her faith by having children, which is harder and harder to do with an optimistic attitude. She says, 'It's just that I want to have children . . . I don't care how rotten the world is, I want to have them anyway. But I'm so far from being able to have them. I'm all involved with you and you're not going to have kids with me. We're not even getting married.' Her frustration is huge, and it is for all the characters. Every one of them is trying to make a connection in a scary environment.

GF: *You gave the scene where Mary McDonnell [as Mack's wife] finds the abandoned baby a kind of mystical glow. It's like a little fairy-tale amid all this urban angst.*

LK: It's the baby-in-the-bulrushes idea. She's achieved what we used to think was an ideal situation – freedom and comfort – but she's not happy. She has invested so much in her husband and her child, and now they don't seem to need her any more. Her kid has grown up and she no longer has anything to do. She sees the baby as her salvation, but she shouldn't need the baby to give focus to her life.

GF: *The scenes in South Central in* Grand Canyon *are not as harshly visualized as some directors have recently shown that neighborhood.*

LK: I thought the film was shot realistically. It's not like a New York picture, where you go into a tenement and see people shooting up. When you go to South Central, you're struck by what a neat neighborhood it is; it's not the South Bronx. If you stand at a distance, it looks like everything is working, but it isn't. LA is very deceptive that way. Simon [Danny Glover], the central black character in the film, is doing his job and succeeding to some extent. He's surrounded by despair but not giving in to it – he's very strong. I think some people objected to the ending of the film, as if it were an upbeat ending, though if people think it's upbeat, then I've failed. To me, the ending is a question: 'I can't do anything to repair the rifts in society, I am mystified by it, I don't know what our role is here, because it's so short and so temporary. We're just visiting this big rock, but what's our relationship to the rock and what are our higher concerns in relation to the planet?' Each character in the film relates differently to different issues; the only one who gets to voice his relationship to the planet is Simon, who has found some kind of philosophical respite from the world – but not a solution, not relief. Maybe that's why people think the ending is upbeat, but it's not. You know Simon and Mack and their families won't stay at the Grand Canyon; they're going back to LA. There is no running away from it. There is no safe place.

GF: *The Grand Canyon is a metaphor for the gulf between rich and poor?*

LK: That's it. That's what the Steve Martin character recognizes when he's in the golf cart on the studio lot. I talked earlier about the distance between the writer/director and his characters – but it's true that the characters do ask questions for the director. I do think that there is a huge problem developing in this country and that a rage is emerging. The images we get on the local news every night are images of violence and murder. Society is rupturing and it creates agony.

GF: *Do you think it's going to reach a cataclysmic point?*

LK: I am hopeful about the change of government in America. For twenty

42 *Grand Canyon*: on the studio lot (Steve Martin and Kevin Kline)

years we had leaders who said that things were all right and consequently nothing got done. Now we have leaders who say that things are terrible, but maybe they can improve them. Whether they succeed or not doesn't matter – what's most important is the *quest*.

If *Grand Canyon* really did have an upbeat ending – which it doesn't in my mind – why would that be so wildly inappropriate in these times? Why does every critic say, 'Oh, it's so Pollyanna-ish!' Does that mean that any kind of optimism about our ability to connect with other people is unjustified? I don't believe that. The press is so cynical and history supports their cynicism, but it's non-productive. What was great about last year's Democratic Convention was that people said with some passion that it still matters that we care about each other. If you don't try, there's no chance. I don't consider myself Pollyanna-ish or cynical, though I've been accused of both. I'm just trying to take it all in.

GF: *Is your film* Wyatt Earp *going to be a revisionist look at Earp's career? It can be argued that Earp and his brothers were no more law-abiding than their rivals, the Clantons and the McLaurys. Their story has never been told on film with any degree of realism.*

LK: No, it hasn't – it's always been idealized. When you know about the actual Earp story, Ford's version, *My Darling Clementine* – which is one of my favorite movies – seems like a fairy story, but a very powerful one. If I could make a film half as good as *My Darling Clementine* is, I would feel my whole life had been justified. Even though there are problems with it, it has images in it that are so sublime that they mesmerize me. No matter how fantastical its treatment of the

43 *My Darling Clementine*

44 *The Man Who Shot Liberty Valance*

Earp story, those images embody what was important to Ford about the American character. When you think of Henry Fonda in that film, his performance was as close to ballet as it was to acting, and that, to me, was as powerful as any image about America and about manhood. If Ford had shown me something grittier or more real, it wouldn't have been more true.

The movie I'm doing is much more about what Earp was like, but it is sympathetic to him in the sense that – and this is my interest in him on this day when we're doing this interview – he had certain ideas about the way life should be, and he stuck rigorously to his notions and it led to tragedy. This is a classic confrontation of legend and fact. There's something to be said for Ford's famous line in *The Man Who Shot Liberty Valance* – 'When the legend becomes fact, print the legend' – because who knows where the truth lies? Do you believe that the recorders of our history, the journalists, are giving us an accurate picture of what's going on now? I do not. So in the enormous amount of research I've done on Earp, reading many varying portraits of him, you wonder what the truth is. Who was Wyatt Earp? You will never know; you will only come up with a story. For me, he is not idealized – the way he was in *Frontier Marshal*, *My Darling Clementine*, and *Gunfight at the O.K. Corral* – but neither is he some horrible guy because, in fact, he wasn't. One reason I love this story is that Earp is a larger-than-life character who does extraordinary things, and yet he's a very human guy with real conflicts between his desires and his ideals.

GF: *Couldn't you say, though, that the Earps were essentially a criminal element – the guys who ran the brothels and the gambling, killers when necessary – who used law-enforcement to suit their own ends?*

LK: They were like that whole class of lawmen who were willing to do a lot of different things, who wanted to be entrepreneurs and tried to make a go of it as saloon-owners and gamblers. They did the basic American thing, which is to try to build up your fortune. But they were only good at one thing, which was being lawmen. A lot of attention has been focused on their involvement in the gunfight at the O.K. Corral in Tombstone, which was a very ambiguous event, but the fact was they had been very successful lawmen in other towns.

GF: *What parts of Earp's life will the movie cover?*

LK: A lot of it. It starts when he was young and focuses on the period between 1871 and 1881, when the gunfight at the O.K. Corral took place. I've never talked about a movie I've yet to make before, and it will be interesting to me to see much how I achieve between now, when I'm just finishing the script, and when I'm done with the whole thing. I don't know what it will wind up to be, because I'm hoping to breathe all that air into it that I was talking about earlier. It's clear to me, at this point, that Wyatt Earp embodied a lot of American problems. No matter what the reality was, when you mention the name Wyatt Earp people think of a lawman cleaning up a town. That is the American idea:

that you can go into Vietnam and clean up the situation, that you can go into
Somalia with 17,000 Marines and clean up the situation there. Time and time
again, you see that it doesn't work, because the situation cannot be cleaned up.
Wyatt Earp found that out, too. He is like an exemplar of a certain aspect of
American society. And was he compromised? Absolutely, as are most people.
He was rigid and unforgiving, and loyal to his friends, and when you were an
enemy he could not see you clearly. That's a real American way.

GF: *What will the shape of the film be?*

LK: It's an epic and that's always dangerous. But I can't think of a better canvas
for an epic than the American West with these men and their women struggling in a harsh but beautiful environment to make some sense out of their
lives. There's the opportunity for incredible images. This was a very brief
period in our history – 1865 to 1890 – what we think of as the Wild West, and
Earp walked right down the center of it. He went west on a wagon train, he
worked as a teamster, hunted buffalo, became a lawman, tried to make it as a
businessman, was a gambler, a miner, lived to be eighty. Anywhere where
things were happening, there he was, but along the way he lost the thing that
was most dear to him – his family. It was a miracle that he lived because he was
in all these gunfights. He just survived. Never got hit.

GF: *Does Doc Holliday function as a foil to Earp in your script?*

LK: Yes, as he really did. Their actual relationship is practically incomprehen-
sible to us now. Holliday, who was dying when they met, just latched on to
Earp, and Earp obviously developed a real affection for him. But their friend-
ship wasn't helpful to Earp at all, because Holliday was an unpopular and
infamous guy. They just connected in some way, right through this dramatic
episode in Earp's life.

GF: *Presumably it won't look too much like* Silverado, *despite your affection for the*
High Noon *look. You'll dress Wyatt and Doc and Bat Masterson in derbies and frock
coats?*

LK: *Silverado* is an imagined West. Hopefully, this will be much more authentic. It was a very beautiful place, though there was enormous squalor in
those towns. They had no garbage disposal, no sewerage systems. I don't know
how much of that I'm going to show, because I'm walking the same line that
Ford walked – legend versus fact – and the Earp legend is terribly important.
But I don't know if I can get a hold of the fact because I don't really believe in
it. I don't know the true story of people living now. I'm not sure I know my own
true story.

GF: *What you're saying is that the mythic resonances are what make the movie worth
making.*

LK: Earp looms larger than he deserves to. The gunfight at the O.K. Corral,
the most famous gunfight in the history of the West, wasn't even a *good*
gunfight. It was a mess, just a street brawl; there was nothing classic or

monumental about it. But it gave us this very powerful image of Earp and his two brothers walking down the street to face the enemy; and standing with them is his friend, this dissipated dentist Doc Holliday, who's a very dangerous guy. Right there, that's a very attractive idea from American folklore. No one really bestrides that era as a giant: Wild Bill Hickok, the other legendary marshal, was a very compromised guy. What you're dealing with is the inter-section between what these guys were and what they came to represent.

GF: Wyatt Earp *is your most ambitious project. Given the mythic elements we've talked about, the casting of Kevin Costner as Earp, and the strong revival of the Western, it has the potential, if successful, to give you substantial creative power. You've expressed, at different times, some disappointment about the general state of Hollywood film-making, but by pursuing personal, humanist and often unfashionable subjects, you've carved a unique place for yourself in mainstream cinema. What, ultimately, has been the key to that – is it in your screenwriting or simply in the desire to do it?*

LK: It's been said that a Buddha is what you do to it. Accordingly, Hollywood is whatever you want it to be – I believe that very strongly. You simply have to have the will. The studios are in chaos and fear, more than most businesses, although most businesses operate that way. If you can convince them that you can give them what they want, if you can repeatedly take care of their need to fill theaters, you can do anything you want. You can have enormous freedom. Film-makers tend to underestimate their own power and overestimate the resistance of the studios to their ideas, and they often give in before the fight. Writing my own scripts has obviously given me enormous leverage because I don't need the studios' stories or scripts, but they've given me the support I need within the system and so I've made Hollywood movies. For me, a lot of the most powerful movies were made within that same system – I include *Lawrence of Arabia* and *The Seven Samurai* in that. And those are the kinds of movies I want to make.

Hollywood Bound

Michael Tolkin writes about interviewing screenwriter Robert Towne, about the screenwriters he admires, how he struggled to become one himself in a town where writers are treated with ambivalence, if not disdain.

In contrast, producer Art Linson tussles with screenwriter David Mamet over The Untouchables.

Quentin Tarantino tells us how he made it by the sheer bravura of his writing. He stunned Hollywood with witty violence and gratuitous humour – a combination that proved irresistible in Reservoir Dogs.

Sally Potter kept a diary of her promotion tour for Orlando. *The major studios fell at her feet with offers but, in fact, none of them would have made* Orlando.

Gus Van Sant offers us a section of his work in progress which he describes as 'a biographical novel with a few movie hints. It's an attempt to pass on some things I have learned working in the cinema to film-makers at whatever crossroads (Stoplights? Watering holes?) they might be in their careers.'

45 Michael Tolkin (photo by Scott C. Schulman)

8   The Struggles of a
Screenwriter
Michael Tolkin

In 1977 I interviewed Robert Towne for the *Village Voice*. I was twenty-seven, and tired of journalism, and tired of the East, where I'd lived since graduating from high school in Los Angeles ten years before. Robert Towne was the most famous screenwriter of the decade, and a hero to every writer I knew. He had already written *The Last Detail*, *Shampoo* and *Chinatown*. His movies were as much about the possibility of what movies could be as they were about anything else, about the times, about society. His credit was equal to his directors'. Probably every writer I knew in those years wanted to direct. We certainly talked more about movies than novels, and I suppose we all secretly wanted to run the show, or even not so secretly, but there was a suspicion, useful to our pride, that somehow the technical and political skills necessary for directing interfered with those rich qualities of character, filled with the silt of experience, that made us writers. Of course, we thought we were good writers and in those days smart writers in their twenties could look to the movies for examples of writers who had not lost their identity as writers, that screenwriting was an achievement by itself, the result of a specific private effort, a discipline. In those days we saw films that seemed to be simultaneously acts of criticism and examples of what the movies could be like if we lived in Utopia. There was Towne, Schrader, Milius, Adrian Joyce, Carol Eastman, Waldo Salt, Paddy Chaefsky, Benton and Newman, Willard and Gloria Huyck, William Goldman. Coppola's first Oscar was as a writer, for the *Patton* screenplay. Even Sylvester Stallone's legend began as the story of a writer who created *Rocky* for himself, and turned down four hundred thousand dollars to let James Caan play the part.

When I went to visit Towne on a trip to Los Angeles, I didn't go just as an interviewer, I was really going as a pilgrim to visit the Master, to feel his presence. I needed to see what he looked like, to see if he was so different from what I thought I could be, a writer in Hollywood.

After a few bad starts in high school, I finished my first script when I was in college. It was about a junk-shop in a Mojave Desert town that dies when the freeway comes by without an off-ramp. My father, a television writer, gave it to his agent. The script, *Curios*, was a kind of spiritual sequel to *Two Lane Blacktop*, and I probably should have sent it to Monte Hellman, but I asked my

46 *Patton*: George C. Scott

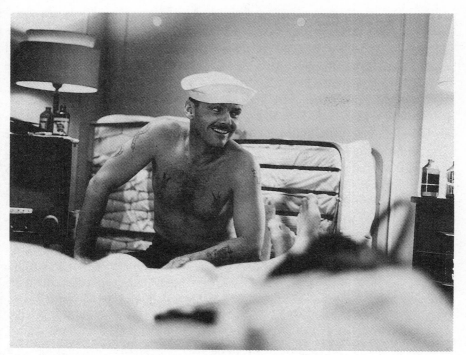

47 *The Last Detail*: Jack Nicholson

48 *Two Lane Blacktop*: Dennis Wilson, Laura Bird and James Taylor

father's agent to send it to Steven Spielberg, because I thought that *Duel*, which had just shown on television, captured something about the desert that I hadn't seen before, the deadpan paranoia. He wrote back an encouraging note, but the script wasn't for him.

I stayed in school and put the script away. After college, I went to New York, and on the subway one day I saw a friend on his way to the race-track, and I went with him and stayed three months and came back with a magazine article and sold it to the *Voice*, and then I was a journalist. In those days, I forgot that I had once wanted to make movies. Journalism was still interesting then, the city was an orgy, and there were stories everywhere. Mostly I wrote about people on the fringes of things, bad comedians, salesmen, swingers. The paper assigned me to write a profile of Tom McGuane after he directed *92 In the Shade* from his own screenplay and novel. The piece was mean and arrogant, mocking him. I was congratulated by senior staff, who were getting tired of me because I needed a lot of editing. A career was forming. McGuane wrote a violent letter to the paper, too long to be published, and everyone there laughed at it, but he was right to feel hurt. He was doing what I wanted to do, he wasn't so much older than I was, he was more accomplished and I had made him unhappy. For what?

Towne, my model, was reluctant to talk because he didn't have a movie in release, but he said that he would meet me if I would include in the article more than just a courtesy mention of his efforts to stop the slaughter of dolphins caught in the long nets of the tuna fleet. He wanted me to help him. I owed a karmic debt after the McGuane article, and I said I would.

He lived on Hutton Drive, a small street leading up a hill in Benedict Canyon. He was just across the road from the first house my parents rented when we moved from New York in 1960. My father's career began in live television, and we left when the industry there died. While my parents unpacked on the day we arrived in Los Angeles, I went outside and saw a monkey, escaped from a back-yard cage, walk along the telephone wire in front of the house that Towne would move into.

I was overwhelmed by the physical reality of this writer's life. His house was smaller than I expected, a one-story ranch house, two bedrooms, I think, with a pleasant living-room looking out on a shaded patio. His Oscar was tucked away in the office, but what I remember after sixteen years were some old architectural drawings of Los Angeles in the thirties, or maybe they were an art director's sketches for movie sets. I got the feeling the drawings had come to him for his work, that someone interesting knew he would like them, that his work had attracted something beautiful and appropriate, that he had them as a reward for his work.

I'm not sure how old he was then, probably a bit younger than I am now, in his late thirties, and he was cautious around me. Since then, I've probably seen him at a distance two or three times. He's a serious man; perhaps the part of him that didn't fit my generic notion of writers or artists was his lack of humor. Through my father, all of the writers I knew wrote comedy and they were always performing, there was always something silly about them, even as they were generous with their humor and shared it with children. Towne was different, but he was also the most important writer I had ever met, and he seemed burdened by his thoughts. He wasn't a wise guy like me.

He had a large Hungarian dog with a thousand white dreadlocks. There's a Writers Guild rule that says if you take your name off a movie you lose all residual payments that might come to you, but you don't if you use a pseudonym. When *Greystoke* came out, after he'd been fired from it first as director and then as writer, Towne refused screen credit and gave it to the dog, P. H. Vazak.

I worried he would guess that my real purpose for the interview was to see him, that everything else was pretext. We talked about his movies. He talked about the dolphins. The fate of the dolphins was a real issue with him now, because the tuna fishermen were killing thousands of them. Towne grew up partly in San Pedro, and knew the Portuguese fishermen in the harbor's tuna fleet. He was talking to them, and he understood how hard it was for a writer to lecture to men who risked their lives about why they should spend money on nets that would not hurt dolphins, but it was something that mattered to him.

Now I can recognize the symptoms of Towne's discomfort with being interviewed, even the source of his sober dignity, because of course everything I asked him he had already been asked a dozen, a hundred times. One wants to be helpful, one wants to set the record straight, one is interested to hear one's alienated voice shape a slightly new twist to an old answer, one would like the journalist with his damaged tape-recorder, his bad shoes and his inappropriate chumminess to evaporate in a mist of his own sulfurous envies.

Three things he said have stayed with me. The first took me a long time to understand, and he said it to a group of film students the next day at an American Film Institute seminar: 'Make movies with your friends.' On the surface, this seemed cruel advice, since his friends were Hal Ashby and Warren Beatty and Jack Nicholson, but of course they weren't when he met them.

The second thing was this: I think I said something to him like, 'You don't know how many writers look up to you.' And then he said, 'By the time success came to me, I was too tired to recognize it.' It seemed almost too coy to me, that a man could have an Oscar in the house and not feel confident about every breath for the next fifty years. This is journalism's weakness, to see ritual instead of struggle.

And then he said that a friend of his told him a story about the women who sew mink coats, and how highly paid they are. And Towne had wondered why, and the answer had been, because the work requires such intense concentration that eventually the seamstresses lose their vision. And this applies to Hollywood. He said that eventually he was going to join the next generation of assholes.

He took a call from Warren Beatty, and they made a date for dinner.

I went back to New York, where my editor wanted to throw out all of the material about the dolphins. I'm sure the rest of the article was empty, and it never ran.

A year later, and I was living in Los Angeles.

By the time I moved here, the new writers to be scared of were Lawrence Kasdan and Oliver Stone. Of course, the press didn't really cover them but writers knew who they were, and the fear their names inspired came from their simultaneous ability to conquer the difficult form of the screenplay and the difficult business of Hollywood. When Oliver Stone won his Oscar for *Midnight Express*, we saw a writer, and his name on *Scarface* guaranteed that we could feel a specific energy in the film that wasn't just De Palma's. Kasdan's name on *Revenge of The Jedi* was an endorsement of the idea of the sequel, that the film was a real movie. And then Stone and Kasdan became directors, betraying everyone who held to fantasies of the writer's power. The generation that came to cultural power in the seventies had enormous influence, and we are still living with the forms they gave us, but other than William Goldman, every interesting writer who was significant fifteen to twenty years ago and who is working successfully today is now also a director.

There's a terrible ambivalence about writers, certainly in the industry, definitely in the entertainment press. When the *Los Angeles Times* prints its annual list of the films expected to be released in the next twelve months, the directors are always cited. Almost without exception, unless the writers are famous, their names are left out.

Why this disdain for writers, the refusal to give them separate attention unless they somehow develop cachet, which is never on a large scale?

In a crowded age, writers are envied for the solitude they need, and in this solitude they are expected to maintain something like a conscience, and when this is betrayed, when they do something that's called 'selling out', they're hated for letting everyone down. One struggles to think of ways that a director can sell out so badly his reputation suffers for ever.

The vulgar notion of the sell-out falls harder, as usual, on writers than on directors. Writers are more quickly accused of selling out than directors. Writers sell out, directors miss. A director can stun the world a few times, then follow his vanity into half-a-dozen miserable lapses. When he returns to glory, the industry forgives what had formerly been reviled, as he sweeps his collaborators' chips from the table and adds them to his own account. Writers are not so richly indulged, but maybe they should be thankful that someone still believes that a moral torch has to be kept lighted somewhere in this world, and the thing that writers have to sell is valued, is real, is precious. If writers are envied for their freedom from physical labor, from commerce with the crowd, they're expected to use this unbelievable luxury well. Then by selling it, they lose something, they have degraded something in themselves and disappointed those who had faith in them. The common wisdom of this concept suggests that once sold, this precious thing can't be regained. It takes a long time for a director with a good reputation to become a hack, and even then, some respect is always there, but writers can fall. John Frakenheimer still works; how many of the writers he started with are still getting their movies made? Directors are given second chances, third chances, fifth chances, whole careers based on a few early hits.

Why do we accuse writers of being hacks more quickly than directors? What is a hack? The problem in selling out is that when you mix your blood with the blood of a bad idea, when you give your best to a bad idea, a process of reflux draws the bad into you. Writers who succeed with their own ideas and then cash in their vision have trouble regaining what was theirs. Fine directors can make commercials, either for money or just to experiment with the camera, but what could a writer achieve by writing the copy for an Armani ad? Yes, it's possible that the director who leaves features for commercials is also harmed by adding noise to the world, but the damage to his art is not so apparent or immediate.

Or look at the problem this way: Other than for the money, I'm not really sure why anyone would want to be a screenwriter now, someone whose ambition it is to write movies but not to direct them. I have to rephrase this. For the screenwriter-who-does-not-want-to-direct, with ambitions to greatness, not just box-office, whose concerns, however inflated with cineastic pretension, take into their sphere of consideration matters of form, film history, sincere competition with heroes, and a need to record something of the complexity of the world, what can we offer?

Are there any screenwriters today, who are not directors, whose careers are followed by anyone other than agents and studio executives? Beyond the pleasant drunken evenings of a film festival, to which writers are only invited when the directors are unavailable, or a few reviews by critics generous enough to mention the writing as something either separate from the director, or something that the director, in this picture as compared to his last picture(s), did not wreck with his usual self-indulgence, what's left but posterity? Are there any screenwriters-who-are-not-directors for people dreaming of writing screenplays to look up to? The artist who waits for election by posterity lives in a vanity so profound that the better word for it is despair. So, for the screenwriters-who-are-not-directors, who are the models today?

Richard Corliss' list of pure screenwriters in the December 1992 issue of

Film Comment embraces Joe Eszterhas, Carrie Fisher, Horton Foote, Lowell Ganz and Babaloo Mandel, Callie Khouri, Craig Lucas, Daniel Waters. Corliss leans towards respectable films; I would add Shane Black and Jeb Stuart. There were a few others, but since then they've become directors. Some of these people only have one or two sole credits, which doesn't really define a career.

Here are some writers with careers:

These are the names of the writers who worked with Kurosawa, together and separately*: Ejiro Hisaita wrote *No Regrets For Our Youth, The Idiot, The Bad Sleep Well.* Ryuzo Kikushima wrote *Stray Dog, Scandal, The Throne of Blood, The Hidden Fortress, The Bad Sleep Well, Yojimbo, Sanjuro, High and Low, Red Beard.* Shinobu Hashimoto wrote *Rashomon, Ikiru, Seven Samurai, Record of a Living Being, The Throne of Blood, The Hidden Fortress, The Bad Sleep Well.* Hideo Oguni wrote *Ikiru, Seven Samurai, Record of a Living Being, The Throne of Blood, The Lower Depths, The Hidden Fortress, The Bad Sleep Well, Sanjuro, High and Low, Red Beard.* And Masato Ite also worked on *Red Beard.*

There's a legend that has Federico Fellini going to the set with the actors and telling them just to count instead of saying dialogue, so that he could make up the story in the editing room. These men worked with Fellini†: Tulio Pinelli and Ennio Flaianol wrote *The White Sheik, I Vitelloni, La Strada, Il Bidone, Nights of Cabiria* (on which Pasolini adapted the Romagnan dialect), and were joined by Brunello Rondi for *La Dolce Vita, 8½,* and *Juliet of The Spirits.* Tonino Guerra, Antonioni's great collaborator (*L'Avventura, La Notte, L'Eclisse*) who also did *Nostalgia* for Tarkovsky, wrote *Amarcord.* Bernardino Zapponi wrote *Toby Dammit, Satyricon, The Clowns,* and *Roma.*

It's obvious from these lists that, as the directors changed writers their movies changed, and the films unified by style or theme represent more than just the director's vision. Stupid to argue against the director's authority in this, but stupid also to deny writers.

The directors also knew that it's almost impossible for one person to write a great movie. Of course, actors come up with good ideas, so do directors, sometimes. It's piggish and disgusting when they don't thank the writers, but it's also the way things have always been and the way things will always be. The scrambling for credit among writers in Hollywood reflects everyone's fear that somehow they'll be thought less of by having to share.

---

*Donald Ritchie, *The Film of Akira Kurosawa*, University of California Press, Berkeley and Los Angeles, 1970.
†Pinelli was a playwright, and Flaiano was a novelist and essayist. Since they wrote the films together, it's impossible to separate their contributions, but Flaiano's book *The Via Veneto Papers* (Marlboro Press), which is part journal and part philosophy, gives a beautiful picture of the fifties and sixties in Rome. I suspect that Pinelli gave the films their solid construction, while Flaiano, a social observer obsessed with hypocrisy, was the ironist and moralist. I can't recommend it enough.

49 *8½*: Marcello Mastroianni

Some writers who don't direct try to protect themselves by becoming producers, but the real work of producing is something few writers understand or have the resources for, in the bank or the address-book. When a writer says he wants to produce, all he's really saying is that he wants an official title that protects him from being fired by the director. Most writers who want to produce negotiate their credit with experienced producers, who have the skill to give their writers the illusion of effectiveness without letting them get in the way of the production, even if that means hiring other writers, and letting the director, finally, have whatever he wants.

If the ambition to write great screenplays can't be separated from directing, then screenwriting is hopelessly devalued as an art in itself. The Writers Guild has made an issue of age discrimination in the Industry, and it's quite clear that, over forty, it's hard to get work these days unless you're established. I'm sure there's obnoxious prejudice on the part of twenty-eight-year-old story editors, but at the same time, since it's so hard to get a movie made, at a certain point it has to follow that people in their forties or fifties are going to be disheartened by the process of getting their work produced, and won't have the craft, stamina, humor or energy to make a studio comfortable about cutting large checks. And what does it really mean to be established? A few strong credits can launch ten years of work with nothing else produced, but to be established now seems to mean having a good seat at the table where the most adaptable novels are handed out, and where the scripts with the best directors and biggest stars are looking for rewrites. At this level, screenwriting is no longer a matter of bringing one's vision to the world, unless the vision is of entertainment. In these conditions, how can any writer hope for posterity's good judgement when the system makes it impossible for anyone, with the exception of comedy writers and action writers, to develop a body of work large enough to secure a reputation and a tangible style that defines a set of themes and obsessions, of marks?

A few years ago Michael Eisner said something about the miracle of Hollywood being the kid from Ohio coming out here with twenty-five cents and a screenplay that will change the world, and that it's not as though the system doesn't know it all begins with the word, but the system doesn't believe, and has no reason to believe, that the word belongs to the writer.

The system makes it almost impossible for writers to find out how good they really are, or what they're really thinking about, what kind of patterns they keep repeating, what parts of their imaginations need to be explored, or how they can learn to improve their sense of structure, how to fit their complicated ideas to a film's need for simplicity and brevity. Maybe this can all be reduced to a simple maxim: it's hard to get better. Directors aren't fired every two weeks. Editors aren't fired off of every picture, but most scripts are rewritten.

And after they're rewritten, the credits are contested, because only credited writers get their production bonuses and residuals, and when the battle is over everyone is drained and no one is really sure of their contribution any more. The strategy of each writer subsequent to the original writer is to erase as many traces as possible of earlier work so as to influence the arbitration committee, which reads every relevant draft of the script to determine who should get credit and in what form. Rewriters may deny this tactic, but changing character names, paraphrasing description and changing dialogue just for the sake of making the script look different are standard practices designed to get a credit award.

The Writers Guild assembles three writers unknown to each other and the contestant screenwriters, who review all of the scripts and then, using guidelines set down in the Guild's credits manual, award the credit. The decisions of the committee are final, although a review board can be assembled if a losing writer finds procedural fault. In the last few years writers who have lost credit, and writers who have been forced to share credit when they felt they deserved sole credit, have complained about the rules. The old manual was a few pages long and assumed that everyone in the process, writers and arbiters, was going to be fair. Drafted at a time when the Guild was smaller and presumably a greater percentage of members were getting their movies made, the rules were loose and the language was relaxed. Now the manual is twice as long and filled with detailed definitions of every term. For example:

Story: The term 'story' means all writing covered by the provisions of the Minimum Basic Agreement representing a contribution 'distinct from screenplay and consisting of basic narrative, idea, theme or outline indicating character development and action.'

Screen Story: Credit for story authorship in the form 'Screen Story by' is appropriate when the screenplay is based upon source material and a story, as those terms are defined above, and the story is substantially new or different from the source material.

Screenplay: A screenplay consists of individual scenes and full dialogue, together with such prior treatment, basic adaptation, continuity, scenario and dialogue as shall be used in, and represent substantial contributions to, the final script.

'Written by': The term 'Written by' is used when the writer(s) is entitled to both the 'Story by' credit and the 'Screenplay by' credit. This credit shall not be granted when there is source material of a story nature. However, biographical, newspaper and other factual sources may not necessarily deprive the writer of such credit.

'Narration Written by': 'Narration Written by' credit is appropriate where the major writing contribution to a motion picture is in the form of narration. The term 'narration' means material (typically off-camera) to explain or relate sequence or action (excluding promos or trailers).

'Based on Characters Created by': 'Based on Characters Created by' is a writing credit given to the writer(s) entitled to separated rights in a theatrical or television motion picture or each theatrical sequel to such theatrical or television motion picture.

Which all leads to this:

RULES FOR DETERMINING CREDIT:
'Screenplay by'
a. Original and Non-Original Screenplays
For purposes of determining 'Screenplay by' credit only, two categories of screenplays
are recognized:

    (1) Original screenplays (i.e., those screenplays which are not based on source
       material and on which the first writer writes a screenplay without there being any
       other intervening literary material by another writer pertaining to the project). In
       the case where a team writes a story, and there is no source material, and one
       member of the team goes on to write a screenplay without there being any other
       intervening literary material by any other writer, the screenplay shall still be
       considered an 'original screenplay'. If a writer is furnished or uses research
       material, the screenplay is still considered an original screenplay; and

    (2) Non-original screenplays (i.e., screenplays based upon source material and all
       other screenplays not covered in (1) above, such as sequels).

Percentage Contribution Necessary to Receive Screenplay Credit.

    (1) In the case of Original Screenplays:

    (a) If there are only two screenplay writers, then the first writer must contribute at
       least 25% to the screenplay to receive credit and the second must contribute
       40% to the screenplay to receive credit.

    (b) If there are three or more screenplay writers and the first writer's contribution is
       at least 40% to the screenplay, then a subsequent writer must contribute 40% to
       the screenplay to share credit;

    (c) If there are three or more screenplay writers and the first writer's contribution is
       less than 40%, then any writer who contributes 25% to the screenplay shall be
       entitled to screenplay credit;

    (d) If there are three or more screenplay writers and no individual writer contributes
       enough to be entitled to screenplay credit under subparagraphs (b) or (c) above.
       then those writers making the most significant contributions to the screenplay
       shall be entitled to screenplay credit, not to exceed four writers.

    (2) In the case of Non-Original Screenplays:

    (a) If there are only two writers on screenplay, then any writer who contributes 33%
       to the screenplay shall be entitled to screenplay credit;

    (b) If there are three or more writers on screenplay, any writer who contributes 25%
       to the screenplay shall be entitled to screenplay credit;

    (c) If there are four or more screenplay writers, none of whom contribute 25% to
       the screenplay, then the most significant contributors to the screenplay, not to
       exceed four writers, shall be entitled to screenplay credit.

The percentage contribution made by writers to screenplay obviously cannot be
determined by counting lines or even the number of pages to which a writer has
contributed. Arbiters must take into consideration the following elements in determining whether a writer is entitled to screenplay credit:

    (a) dramatic construction or structure (i.e., the ordering or internal structuring of
       scenes so as to affect dramatic values). The ordering or structuring of scenes
       affecting basic narrative line should be considered a contribution to the story,
       not the screenplay;

    (b) original and different scenes;

    (c) point of view, style or attitude;

    (d) characterization or character relationships; and

    (e) dialogue.

I've been a judge three times and I've been judged twice. On *Gleaming The Cube* I won an arbitration. On *Deep Cover* there was a forced arbitration because the other writer was a producer; there was an ugly fight, but we finally settled out of court. And I was the ugly one. The battles are wretched. The contestant writers send in letters detailing their contributions and proving that they deserve credit. The first writer always tries to show how little was changed from the last draft he worked on. At the time when a writer should feel a little bit of triumph, he's scrambling for crumbs in the mud. In the past, in the case of original scripts, subsequent writers had to contribute more than 50 per cent to get credit, and in the case of scripts based on other sources, 33 per cent. Under the new rules it will be easier for contributing writers to get credit. Composed as guidelines for the arbiters, the rules are also a brilliantly clear instruction manual for rewriters, as the race to get a movie made turns into a race to get a first position in the credits.

It would be pretty if everyone accepted the notion of movies as collaboration, which is a nice concept – the film as Swedish automobile, assembled by a team – but of course the game is much harder than that, more emotionally brutal. If you're writing on assignment, if you've been hired by the studio to adapt a book, and they fire you and hire someone else because they didn't like what you wrote, it's easy to rationalize the failure as being on the part of dense producers. But to be fired from an original idea is a much more painful event, to be told that you're not as good as your own idea, that you didn't realize your own potential. And these days it's hard to keep it secret that you've been dumped, because almost every day there's a filler item in the trade papers saying that an. original writer has been replaced. And looking at careers over the last few years, the non-directing writers who thrive are usually the best rewriters, not the people with the most interesting original scripts.

The original writer, if he's going to continue to write without feeling punished or diminished by having been fired from his script, has to be someone with an inhumanly clear sense of his own contribution, and a generous regard for the contributions of the other writers. No wonder we drink.

I was at the press conference for *The Player* in New York, in a hotel ballroom where a hundred reporters, flown in from around the country, were sitting at round tables, about eight or nine at each one, with the microphones all pointed to an empty seat, a happy Passover table confident of Elijah's return. Every twenty or thirty minutes a bell rang, and like that scene in *Darling* where everyone on the beach turned over to even their tans when the alarm clock went off, we left our tables and marched to the next. I was behind some of the cast, and though I'd been interviewed about the movie a few times already, and I knew most of the questions – which were usually about how we got the stars to play themselves, and is Hollywood really like this? – in that ballroom the first question at every table was new: 'The actors are saying they improvised the movie. How do you feel about that?'

Well, I'd had casting approval, but it was a little too late to invoke that privilege. I mumbled a few things about film being collaborative, but in the middle of my triumph I felt sick, defeated, and betrayed. I wanted to scream, 'Did these actors improvise their way into the movies? Did these actors improvise their characters? Did they improvise locations? Did they improvise the story? So these actors play with a few lines and they think that qualifies them as writers? Doesn't anybody know how movies are made? Don't you know that writers have to be kept off the set, not because it's bad for the director, but to protect the writer? That keeping the writers off the set is as necessary for their health as using general anesthesia during open-heart surgery, with the same end, to reduce the pain? So the writers' cries don't end up on the sound-track? Don't you know that?'

I kept my mouth shut.

(Michael Tolkin's screenplays of *The Player*, *The Rapture* and *The New Age* are published by Grove/Atlantic Monthly Press.)

9 The Perils of Producing
Art Linson

I am trying to figure out what lesson one could learn from reviewing my journey with David Mamet as he was hired to write *The Untouchables*. Just remembering it has caused me such anxiety that the only conclusion I can draw is that it has taught me the need for patience, humility – some might say groveling – and, in the end, improvisation. It has also taught me to use the expression, 'I don't care, you are bought and paid for.'

As I was driving down Seventh Avenue toward the Chelsea District in Manhattan, I was considering how to persuade Mamet to write *The Untouchables* for Paramount Pictures. I was never a big fan of the television series, but I loved the subject matter. Al Capone, Eliot Ness, bootlegging, machine-gun violence, Chicago in the 1930s were a significant part of American folklore. I knew that if we could take the high road, the movie could be great. I wanted a high-priced writer who would distinguish the movie, rather than approach it as another trashy remake chasing a famous title.

Ned Tanen and Dawn Steel offered no resistance.

At the time, Dawn was the most powerful female movie executive in Hollywood, but she did report to Tanen. She was volatile, ambitious, supportive and had long, thick hair. Mamet, who had established himself as a major playwright with *American Buffalo* and *Glengarry Glen Ross* (for which he won a Pulitzer Prize) and as a major screenwriter with his adaptation of *The Verdict*, was at the top of our list. He and I had yet to meet, but I knew he was from Chicago, Al Capone's stomping ground.

When he climbed into my limo, he reminded me of a Jew with a buzz cut trying to impersonate a biker. Judging from his play *Speed-the-Plow*, which he later wrote about Hollywood, I must have reminded him of a clammy rag salesman in casual clothes. I immediately liked him. He, however, remained suspicious.

We went to a small Italian restaurant in SoHo. I waited until we were seated to discuss the inevitable. I thought that the best approach would be to mention the historical significance of the project, to emphasize the intrinsic value in portraying American icons in a meaningful context. It would be a chance for him to re-create his hometown in a legendary way. My head was overtaxed with facts about Al and Eliot. I had committed to memory laborious details of

50 Art Linson (photo by Deborah Feingold)

all the plays and scripts Mamet had written, trying to find some connections that would coax him into taking on this assignment.

I was prepared.

The waiter inquired if we wanted anything to drink. I ordered a bottle of wine. I stared at Mamet for a pregnant moment, grinning. Overloaded with so much information, I didn't know where to begin. Mamet just looked at me curiously. I didn't realize it at the time, but the concept of Hollywood coming to visit him always gave him a twisted thrill. It was time to say something.

'Dave, don't you think that the best career move for somebody who just won the Pulitzer Prize would be to adapt an old television series like *The Untouchables* for a *shitload* of money?' I asked. This was the best I could come up with.

Without a beat, he said, 'Yes, I think so.'

I said, 'Great, let's eat.'

That was it.

Within four weeks after the deal was closed, Mamet turned in his first draft. Some writers take four months, and many can take up to a year to hand in a draft. This was quick. My cynicism was kindled. Was he taking the money and running, or was he just flat out fast?

When I read it, I did have some initial concerns: Capone seemed sparsely drawn, and the plot contained some confusions, but the basic elements that made the movie special were all there. The brilliant invention of the Malone character (Sean Connery) as the reluctant teacher of Ness, who helps to clean up Chicago and dies for it, was breathtaking.

MALONE: You want to get Capone? Here's how you get him: he pulls a knife, you pull a gun; he sends one of yours to the hospital, you send one of his to the morgue.

When Capone was finally put away for income tax evasion and bootlegging, Mamet's true-blue, straight-talking Ness provided the only irony in the movie.

REPORTER: They say they're going to repeal Prohibition. What will you do then?
NESS: I think I'll have a drink.

For me the screenplay was emotional, witty, and filled with unexpected, memorable exchanges that would distinguish it from the television series. But I felt that there was still work to be done. Two problems, however, had to be confronted: David hated to do rewrites (particularly if they took more than two days), and the studio didn't warm to this first draft, especially after it had been sneaked to a couple of A directors who turned it down.

This is how the process works. A screenplay is turned in to the studio, and it is read not only by the heads of the Motion Picture Department (in this case Tanen and Steel) but also by the rest of the staff, which can include as many as ten junior executives. Of course, some of them have more say than others, but in their weekly staff meetings a comprehensive discussion of the merits of new submissions will occur. Those at the top can be influenced by the junior executives, because knowing 'what is good' is disturbingly subjective. Needless to say, trying to please a dozen people – many of whom are so inexperienced that they've never been involved in the making of a movie – with an unconventional screenplay can be a very formidable and troublesome affair.

To compound the difficulty, Mamet's screenwriting style is quite different from others'. Executives, who claim to read dozens of scripts each week, get used to a particular format. Screenwriters learn to write screenplays by reading other screenplays. I assume that when you are confronted with something different the natural instinct is to think it's wrong. You know, sort of like the white baby chicks pecking out the eyes of the black chick for being different. The first thing you notice about Mamet is that the characters do not always sound conversational in the way we are used to. I call it Mametese, and, believe me, it has turned off more than a few executives.

When the mother of the little girl who gets blown up at the beginning of the script visits Ness, she says:

MRS BLACKMER: It was my little girl they killed with that bomb. (*Beat.*) You
     see, because I know that you have children, too. And this is real to you.
     That these men cause us tragedy. (*Beat. She nods.*) I know you will put a
     stop to them. (*She nods again.*) And now you *do* that, now.

Is it poetry or is it awkward? Will audiences respond to it, or will they think
it's stilted? Will the goody-goody approach to justice be laughed at, or will it be
considered a fable? These are some of the questions that ran through the
execs' minds, but after getting a couple of director rejections, their first instinct
was to retreat and to change the script. There was even talk of getting a new
writer and starting all over.
     Mamet did one brief set of revisions when he came to LA. He sat down at
the typewriter in my secretary's office and wrote the baseball bat scene:

CAPONE: A man. A man stands alone at the plate. This is the time for what?
     For individual achievement. There he stands alone. But in the field, what?
     Part of a team. Looks, throws, catches, hustles, part of one big team. He
     bats himself the livelong day, Babe Ruth, Ty Cobb, and so on: if his team
     don't field . . . you follow me? What is he? *No* one. Sunny day, the stands
     are full of fans. What does he have to say? I'm going out there for myself.
     But I get nowhere unless the *team* wins!

Capone proceeds to bash in the fat man's head.
     Even with this scene, Tanen and Dawn were getting a lot of resistance from
their staff. Feelings about the script were still very mixed. When I tried to get
David to do more work based on executive notes, he howled. He said he
weighed them before he threw them away.
     Tanen even went so far as to say, 'Linson, if one person tells you that you
are wrong, maybe you aren't, but when they start to line up and take numbers,
like they're at Baskin-Robbins, just to tell you a script doesn't work, then
maybe you should listen.' My only response was, 'I have seen those people at
Baskin-Robbins. Maybe you should send them home.' Things were getting
fragile.
     If the next director couldn't make sense of this, the new version of *The
Untouchables* would be headed toward the warmth and comfort of familiar
mediocrity. Written by committee and certainly without Mamet.
     Brian De Palma, the next batter up, committed.
     I will go into greater detail later about the influence that additional elements
have on the studio as you get closer to production, but, for now, suffice it to say
that the inclusion of De Palma took the studio's executives off the script. Now
they had a 'package.' Particularly after the expensive *Scarface*, they started to
focus on and fret over the cost of production. Brian and I wanted some script
changes, but we were both savvy enough to try to collaborate with Mamet on

our own. I was expecting this next phase to be interesting. Neither of these guys had a reputation as a doormat.

Mamet, being a playwright, is used to retaining enormous power over the execution of his work. He has been known to sit in the back of a rehearsal and close his eyes, not even look at the actors, so he could just listen to the cadence of the dialogue. Each pause, each stutter he would account for. Not a line or a word could be changed without David's consent. He would revel in its sound. He was in complete control.

Well, movies are not plays.

Screenwriters will tell you that the control shifts to the director once he is on board. This ain't Broadway. You can either serve the director or face some interesting mental cruelty as your work gets rearranged. Of course, another option for the writer is to walk, to wish everyone well and ask to be invited to the cast and crew party. Rarely is this option considered.

The initial meeting between the three of us, at the Sherry Netherland Hotel in New York, was like a diplomacy gathering between Arabs and Jews. Testosterone was spilling on the rug. We just didn't know how to get started.

'So, how was the cab ride to the hotel?' I said to Mamet. How was that for inane small talk?

De Palma would have none of it. Before David could even respond, he opened the script and said, 'David, there were a lot of plot points that simply do not make sense.' Brian was never much of a diplomat, and small talk is beyond him.

'Uh huh.' David glanced at me as if to say, Why don't I just bend over and be done with it?

'We are here because we think the script is great' is the line I like to start with, but it was too late for that. Swords were drawn. David quickly saw that he wasn't going to be sitting behind the camera with his eyes closed on this one. For him this was not going to be some great religious experience.

The fact is that De Palma and I had some legitimate concerns. Capone, at this stage, was in only three scenes. We wanted to be able to build up the cameo role, if for no other reason than to get a big actor to commit to it. With regard to the technical aspects of the plot, there were some confusions over the discovery of the income tax evasion evidence as it related to the accountant, and the relationship between Capone and Nitti was very vague. Brian also felt some of the climactic moments could be staged in more dramatic settings, adding a more powerful visual interpretation of the script.

Before David excused himself from the meeting, the only thing he said was that he thought the room service at the Sherry could be improved.

One week later, we received the next draft. It was the last set of revisions that David owed us under his deal. If we needed him for more work, we would have to pay him more money. The plot problems for Brian, however, remained. The good news was that David had added more Capone. The work was sterling. Here's just a taste:

CAPONE: AM I ALONE IN THE WORLD . . .? DID I ASK YOU
    WHAT YOU'RE TRYING TO DO . . .?
OVERCOAT: No, Al, I –
    (CAPONE *goes to* OVERCOAT *and hits him in the face. Pause. He's bleeding profusely. Beat.*)
CAPONE: (*Beat; calm*) I want you to get this fuck where he breathes, I want you to find this nancy-boy. Eliot Ness. I want him dead. I want his family dead. I want his house burnt to the ground. I want to go there in the middle of the night and piss on his ashes.

Well, this kind of stuff gives producers wet dreams. I asked David why the rewrite took an entire week, and he told me that it got delayed in typing.

As Brian and I got deeper into other phases of production (some of which will be discussed later), we tried to go back for a third set of revisions. David was being difficult, and who could blame him? The studio was reluctant to give him any more money, and Mamet was about to start directing his own movie. Every time I would call, beseeching his help, he would politely wish me lots of luck with the movie. By this time we were well settled in Chicago, it was four weeks before shooting, and we desperately needed some work done that only David could do.

The problem with rewriting Mamet's scripts is that no one can match his dialogue. It has a different rhythm, a different feel to it. When Brian and I tried to fix some of the problems ourselves, it just never sounded like it was from the same script. Nevertheless, there were two specific things to be done: We needed a scene that tied Capone to the murder of Malone (Connery), and we needed a more exciting climactic scene to catch the accountant. We needed them now.

'Mamet, I need your help,' I said on the phone to Seattle, where he was shooting *House of Games*.

'Art who?' was his response, but I could tell he was warming to my call.

'Look, we are up against it. If I come to Seattle, you could do this rewrite in one hour.'

'Come to Seattle. I'd love to see ya,' he said.

Upon arriving at the airport, I was driven directly to the set. I approached Mamet during his lunch break. He had a new look in his eye. It was the look that most directors get when they are in the full bloom of exercising total control. He smugly pointed out his producer, who was doubling as the still photographer.

'See, this guy knows how to make himself useful,' he said.

I suggested that we go where there was a typewriter.

'Why?' he asked.

'Why!' I said. This was getting uglier than even I could have realized. I told the driver to start the car and get ready to go back to the airport.

'All I said is that I would love to see you. I meant it. By the way, where did you get that jacket?' he asked.

'Armani.'

'Nice.'

'Do you have any suggestions?' I asked, thinking that maybe I should drop to my knees and beg.

'Yeah, tell that greasy bastard that if he gets into trouble, to use that scene from *Carrie* where the hand comes out of the coffin and grabs Ness by the throat.'

Back in Chicago, Brian came up with the Potemkin 'steps' scene to dramatize the railroad station, and then we discussed using an opera sequence whereby Nitti could tell Capone about Malone's death. In looking back, I still think our solutions were quite ingenious. Neither scene required dialogue that could be heard. In the opera, when Nitti whispers into Al's ear, it is drowned out by the clown's aria, but Bob De Niro's priceless expression tells us everything. Capone ordered and took relish in the murder. We narrowly escaped having to match Mamet's poetic but very idiosyncratic cadence.

When Mamet first saw the opera sequence at an early screening, he was caught by surprise. As he instinctively started to sink in his chair, I turned and whispered, 'Be a good sport, you are bought and paid for.'

(Extract taken from *A Pound of Flesh: Perilous Tales of How to Produce Movies in Hollywood,* which is published in the UK by André Deutsch, and in the US by Grove/Atlantic Monthly Press.)

10   Answers first, questions later
Quentin Tarantino interviewed by Graham Fuller

Introduction Graham Fuller

Quentin Tarantino was born in Knoxville, Tennessee, in 1963, the year when Monte Hellman's *Back Door to Hell* and *Flight to Fury*, Don Siegel's *The Killers*, and Sergio Leone's *A Fistful of Dollars* were also in gestation – as Tarantino himself could probably tell you. The writer/director of *Reservoir Dogs* (1992) and writer of *True Romance* (1993) and *Natural Born Killers* (1994), Tarantino is the most extreme instance of a movie-struck kid who has parlayed his obsession with cheap thrillers and Westerns into a career at a time when both forms are being reinvented and revitalized by Hollywood.

Tarantino was raised by his mother in Southern California and received his movie education at the Carson Twin Cinema, Scottsdale, and later as an employee of Video Archives, Manhattan Beach, where he worked while training as an actor. His scripts pullulate with references to his movie diet during those days. The story of two kids, Clarence (Christian Slater) and Alabama (Patricia Arquette), on the run with a cache of cocaine they've offloaded from the Mob; *True Romance*, directed by Tony Scott, is set up by Tarantino as a self-conscious analogue to Terrence Malick's *Badlands*, replete with the same Erik Satie theme and a gauche voice-over by the female lead.

The point is that Tarantino is not so much a post-modern *auteur* as a *post*-post-modern one, for he is feverishly interested in pop-cultural artefacts and ideas (television, rock music, comics, and junk food, as well as movies) that themselves spring from earlier incarnations or have already been mediated or predigested. Because *Badlands* was made with *They Drive By Night*, *You Only Live Once*, *Gun Crazy*, and James Dean in mind, *True Romance* has a double frame of reference. In *Reservoir Dogs* – Tarantino's update on Stanley Kubrick's *The Killing* and/or Larry Cohen's *Q* – the pre-heist debate about the possible meanings of Madonna's 'Like a Virgin', as implausible as it is funny, is an anti-intellectual demystification of Madonna's much chewed-over status as a post-feminist icon in books like *Madonnarama: Essays on Sex and Popular Culture*. It's not Madonna that concerns Tarantino in this scene – but what Madona has come to represent.

All of which might seem like mere dressage for Tarantino's tough, cynical,

51 Quentin Tarantino (photo by Paul Joyce)

52 *Badlands*: Sissy Spacek and Martin Sheen

and exuberantly amoral genre-bending scripts. Except that his appreciation of pop ephemera is as central to his movies – you could say it is the world they move in – as their rabidly talky flow, their intricately structured plots, their casual explosions of violence, and their reverse psychology. (Brought together in anonymity, for example, *Reservoir Dogs'* hoods form immediate allegiances, while the coolest among them turns out to be a psychopathic killer and the angriest the most professional.) That delight in contradiction is really Tarantino's calling card, for he writes pulp movies for audiences who want more than mere visceral thrills, who may not have read much Tolstoy, and even less Michael Crichton or John Grisham, but who might figure out how bloody a 'Douglas Sirk steak' can be, or the qualitative difference between *Bewitched* and *I Dream of Jeannie* – to cite Tarantino's *Pulp Fiction*. This was the script he had just finished writing, for himself to direct, when we talked, in May 1993.

GRAHAM FULLER: *When you started writing scripts, was it as a means to becoming a director or because you had specific stories you wanted to tell as a screenwriter?*
QUENTIN TARANTINO: I've never considered myself a writer writing stuff to sell, but as a director who writes stuff for himself to direct. The first script I ever did was *True Romance*. I wrote it to do it the way the Coen Brothers did *Blood Simple*, and I almost directed it. Me and a friend, Roger Avery, were going to raise about $1.2 million from a limited partnership and then go off and make the movie. We worked on it for three years, trying to get it off the

53 *True Romance*: Patricia Arquette and Christian Slater

54 *The Killing*

55 *Reservoir Dogs*: Michael Madsen as Mr Blonde

ground like that, and it never worked. I then wrote *Natural Born Killers*, again hoping to direct it myself, this time for half-a-million dollars – I was shooting lower and lower. After a year and a half I was no further along than at the beginning. It was then out of frustration that I wrote *Reservoir Dogs*. I was going to go really guerrilla style with it, like the way Nick Gomez did *Laws of Gravity*. I'd lost faith in anyone giving me money – and then that's *when* I got the money.

GF: *What was your response to relinquishing* True Romance *and* Natural Born Killers *as scripts you would direct yourself?*

QT: After *Reservoir Dogs* I was offered both of them to direct. The producers who had *Natural Born Killers* – before Oliver Stone acquired it – tried like hell to talk me into directing it. Tony Scott and Bill Unger had *True Romance*. I had convinced Tony to direct it, but Bill was saying, 'Look, Quentin, would you be interested in doing this as a follow-up to *Reservoir Dogs?*' And my answer was no. I didn't want to do either one of them because they were both written to be my first film and by then I'd made my first film. I didn't want to go backwards and do old stuff. I think of them as like old girlfriends: I loved them but I didn't want to marry them any more. The thing that I am the happiest about is that the first film of mine produced was one that I directed.

GF: *How had you originally gone about positioning yourself in the industry?*

QT: During the time I wrote these things, I wasn't anywhere near the industry. Eventually, what got me inside was moving to Hollywood and making some friends who were film-makers. One of them was Scott Speigel, who had just written the Clint Eastwood movie. *The Rookie* [1990], and people were calling him to write things he didn't have time to do, so he would suggest me. The next thing I knew, I was sending out *True Romance* and *Natural Born Killers* as audition scripts and, little by little, I started doing a little rewrite at this company, doing a little dialogue polishing at that one.

GF: *You say you're not a writer, but the narratives of each of your scripts is very carefully crafted and rich in imagery. You establish your characters very fast.*

QT: I'm not trying to be falsely modest. I am a pretty good writer – but I always think of myself as a director.

GF: *In the* Natural Born Killers *script you wrote in a lot of the camera directions, so it was clearly a blueprint for a film you'd direct yourself. I remember Ken Russell saying he gets irritated when he sees scripts telling him where to put the camera.*

QT: Writing for somebody else and writing a movie for yourself to do are completely different. I'm not bagging on screenwriters, but if I was a full-on writer, I'd write novels.

GF: *You've talked about directors that have influenced you – including Samuel Fuller, Douglas Sirk, and Jean-Pierre Melville – but were you also influenced by specific screenwriters or novelists?*

QT: I think Robert Towne is one screenwriter who deserves every little bit of

56 *His Girl Friday*: Cary Grant and Rosalind Russell

the reputation he has. I'm also a fan of Charles B. Griffith, who used to write for Roger Corman. But most of my writing heroes are novelists. When I wrote *True Romance*, I was really into Elmore Leonard. In fact, I was trying to write an Elmore Leonard novel as a movie, though I'm not saying it's as good.

GF: *What about earlier writers? Is your script for* Pulp Fiction *modelled on Cain, Chandler, and Hammett?*

QT: I don't know how much I am actually influenced by those guys, but I have read them all and I like them. The idea behind *Pulp Fiction* was to do a *Black Mask* movie – like that old detective story magazine. But I just finished the script and it's really not like that at all; it kind of went somewhere else. Two other writers I'm crazy about are Ben Hecht and Charles MacArthur, both as playwrights and as screenwriters. In fact, on the first page of *Pulp Fiction*, I describe two characters talking in 'rapid-fire motion, like in *His Girl Friday*'.

GF: *How do your screenplays evolve?*

QT: One of the main things I like to do with my scripts is monkey with structure a little bit. I always know the structure I am going to employ in advance, and all the whys and the wherefores of the story when I start writing, but there's always some unanswered questions, ideas I want to explore. I don't know how effective they're going to be, but I want to try them out. When I start writing I let the characters take over. If you read my scripts, you'll see that the dialogue scenes just go on and on and on. I never went to a screenwriting or creative writing class, but I did study acting for about six years and I actually approach writing the way an actor approaches acting.

GF: *Do you write in a linear way?*

QT: I have to write from beginning to end because the characters are kind of telling the story.

GF: True Romance*'s narrative is linear, but with your script for* Natural Born Killers, *you move in a lot of flashbacks and a long sequence involving a tabloid-TV-film-in-progress. Then you made another leap forward with* Reservoir Dogs, *which has a kind of dovetailed structure.*

QT: *True Romance* had a more complicated structure to start with, but when the producers bought the script they cut-and-pasted it into a linear form. The original structure was also an answers-first, questions-later structure, like *Reservoir Dogs*. Thinking back on it, that version probably wasn't the most effective script that I've done, but I still think it would have worked. Tony [Scott] actually started putting it together that way in the editing room, but he said it didn't work for him.

I guess what I'm always trying to do is use the structures that I see in novels and apply them to cinema. A novelist thinks nothing of starting in the middle of a story. I thought that if you could figure out a cinematic way to do that, it would be very exciting. Generally, when they translate novels to movies, that's the first stuff that goes out. I don't do this to be a wise guy or to show how clever I am. If a story would be more dramatically engaging if you told it from the beginning, or the end, then I'd tell it that way. But the *glory* is in pulling it off my way.

GF: *When you sat down to write* Reservoir Dogs, *did you have a structure or a stratagem in your head?*

QT: Definitely. I wanted the whole movie to be about an event we don't see, and I wanted it all to take place at the rendezvous at the warehouse – what would normally be given ten minutes in a heist film. I wanted the whole movie to be set there and to play with a real-time clock as opposed to a movie clock ticking. I also wanted to introduce these guys in a series of chapters. Like, when you're reading a book, you're reading about Moe, Larry and Curly doing something in chapters one, two, and three, and then chapter four is about Moe five years before. Then, when that chapter is over, you're back in the main thrust of the action again, but now you know a little bit more about this guy than you did before.

GF: *Did* Reservoir Dogs *go through rewrites?*

QT: Not really. I wrote it real quick, and six months after I wrote it, we were shooting it. After I did the first draft, the big change I made was to include the scene where Mr Orange is in the bathroom telling his story – that whole undercover-cop training sequence. I had written it earlier and then, when I was putting the script together, I'd think, 'No one cares about this; they want to

57 *Reservoir Dogs*: Mr Orange (Tim Roth) and Mr White (Harvey Keitel)

58 *Reservoir Dogs*: the standoff (Steve Buscemi and Harvey Keitel)

get back to the warehouse.' So I left it out and put it in my drawer. But when we were trying to get the movie made, I dug it out and read it and I went, 'Quentin, are you insane? This is really good. You've got to put this in.' That was the only major change to the second draft.

I also kept changing who said what in the opening scene. That was the thing that went through the most metamorphosis. At one time, Mr Blonde made this speech, and another time Mr White said it, and so-and-so said this and so-and-so said that. I just kept switching speeches all the time. It's really funny, because when I look at it now, it doesn't look like it went through all that. But maybe it was good that it did – because all the right people ended up saying all the right things.

GF: *Did you have to fix things during shooting at all?*

QT: The only thing I did was a little polish after auditions, because auditioning shows you what lines don't work. So I got rid of them. Also, actors will come in and either improvise deliberately or they'll accidentally say something and it's funny.

GF: *I don't know if you've ever seen Michael Powell and Emeric Pressburger's* The Life and Death of Colonel Blimp . . .

QT: I never have – I've always wanted to.

GF: *The key event in the first half of the film is a duel between Roger Livesey and Anton Walbrook. There's a great deal of rigmarole leading up to it concerning the rules and codes of duelling. Then, just at the moment the duel is about to start, Powell cranes away from it and you never actually see it. It functions in the film in the same way the heist functions in* Reservoir Dogs. *My question is: do you consider omission part of the art of screenwriting? Is what you leave out as crucial as what you put in?*

QT: I completely think so. To me, it even applies to the way you frame a shot. What you don't see in the frame is as important as what you do see. Some people like to show everything. They don't want the audience to have a second guess about anything; it's *all* there. I'm not like that. I've seen so many movies that I like playing around with them. Pretty much nine out of ten movies you see let you know in the first ten minutes what kind of movie it's going to be, and I think the audience subconsciously reads this early ten-minute message and starts leaning to the left when the movie is getting ready to make a left turn; they're predicting what the movie is going to do. And what I like to do is use that information against them.

GF: *You do that in your* Natural Born Killers *script, which opens with a lazy coffee-shop scene that suddenly turns into a massacre.*

QT: Also the scene in *True Romance*, when Alabama has a terrifying fight with the hit man. One of the reasons that I think that scene is so exciting is because dramatically, in the context of where it falls in the movie, Alabama could get killed. We like Alabama, but it's getting towards the end of the movie and it would make a lot of sense for her to die. It would give Clarence something to do for the last fifteen minutes.

GF: *To avenge her, you mean.*

QT: Yes. I once saw this Stephen King movie called *Silver Bullet* [1985, directed by Daniel Attias] with Gary Busey, who's really entertaining in it. It's got this little kid [Corey Haim] in a wheelchair and this young girl (Megan Follows] who's narrating the story. At the end, there's a big fight with a werewolf – and I was so scared for Gary Busey! I knew they weren't going to kill the little kid in the wheelchair or the girl because she's the narrator, but Gary Busey *could* die. Dramatically, they could have killed him – and so it was really scary. My sympathy was with him, because he was perishable. The point is, I didn't know what was going to happen.

GF: *In your own scripts, you tend to be unrelenting. The Mob execution of Clarence's father in* True Romance *comes as a major blow. Even the deaths of the cops played by Tom Sizemore and Chris Penn are surprising, because in the short time they're on screen we get to like those guys.*

QT: Throughout *True Romance*, Clarence and Alabama keep running into all these people, and when they do, the movie becomes the story of the people they meet. When they're with Clarence's father, I treat him as though the whole movie is going to be about him. When Vicenzo Coccotti, the gangster that Christopher Walken plays, comes in, the whole movie could be about him. The same thing with Drexl, the Gary Oldman character. But particularly the father – you just figure he's going to play a central role. One of the things I don't like about comedy-action films is comic villains. They're never a threat; they're usually just buffoonish. The villains in *True Romance* rub Dennis Hopper out. That's a shock. All right – so now these guys are really, really scary, and every time they come in you think the worst thing in the world could happen.

GF: *At the end, Alabama cradles Clarence in her arms and you think he's dead, but he's not. Did you actually think of letting him die?*

QT: In my original script, Clarence gets killed. If I were to write a script and sell it now, I would make the provision that they couldn't change anything. I can do that now, but at the time I was selling *True Romance* to get the money to make *Reservoir Dogs* it never occurred to me it would get changed. When I read the new ending, in which Clarence survives, I felt that it worked – I just didn't think it was as good an ending as mine. My ending has a symmetry with the whole piece. At first, I was really distraught about it; in fact, I was talking about taking my name off the film. I had a lot of faith in Tony Scott – I'm a big fan of his work, especially *Revenge* – but where I was coming from, you just couldn't change my ending, you know?

Anyway, we got together and talked about it, and Tony said that he wanted to change the ending in particular, not for commercial reasons, but because he

59 *True Romance*: father and son (Dennis Hopper and Christian Slater)

60 *True Romance*: the standoff

really liked these kids and he wanted to see them get away. He said, 'Quentin, I'm going to defer to you. I'm going to shoot both endings, then I'm going to look at them, and then I'll decide which one I want to go with.' As much as I didn't want my ending changed, I figured I couldn't really ask for more than that. When it came to it, he really liked the happy ending and went with it.

GF: *Oliver Stone has substantially reworked your script of* Natural Born Killers.

QT: Yes.

GF: *Whereas your* True Romance *script was pretty much left alone.*

QT: Yes. Except for the ending, Tony did my script. Aside from that, I am really proud of the film. *True Romance* is probably my most personal script because the character of Clarence was me at the time when I wrote it. He works at a comic-book shop – I was working in a video store. When my friends from that time see *True Romance*, they get melancholy; it brings back a certain time for us. It was weird when I first saw the movie because it was like looking at a big-budget version of my home movies, or memories. What happened with that film was exactly what I wanted to happen, in that I saw my world through Tony Scott's eyes. As I say, I'm a big fan of Tony as a director and I knew I would probably never be in a situation where I would be writing anything for him to do again, so *True Romance* was my one chance. Oddly enough, our aesthetics are similar. Tony keeps trying to do darker things and then keeps bumping up against the studios and having his rough edges rounded off. I remember when he was editing *The Last Boy Scout*, I showed him *Reservoir Dogs* and he was depressed. Because here I was doing this little no-budget movie with all its sharp edges intact, and here he was doing this big-budget movie, watching the studio round him off.

But if our natural instincts are similar, his shooting style is completely different to mine. I love the way he shoots; it's just not my way. He uses a lot of smoke and I don't want any smoke in my movies. I have a lot of long takes, whereas for Tony a long take is twenty seconds. But I like the idea of seeing my world look like that, through someone else's eyes.

GF: *What, though, is your stance on a situation where you sell a script and effectively lose control of it?*

QT: I think it's a really thankless situation. That's one reason why I wouldn't be a screenwriter – it just seems like it would lead to ulcers. You can make more money than a novelist will probably ever make, unless you're Stephen King, but ultimately your work has to stand on its own. Everyone thinks that people just rewrite screenwriters' work and that's the way it has to be, but it isn't. You could do a script and put in the contract that they can't change a word of it unless you say so. It can be argued that nobody would then buy the script, but that's not necessarily true. If you wrote a very good script and a studio thought they could make money from it, they'd buy it. It would be a pretty revolutionary thing if some unknown writer tried to do that. In making the deal for *Pulp*

Fiction as a writer-director, I realized that a studio has no right to bring in another writer to do any rewriting at all. My lawyer put such a proviso in there and he thought he was going to have to fight for it, but he didn't have to.

GF: *Do you feel that* Natural Born Killers *will still, in some way, be a Quentin Tarantino film?*

QT: Not even remotely. I had bad feelings about *Natural Born Killers* for a long, long time, but I've come to terms with them now. I got together with Oliver Stone recently. I haven't read his version of the script but in the course of talking to him, I realized something that helped defuse my feelings about it. Where you can see some affinity between Tony Scott and me, there's really none between Oliver and me in terms of what I am trying to do with my movies and what he's trying to do with his, except that he's a really cinematic director, too. I don't show you events. I like things to be ambiguous. Constantly people will ask me, 'Why did Mr Orange tell Mr White that he was a cop at the end of *Reservoir Dogs*?' And my answer to that is, 'If you have to ask that question, you didn't get the movie.' I doubt Oliver would ever let a question like that be asked in one of his movies. He wants you to know exactly where he's coming from and his movies are making *points* and going for big emotions. He doesn't want ambiguity. He twists emotions entirely and he's hammering his nails in. He wants to make an impact. He wants to punch you in the face with this stuff and when you leave the theater, he wants you to leave with a big idea. I'm more interested in telling the story. It's not better or worse in the grand scheme; it's just two completely different styles. When we were talking, he goes, 'You know, Quentin, you're like Brian De Palma or John Woo. You like making movies. You make movies and your characters are movie characters – I am making *films*.' And it's true. I am not into making *films*. To me, Oliver Stone's films are very similar to the kind of films that Stanley Kramer used to make in the fifties and sixties, the big difference being that Stanley Kramer was kind of a clumsy film-maker and Oliver Stone is cinematically brilliant.

GF: *Are you going to take screenwriting credit for* Natural Born Killers?

QT: As of now, yes, and I wish the movie well. It's not going to be my movie, it's going to be Oliver Stone's, and God bless him. I hope he does a good job with it. If I wasn't emotionally attached to it, I'm sure I would find it very interesting. If you like my stuff, you might not like this movie. But if you like his stuff, you're probably going to love it. It might be the best thing he's ever done, but not because of anything to do with me. Apparently, he's planning stuff that's going to put *J.F.K.* to shame as far as experiments. I actually can't wait to see it, to tell you the truth.

GF: *It will be curious to see which aspects of your original screenplay will emerge.*

QT: I have no idea when I will raise my ugly head in the course of that movie! I am not expecting to do it much, but when I do, it will make it all the more interesting. If *True Romance* was my world through Tony Scott's eyes, this is my idea in Oliver Stone's world and through Oliver Stone's eyes.

GF: *Do you feel that your screenplays provide a kind of legitimate forum for violence?*

QT: I don't quite look at it like that. I don't take the violence very seriously. I find violence very funny, and especially in the stories that I've been telling recently. Violence is part of this world and I am drawn to the outrageousness of real-life violence. It isn't about people lowering people from helicopters on to speeding trains, or about terrorists hijacking something or other. Real-life violence is, you're in a restaurant and a man and his wife are having an argument and all of a sudden the guy gets so mad at her, he picks up a fork and stabs her in the face. That's really crazy and comic-bookish – but it also *happens*; that's how real violence comes kicking and screaming into your perspective in real life. I am interested in the act, in the explosion, and in the entire aftermath of that. What do we do after this? Do we beat up the guy who stabbed the woman? Do we separate them? Do we call the cops? Do we ask for our money back because our meal has been ruined? I am interested in answering all those questions.

GF: *What about the visual aesthetics of violence, which seem to be writ large in your films? You mentioned John Woo. In his films, the violence in them is pleasurable to watch if you accept it as stylized comic-strip violence.*

QT: Well, like I say, I get a kick out of violence in movies. The worst thing about movies is, no matter how far you can go, when it comes to violence you are wearing a pair of handcuffs that novelists, say, don't wear. A writer like Carl Hiassen can do whatever he wants. The more outrageous, the better for his books. In movies, you don't really have that freedom.

GF: *When I asked you if your films provide a legitimate forum for violence, what I meant was that – within reason, obviously – it can be acceptable to see on screen that which is unpalatable in real life.*

QT: Oh, I completely agree with that. To me, violence is a totally aesthetic subject. Saying you don't like violence in movies is like saying you don't like dance sequences in movies. I do like dance sequences in movies, but if I didn't, it doesn't mean I should stop dance sequences from being made. When you're doing violence in movies, there's going to be a lot of people who aren't going to like it, because it's a mountain they can't climb. And they're not *jerks*. They're just not into that. And they don't *have* to be into it. There's other things that they can see. If you *can* climb that mountain, then I'm going to give you something to climb.

GF: *Conventional notions of morality are made complicated in your films. You give your characters a license to kill.*

QT: I'm not trying to preach any kind of morals or get any kind of message across, but for all the wildness that happens in my movies, I think that they usually lead to a moral conclusion. For example, I find what passes between Mr White and Mr Orange at the end of *Reservoir Dogs* very moving and profound in its morality and its human interaction.

GF: *In the same way that Tony Scott wanted Clarence and Alabama to survive* True Romance, *do you suppose audiences might want Mickey and Mallory, the serial-killing couple in* Natural Born Killers, *to escape? I feel that the point you are making is that the world they are seemingly intent on blowing away is so sleazy that it almost warrants it. Perversely, it's almost as if they are a moral force.*

QT: In writing *Natural Born Killers*, though, I didn't necessarily want the audience to sympathize with Mickey and Mallory. I want the audience to enjoy them, because every time they show up on the screen they create mayhem that is exciting to watch. You watch that opening scene, and you think, 'Yeah, that was really neat, that was really fun.' You see them posturing and being cool and surly, and they're romantic and they're exciting. Then you see them killing people that you know *don't* deserve to die and, hopefully, the audience will turn back on it and say, 'Wait a minute, this isn't fun any more. Why aren't I having fun? And, more important, why was I having fun at the beginning?' But Mickey and Mallory will still be charismatic. By the end, when Mickey is doing the big TV interview, the audience won't know what it feels about these guys or what it wants to happen to them – which, actually, is my problem with serial killers. I don't believe in the death penalty. I don't believe the government should have the right to kill people. However, I find serial killers so *foul* that, in my heart, I wish they could just be executed. The trouble with that is that it's making me go against what I believe in. I don't even know if that worked itself into the writing. At the time I wrote it, I was kind of fascinated with serial killers and I got sick of Mickey and Mallory really quickly. In fact, to this day, people who've read the script come up to me and start talking to me like I'm some serial-killer nut and I go, 'Oh, you're talking to the wrong guy.'

GF: *The Belgian documentary spoof* Man Bites Dog *[1991, directed by Remy Belvaux, Andrei Bonzel, and Benoit Poelvoorde] starts out as a very funny satire about a serial killer, but as it becomes more graphic, it makes you question what you are watching and how you are responding to it.*

QT: Exactly, but the serial-killer guy never stops being funny. *Man Bites Dog* does exactly what I was trying to do in the original *Natural Born Killers*.

GF: *Why do you think pop culture, comics, and movies themselves proliferate in your scripts?*

QT: I guess it just comes from me, from what I find fascinating. If I have an interesting take on it, it's not that I'm necessarily lacing it with irony or showing it to you so you can laugh at it. I'm trying to show the enjoyment of it.

GF: *Junk food, too.*

QT: Cap'n Crunch cereal or whatever! It's funny, because I'm actually getting on a more nutritious diet myself. I started writing down this list of bad fast-food restaurants I'd go to to eat a bunch of stuff that I really didn't want to eat. I'm looking at it right now in my apartment and it says, 'Stay away until you absolutely have to go there. Then enjoy it. But don't get used to it.' Then there's a list that says, 'Hanging out with Scott, Roger, and this group of guys!'

GF: *Scott and Roger being the prototypes for the TV crew guys with those names in* Natural Born Killers?

QT: Yeah. And then underneath it says, 'I want to still do that, so I must not do it frequently, and cut down in other areas, so I can still have fun with those guys.' And then another bad place: 'The kitchen at the office' – Cokes and cookies and stuff like that; stay away from there. Empty calories.

GF: *Do you see yourself writing scripts in a more classical style, perhaps less charged with pop-cultural references, and perhaps less frenetic. A period film?*

QT: I don't necessarily want to make anything less frenetic. Not right now. I'll give you an example. L. M. Kit Carson let me read his script for *The Moviegoer*, and indicated that it would be cool by him if I wanted to direct it. I read it and I liked it a lot, but I told him, 'I'm not mature enough to make this movie right now.' Not that the work I'm doing is immature, but I'm still on my own road. Eventually, I'll get off it and want to go in a different direction, or do somebody else's work. As far as a period piece is concerned, I want to do a Western.

GF: *Were you influenced by Sam Peckinpah at all?*

QT: Not as much as people think I am.

GF: *Sergio Leone?*

QT: Oh, very much so. But if I had to pick my three favorite Westerns, they would be *Rio Bravo*, number one; *The Good, the Bad and the Ugly*, number two; and *One-Eyed Jacks*, number three.

GF: *There are references to* Rio Bravo *in* True Romance.

QT: And *Natural Born Killers*. When Mickey kills Wayne, he goes, 'Let's make some music, Colorado.'

GF: *What has changed about your writing since you began?*

QT: I think it's more sophisticated. I am not chasing it as much. I know the effects I'm after, and I eventually get them. I trust myself more that it will all work out – just keep the characters talking to each other and they'll find the way. After you've done it a few times, you fly blind for a little while, not knowing how you're going to wrap a script up, and then at the last minute something really cool happens. Constantly, what happens in my scripts is that the characters will do something that just blows me away. With regard to the torture scene in *Reservoir Dogs*, I try to explain to people that I didn't sit down and say, 'OK, I'm gonna write this really bitchin' torture scene.' When Mr Blonde reached into his boot and pulled out a straight razor, I didn't know he had a straight razor in his boot. I was surprised. That happens all the time when I'm writing. I equate it to acting. If you're improvising, all of a sudden you say or do something that puts this charge into a scene. That's what it's like writing. The other thing I've learned through acting is that whatever's affecting you that day needs to find a way to be filtered into the work that you're doing. Because if it doesn't, you're denying it.

61 *Rio Bravo*: Walter Brennan, Dean Martin, and Ricky Nelson

62 *The Good, the Bad and the Ugly*: the showdown

63 *One-Eyed Jacks*: Marlon Brando

   Basically, I don't come up with any new ideas. I have a stockpile of ideas in my head that goes back five or six years, and when it comes time to write another script or to think about what I want to do next as a writer, I flip through them and find the right one. They're incubating. I'll come up with one of them and say, 'OK, it's not this one's time yet. Let it just sit here and get a little better. Let's do this one instead.' I want to do them all eventually; I know I never will.

GF: *Do your stories come fully formed?*

QT: I always start with scenes I know I am going to put in and scenes from scripts I never finish. Every script I have written has at least twenty pages that are taken from other things I've done. I had the idea for *Pulp Fiction* a long time ago and then I came up with the idea of how to do it in the editing room when we were cutting *Reservoir Dogs*. I thought about it and thought about it, way past the point I normally do. Normally when I can't think about anything else but the script, then I write it. I couldn't do it while I was in the lab but I finally moved to Amsterdam for a couple of months and started writing *Pulp Fiction* there. After thinking about it for six or seven months straight, suddenly what I was writing was completely different. Even though the movie takes place in Los Angeles, I was taking in all this weird being-in-Europe-for-the-first-time stuff and that was finding its way into the script. So some genre story that I'd had for five years started becoming very personal as I wrote it. That's the only way I know how to make the work any good – make it personal.

GF: *How many drafts will you do before you hand it in?*

QT: When I hand in the first draft of a script, it's probably my third draft of it. That's why I'm pretty comfortable with it and can say, 'If you don't like it, then you don't want to do it, because this is what I'm going to do.'

GF: *Do you revise as you proceed, or do you go back and redo the whole thing?*

QT: I revise scenes as I go along, minimally. Usually, I'm just trying to keep going on it.

GF: *Do you write overnight?*

QT: I write into the night.

GF: *On a word processor?*

QT: No, I don't know how to type properly. When I know I'm going to do a script, I'll go to the stationery store and buy a notebook with eighty or a hundred pages in it, where you rip the pages out of the ring file, and I'll say, 'OK, this is the notebook I'm going to write *Pulp Fiction* or whatever in.' I also buy three red felt pens and three black felt pens. I make this big ritual out of it. It's just psychology. I always say that you can't write poetry on a computer, but I can take this notebook places, I can write in restaurants, I can write in friends' houses, I can write standing up, I can write lying down in my bed – I can write everywhere. It never looks like a script; it always looks like Richard Ramirez's diary, the diary of a madman. When I get to my last stage, which is the typing stage, it starts looking like a script for the first time. Then I start making dialogue cuts and fix up things that didn't work before.

GF: *Do you enjoy the process?*

QT: I usually think it's going to be horrible, but I always have a great time.

GF: *Does it pour out?*

QT: If it doesn't, then I just don't do it that day. If I can't get the characters talking, then I ain't gonna do it. If it's *me* making the characters talk to each other, then that's phoney baloney. It becomes exciting when a character says something and I'm like, 'Wow, he said this? I didn't know that he had a wife or I didn't know he felt like that!'

GF: *So it's a process of discovering what's locked away inside there?*

QT: Very much so. That's why I could *never* do a script treatment where you take the story from beginning to end. I'm not that kind of a writer. There's questions I don't want to answer until I get to writing.

64 Sally Potter (photo by the Douglas Brothers)

11 On Tour with *Orlando*
Sally Potter

Introduction

I first read *Orlando* as a teenager, round about the time I made my first 8mm film and fell in love with film-making. In 1984, shortly after my first visit to the USSR, I wrote the original treatment of *Orlando*. However, it was not possible to find anyone who shared my enthusiasm for the idea, so I put it away in a drawer.

In 1988 I decided it was a film I had to make, and thus began the four-year struggle sometimes known as 'development'. Finally, in February 1992, the cameras turned on the ice in St Petersburg.

Since completing *Orlando* in August 1992, I have been travelling round the world promoting the film as it opens in different territories. The diary which follows covers a ten-day period, typical of my working life over the past year.

May 1993

Thursday 29 April 1993

Straight off the plane in Vienna into seven interviews – four of them radio. It's a tough discipline: trying to find immaculate phrasing in easily translatable bites which nonetheless will neither dilute nor compromise intention or desire.

Remaining interested in my own opinions on the subject of *Orlando* after months of similar interviews in different countries is the toughest part, for I am longing to move on. Longing *not* to speak, but to write again and dream another film.

At the 'gala' screening I am gently and formally accosted by autograph hunters with a very particular style. Each comes armed with a small stack of immaculate white cards which I am to sign, please, with the date and Vienna written on it, and this one, please, to Hansi. A stiff nod, and the next one takes his place.

After the screening, a formal dinner at the Hilton. I am seated at the head of a table, the British Ambassador on my right, the Viennese Minister for Culture on my left. They clearly detest each other. He is a conservative diplomat, skilled with language, concerned with Waldheim's 'unjust' treatment; she is a socialist, an ex-philosophy student who used to run the Vienna Theatre Festival. They both claim Virginia Woolf for their own and wish for my exclusive attention. I have not yet learnt the diplomatic art of portioning my time and gaze, and my neck becomes stiff and my smile more studied as I swivel from one to the other.

In any case, my attention is really on the appalling print I have just seen, which lacked any colour density until the fourth reel, when it suddenly burst into contrast – but also looked as if it had been re-graded. The German (and Austrian) prints were struck from an inter-negative provided by Metrocolor in London, and should have been printed at one light.

Some of the ice scenes, which should have an icy blue quality – in particular, the shot where the sledge comes rattling across the ice towards us out of a blue mist – had been flattened to a dull grey. Another scene (shot day for night) had been mistakenly re-graded as day. The experience reconfirms my conclusion that it is impossible to leave anything, anywhere, unsupervised without risk of disaster.

But how is it possible, with the resources at my disposal, to keep tabs on every aspect of post-production and distribution in so many different countries? Does a larger company have someone whose job it is exclusively to check all technical aspects of the film world-wide and to ensure that the film is released in the form it was made? As it is, the producer Christopher Sheppard and I handle everything between us, and can barely keep up with it all. But then, that's the story of the evolution of this film. Low overheads, high commitment, every penny on the screen.

By 3 a.m. I have circulated round the room and met the thirty or so guests for dinner one by one. At the last table I meet Peter Konlechner, the director of the Austrian Film Musuem. Praising the economy of the script, he asks me about my cinematic history. When I talk about the London Film-makers' Co-op and the disciplines of low-budget or no-budget independent film-making as I experienced it in the seventies, he says it shows, as a strength, in *Orlando*. I am pleased that he sees the economy of means, because so many are seduced by the lushness of the imagery. For me, the driving force through the shoot was economy, even austerity, certainly not richness – though of course there is a visual wealth, but I don't think we linger on it. Rather than indulging in beauty, my energy was driven by the necessity (partly because of lack of time) to tell the story in the simplest possible way, in the minimum number of set-ups and takes. This became the style of the film – the tension between visual complexity and structural simplicity.

Anyway, the conversation led us to the Austrian 'underground' cinema, especially Peter Kubenka. I remembered watching *Arnulf Rainer* for the first time (in 1969), my heart racing at the audio/visual audacity of it – just white and black leader cut together with great rapidity and the sound: the biting, grating shock of the jump of the cuts on the optical track played very loud. That's how I remember it. Pure rhythm. So, we talked excitedly about that kind of film-making: skeletal, no waste, minimalism.

Throughout the conversation, however, his wife or partner sat silently nodding, talking only with her eyes when I looked at her. Even when I addressed a remark to her, he answered. It reminded me of the early days of the London Film-makers' Co-op and the 'underground' film festivals – the curious blend of formalism and sexism. She got her revenge, however, with her clothes. She was wearing an intensely vibrant pink outfit which drew the eye with its lurid extremity. Silent, but seen.

Friday 30 April 1993

This morning *Orlando*'s production executive Linda Bruce, who was working in Vienna as Production Supervisor on the Disney version of *The Three Musketeers*, took Christopher Sheppard and me to the set. A beautiful morning, clear blue sky, soft early summer air, the trees in fresh leaf, scented lilac hanging heavily in the Burgarten, which was being dressed as a location. 'Like filming in Buckingham Palace' was how Linda expressed it, and it certainly had the atmosphere of money spent liberally – not *necessarily* wastefully. But being used to a situation where every financial decision is made with stringent care, the choice of filming in such an expensive city, let alone paying to monopolize a big tourist spot, seemed, well, profligate.

But how seductive a film set is: The sheer human energy spent, with acute attention to detail, on something so *impermanent* in the real world, in order to become permanent on celluloid.

I stagger off the set into a car to speed (because we're late) to the airport – steeped in the longing to shoot again.

Saturday 1 May

Another car, back to Heathrow, to go the States for a third promotion/ publicity trip there, and to receive an award in San Francisco. On the plane (Club Class, courtesy of the San Francisco Film Festival) I watch three movies: *A Few Good Men*, *Sister Act* and *The Third Man* (for the umpteenth time). I am surprisingly impressed by the screen-writing of *A Few Good Men*, especially the Jack Nicholson part. It is an object lesson in building with loving care the argument you *disagree* with in your script. Make sure the villain is not a cipher, and then the victory of rightness (of your hero or heroine) will be that much stronger.

Sister Act is running simultaneously with *The Third Man*. As I have seen the latter so many times, I assume I will watch the former. But I find myself zapping between the two, and finally staying with *The Third Man*, astonished by its jewel-like precision and freshness. On this viewing I am struck by two things – how did Carol Reed decide when to do a camera set-up raked at an angle, and when it should be level?

The interplay between diagonal lines and vertical/horizontal lines on the frame is so daring. One could happily watch the whole film looking *only* at the geometrical shapes created by the camera angle, and how that speaks to us. The tilted camera does not just say 'danger', it also creates triangles (the diagonal lines in relation to the frame) as opposed to the rectangles we come to expect when we see buildings framed.

I am also struck, as always, by the cutaways to faces we never come to know or repeat. I am reminded, sorely, of the opportunities we missed in *Orlando* to pick up such shots. There was always the desperate struggle simply to cover the scene. I wanted so much to film the faces of the twins in the background in Uzbekhistan. No one ever notices they are there – except perhaps subliminally.

Sunday 2 May

New York. The day after our arrival. I wake at 5 a.m., mournful, consumed by exhaustion and jet-lag, and lie, tired yet wide awake, tossing and turning in an agony of doubt about life, work, love, and bad prints. Rerunning conversations, staring fixedly into my imagined future to see if I can see what I will do next. Every journalist asks me, and I answer in a number of ways: truthfully ('I have written another script'); evasively ('I have written another script'); and untruthfully – because although I do have a script, it's not yet what I want to do. I talk about doing a musical, but know that they don't know what kind of musical I have in mind.

The early stages of invention feel delicate and elusive, and I need a structure of protection, whereas interviews are a performance of revelation. At times I feel trapped in performing myself. Perhaps I should learn from Quentin Crisp, who says he has spent eighty years learning how to play the part of Quentin Crisp and hasn't got it right yet. I feel more like Mel Brooks, who said acting is all about sincerity – if you can fake that, you've got it made.

I find myself described variously as 'low-keyed, unpretentious and self-assured' (the *New York Times*) which I found curiously irritating as a description until I read some of the others ('small and intense in designer knitwear', for example).

One thing is sure – an interview is a construct in which you collude without ultimate control. But as Hank Bull of the Western Front said to me years ago, 'Fame allows you to be so *nice*!' Even limited fame, which I guess is what I'm currently experiencing, gives you the opportunity to practise being, or at least sounding like, the person you would like to be – or perhaps really are.

But I wonder if the positivism I try to exude (to contradict the awful complaints of so many artists who've been, as I have, through Hard Times) is the real me, or a mask to cover the despair which surfaced in private so often on the long, long road to making *Orlando*, when I felt I would never be able to offer my life's work to the world – couldn't even get a foothold, a toehold.

Feeling the invisible ceiling holding me down to a life of disappointment and broken dreams, which I had witnessed with my mother and grandmother – despite pitching relentlessly on with every fibre in my body till I felt I might *die* of frustration, exhaustion and rage as the years slipped by and the rejections piled up and the doors closed, one after another, in my face.

But now I've done it, and arrived, and broken through the ceiling – and I feel that at least in the public eye there is no place for my secret world of sadness and wasted time. I'm forty-three and have made one film in the way I've wanted to and with a team the calibre of which my male contemporaries have taken for granted for years. I've kept the silent scream of my life in the last two decades out of the film and out of my interviews.

The only cure for the miserable frustration of not working is to work. Just do it. Just get *the opportunity* to do it.

Later in the day, I venture out into the sunshine, which instantly melts some of the melancholia.

Riverside Park is full of people at play.

I am struck by the unselfconscious comfort in their choice of clothes. Lots of pale, bare, wobbly legs on display in shorts. Everyone has a project – a radio to fiddle with, a book to read, a game to play, new roller skates to try out with all the requisite trimmings of knee, elbow and wrist protectors. There does not appear to be a culture of just sitting and *looking*, as in Europe. Nor one of being looked at. People are not really parading, they're practising. Acquiring skills – faces concentrated, or contorted in the case of the joggers.

A woman jogs slowly round a small tarmac track in pointy little street shoes, carrying a handbag. Meanwhile, the junior baseball league is holding a series of games at one end of the park, all dressed in full kit, each team in different colours. At the other end of the park a ramshackle group of adults of both sexes is playing softball, laughing and screaming encouragement at each other while their mates lie on the grass with their dogs.

The contrast between the adults and the junior league is striking. The junior league is a serious training ground not only for the sport but also for life. That becomes clear watching the coach yelling at the little boys, wiry or plump, as the bat, pitch, run. Here they are trained to compete, to learn to cope with failure, to push beyond limits, to carry the torch for their dads. One child, Danny, is practising batting to one side. When his turn comes a cluster of relatives (including, embarrassingly, his mother) suddenly appear with cameras and yell out inappropriate encouragement. He hasn't a chance and is out within seconds. His family wilts with disappointment, his little face is crushed. Pressure.

There is a moment's excitement when I think I spot a little girl in the team – the star pitcher. But no, he just has some long hair poking out under his helmet, and a delicate build. I look around and see somebody's little sister sitting listlessly to one side, encumbered by a substantial ribbon dangling in her hair. Bored. Her little body is already softening for lack of physical challenge. Her mother is called to provide water for the boys. All fascinatingly predictable, unremarkable.

Strolling back, I am attracted by the promise of a 'Russian Concert' in a local school with authentic Russian snacks. The concert is nearly over in the little yard, with an audience of perhaps twenty White Russians, misty-eyed with nostalgia for the old country. The soloist sings out mournfully, across tables littered with cake crumbs. We have missed the snacks.

Monday 3 May

The interviews today include a photo session, where I juggle, as usual, with artifice and naturalism in the attempt to look like myself. Is this what a film director is supposed to look like, I silently ask myself, as I swivel about in a chair in a park, casually leaning back, intensely leaning forward, trying to direct myself to unencumber my face of its habitual tensions. I feel both naked and hidden.

The radio interviews, as usual, feel as if they are disappearing into thin air (which they are) and I wonder if my language is plain and juicy enough. I suddenly sound very English – I construct my sentences formally, I strive for correctness, but I suspect a more relaxed tone would be more appropriate. By the fourth radio interview I've improved a little.

I move hotels for a night in the quest for the perfect New York hotel bedroom. (No wonder so many film-makers make films set in hotels or on the road.) I fall asleep watching, for the first time, *It's a Wonderful Life* on video, but wake early and finish watching it in the grey early morning light. The tears roll down my face as this wholesome, honest-to-goodness tale of the American Christian socialist dream of small-town America unfolds.

The gentle appreciation of the degrading effect of poverty stirs my own early childhood memories, and I am reminded of the effort it took to imagine myself into the wealth of the background portrayed in *Orlando*. I really had to step out of my own long-held resentment of aristocratic privilege in order to create an innocent on screen – a lovable being as trapped by wealth as others can be by poverty.

I was also moved by the way some scenes in *It's a Wonderful Life* worked *entirely* on subtext. For example, the scene where James Stewart and Donna Reed are on the phone, apparently conversing about plastics and factories – whilst their faces tell us everything about what is *really* going on. Then the ease with which the Angel enters the story – into a genre of realism. The writing and directing seem so integrated. I run back the tape to check the writing credit – yes, Frank Capra gets third screenwriting billing. There is a director's hand in the writing.

Later in the morning, Christopher and I meet Tom Bernard and Michael Barker from Sony Pictures Classics to discuss the game plan and other bits and pieces. Everyone is concerned about the inadequate distribution of the sound-track CD. Christopher Sheppard is concerned about the heaviness of my schedule in Los Angeles and San Francisco. A fax has also arrived with an *intensely* heavy publicity schedule for Australia next month. In between I will have been in Cannes, where I hope to *watch* some films for a change (I've hardly seen a film at the festivals I've been at with *Orlando*).

After Australia it's St Petersburg and Moscow, to complete the psychic circle, as it was the Russian connection that really made *Orlando* possible. It is also where Christopher Sheppard and I met each other at the film festival in 1987. The festival was alive, pulsing with the immediate post-*glasnost* excitement. Non-Russians were falling in love with Moscow and with themselves for being there. We all bumped into each other in the endless corridors of the Rossiva Hotel (5,000 rooms). It was hot and muggy outside. I remember seeing David Puttnam queuing for breakfast in his shirt-sleeves. I was shooting *I Am An Ox* in the day, but couldn't resist staying up late at nights in the crowded festival bar, soaking up the energy released by the dissolving of the Iron Curtain.

In subsequent years I longed for the days before the advertising hoardings went up and felt a useless nostalgia for how it all was before, even for the massive social realist statues of idealized working men and women, and Lenin and Marx. In such a pervasively conservative climate, *It's a Wonderful Life* now seems positively Marxist in its values; unafraid to speak out against the big capitalist (even though he is *too* evil in the film, too obviously the work of the Devil, whereas our hero and heroine are the children of God in a much more complex way.)

But it was such a relief to watch a story so committed to *goodness* and so against the profit motive. Even the family values which I usually find so nauseating are somehow redeemed by their function in the film. The family is a place of real love and support in the face of desperate adversity and the wife/mother is a woman of initiative and courage.

Tuesday 4 May

Manage to watch half of *The Grapes of Wrath* whilst packing to leave the hotel for the airport for LA. Again the now-hidden voice of radical America, laying bare the destructive machination of gross, big-company policies on the lives of working people. It reminds me of how for hours as a child I studied the photographs of Dorothea Lange and Walker Evans, looking into the faces of the Depression. The book was called *The Family Of Man*, and I returned to its stark images time and time again, finding more and more as I looked and looked.

In many ways I think it was still photography that first drew me into film. Particularly Cartier-Bresson and Lartigue. The power of the face, described in light, captured in time, made iconic, graphically framed. The conjunction of the abstract principles of draughtsmanship and composition, with a passionate, compassionate look at lived experience. A story in every frame. A reminder that narrative works in revelatory flashes as well as linearly through time.

Half an hour later I am gliding, bumper to bumper, in a squishy seat in the back of a gold Cadillac towards JFK. Little strips of grass struggle for survival between decaying rubble-strewn concrete roadside verges. But it's early summer (May) so the grass is green and softly dotted with yellow dandelions.

In the last week I've looked out of speeding cars at roadside dandelions in France, Wales, Austria, England, and now the USA. How did they all get there? What kind of energy makes them persist? On the way to Heathrow we passed a small dandelion field by the motorway that had a scattered group of people inexplicably all staring in the same direction, some with picnic tables and folding chairs. They seemed to be intensely watching an invisible scene. The driver explained that they were plane spotting. Is it only possible in England?

At Los Angeles airport I find General Patton, in the form of George C. Scott, standing behind me waiting for his suitcase to come off the luggage conveyor.

The LA reps have sent a *very* long stretch limo. It seems an appropriate way to enter the city.

At the Bel Age Hotel I meet my agent Alexandra Cann who has already been 'doing meetings' on my behalf for two days with agents and producers. We go into a dining room in the hotel to talk over some food. A tired but distinguished-looking man is playing a balalaika, very beautifully. When the waiters come and place blinis with caviare in front of us I realise we have unknowingly entered a 'Russian' restaurant. There is a card on the table which informs us that the balalaika player is the foremost player of the instrument in the world; that he has played in Carnegie Hall and as a soloist with the Philharmonic and other orchestras, and that the management is 'pleased and honoured' that the Bel Age is his home in the US. So now he is playing for his supper in a half-empty hotel restaurant in LA. What a fate. It makes me want to weep. Alexandra is clearly enjoying buzzing around LA in her hired convertible meeting the great and the powerful. We discuss whether in the tiny gap in my schedule on Thursday I should meet with any of these people or not.

Wednesday 5 May

Rising early with the sun, I go up to the roof pool and swim; easing the muscles slackened through long hours spent flying and sitting in interviews. Then the first LA press day begins in earnest, and continues in a blur through till 6 p.m. – a mixture of print, radio and TV.

There are a couple of hours before a Q&A session in the evening at UCLA, so I ask Christopher Sheppard to drive me (in *his* hired convertible) along Sunset Boulevard to the ocean at Santa Monica. It's a relief to get out of the hotel suite. We meander off the road once or twice into the Hollywood hills to look at the houses set in intensely lush tropical greenery.

At the beach in the early evening the display of people intensely concentrating on becoming or maintaining fit, lean, tanned and perpetually youthful bodies is impressively consistent. Roller-skating seems the preferred way. One woman in teeny shorts is doing it speed-skating style, hands clasped behind her back, bent right over, head down, swaying rhythmically from side to side. Beautiful. Another lady dressed all in black but wearing a white hat is skating along with a tiny, excited black dog on a leash.

When we arrive at the theatre on the campus of UCLA, I am taken aback to find that the 'film class' is an enormous hall full of hundreds of students. We catch the last couple of reels of the film and the projection and sound system are excellent.

I find myself driven to make the audience *laugh* as often as possible during the Q&A. As usual, I experience it as a performance: working the audience, playing to them, timing and pitching my answers in relation to their responses in the auditorium. Since observing Quentin Crisp's practice of repeating (very effectively) a good line once he's found one, I now shamelessly hone and repeat my gags to audiences round the world. I used to feel that it was cheating to answer the same question in the same way twice, and still try not to for the press interviews (for a start, identical answers appearing in print in different publications really can look bad) – but it takes a real effort of will not to quote oneself once a reasonably clear answer to interminably similar questions has been arrived at.

But it's nice to find that certain lines – gags – work everywhere. And the Q&As are an opportunity to practise condensed thinking in public, to experience the glow of audience attention, to find an entertaining language to express

dry thoughts and to see the whites of the audience's eyes, rather than just the
backs of their heads in the auditorium.

Thursday 6 May

The second, heavier press day begins. I talk for eight and a half hours
continuously, as one journalist is shuffled out and another in. One of my
favourites is (as he put it) the 'token Spanish' from *La Opinion*, a newspaper for
the Spanish-speaking population. He is an immensely strongly built bear of a
man, with a very pronounced limp and wearing an ear-ring and a stripey
T-shirt which makes him look vaguely like a swashbuckling pirate.

We talk very intensely and finally he asks me to explain a quote from an
earlier interview: Why do I want to make films that generate 'release, relief and
hope'? Release – of tears and laughter, the healing power of entertainment,
because it fuels fresh thinking; relief – at having unspoken, hidden experience
made visible up there on the screen to help people feel less isolated and mad
(he nods agreement vigorously and talks about feeling recognized as a gay man
in the film and how he was able to identify with Orlando both as a man and a
woman); and hope – because we are all secretly carrying such discouragement,
disappointment and despair and need hope to help empower us to dream and
take action in our lives.

We embrace warmly at the end of the interview. I am enveloped in his big
arms and feel the warmth of solidarity across our cultural, language and
gender differences.

At the end of the day I look in the mirror and a pale, tired face peers back at
me. Wasted. And I have half an hour to get ready to meet Jeff Berg and Martha
Luttrell from ICM.

A quick bath, a cup of tea, and the power of fresh clothes to revive
astonishes me. I walk perkily down to meet Alexandra and we speed off.
Impressively, she has been driving everywhere in her frantic schedule, criss-
crossing the city with only a tiny map in her Filofax to guide her.

Martha Luttrell and Jeff Berg are both in smart suits. After a preliminary
hard sell of ICM to both of us, Alexandra speeds off to her next meeting
leaving me with them, and they visibly soften. I had been warned by Alexandra
to expect them to promise the universe, but not to believe it – but she had
obviously primed them well on my main concerns.

When I raised the spectre of total artistic control, Jeff Berg replied in terms
of ownership – of rights (he said the future in the film/media industries will all
be about rights), but also implied that the way to maintain control is to spread
the financial investment. Find an American partner who could work with
European financial sources. All this was fairly standard, but this was a clever
man. He managed to do three things which appealed very deeply. One – he

talked about the twenty-five-year view of my career. Now that's a good alternative to the one-project-at-a-time-never-look-further-than-a-year-ahead struggle. Second – he managed to make me laugh (describing Mel Gibson coming into his office and announcing he wanted to do *Hamlet*. Third – when I was having trouble co-ordinating my next meeting (with Tony Safford of Miramax) he got on to the mobile phone and called around announcing himself as 'Sally Potter's secretary'. Now that's style from one of the most powerful men in Hollywood.

Friday 7 May

Alexandra and Christopher tiff heatedly on the plane about the desirability or otherwise of American agents, and the possibility or otherwise of American finance. Christopher counsels against tying me down to a specific genre in advance – after all, what genre is *Orlando?* As usual he enjoys setting almost impossibly high goals – such as an open cheque with no strings attached – and Alexandra appears to be counselling greater 'realism'. In fact, they are in agreement. I get tetchy with them both and we all realize we are a little frayed from the Hollywood experience.

We arrive in San Francisco to brilliant sunshine and a packed schedule. After a quick change at the hotel, which has a magnificent view from my room on the fortieth floor of the bay and both bridges, we are whisked off to an EFDO reception at the German Embassy. A few stiff speeches from our hosts and much hand-shaking later I stagger back to the hotel, a hot bath and a massage which knocks me out into a profound, dreamless sleep.

Saturday 8 May

In the morning I read the first San Francisco review of *Orlando* in the morning paper immediately before I am due to be interviewed by its writer. I seize the opportunity to confront him with his choice of words to describe my directing style – 'cold and austere' – and become bitingly articulate in what I realize is an expression of my accumulated anger at careless or ill-considered journalistic writing. He seems taken aback that I have read his review so closely, and that I take issue with it at all. When I tell him that I assume he chooses his words with the same care as I choose mine, and that therefore I take them very seriously, the discussion becomes more heated. Eventually I apologize for reviewing his review to him, but he thanks me for my honesty and for showing him how his work affects the film-maker as well as its audience.

Lunch is at 'Chez Panisse' with Mr and Mrs Mukerjii, the sponsors of the Satyajit Ray award which I am being given. They are charming, delightful company, exuding a love of cinema and a love of California in equal portions.

On being questioned about the origins of their love for film they describe their early cinema-going experiences in Calcutta. Apparently one dressed formally to go to the cinema, where it was possible to view a mixed bag of Ealing comedies, American classics and, of course, Indian films. They are surprised that I am familiar with, and enamoured of, Indian musicals. We have a lively discussion about the relative merits of *Man in a White Suit, Kind Hearts & Coronets* and *Paper Flower* – the extraordinary classic black and white Indian musical which I had seen when on the jury at the Third World Film Festival in Nantes some years back, and which had the most stunningly languorous opening sequence I could remember.

The food is as fresh and delicious as expected and when the chef, Alice Waters, comes to the table she seems fresh and wholesome herself. The atmosphere is more relaxed and informal than its English counterpart would be.

A couple of hours later I am driven to the famous Castro Theatre for a presentation of the award prior to the *Orlando* screening. The queue stretches into the distance outside the cinema and the atmosphere is electric.

I am taken into the upper circle of the auditorium to look at the theatre – it is absolutely stunning – a gloriously preserved monument to the big screen experience. Lush glowing murals; gilt decoration; red plush seats; and sheer size. It's enormous, and it's sold out.

As I wait in the balcony area, Otar Iosseliani stumbles up to me, clearly in the midst of a long drinking spree, and thrusts some spindly daisies into my arms.

Finally everyone is seated, but it's late and the slow handclapping begins. Peter Scarlet gives an introductory speech explaining the origins of the Satyajit Ray award, then Mr Mukerjii, his arm in a sling, takes the podium. A frisson of disbelief ripples through the theatre when he refers to me as becoming a 'living legend'. I start to break out into a sweat at the hubris implied, but then am invited on to the stage to accept the award.

As I move to the microphone, Mr Mukerjii puts out his hand and says, 'Just a moment. For a long time I have waited for the opportunity to say "the envelope please"', and Peter hands him the envelope which is duly handed to me. I speak briefly of the awesome sensation of being associated with Ray – and of how when I first saw the Apu trilogy I had the sense of how film can work in the same way as the greatest music – to manifest in images the unseeable world of the spirit. I also say that another reason I find the award moving is because as a female film director I consider myself a natural ally of film-makers of colour.

Then the screening begins; wonderful projection, huge sound, an alert, buzzing audience which laughs, and, it later transpires, cries in all the right places.

Afterwards there is a long standing ovation and a relatively crisp Q&A session. At least I *try* and keep it crisp. I enjoy making such a huge audience laugh with my more pithy replies, and usually regret the longer ones.

In the limo afterward on the way to the reception, Mr and Mrs Mukerjii are high on the film and the award they have created. I am both moved and discomfited by his continued exuberant praise. He calls *Orlando* 'one of the great films of all time'. I blush and stumble out a suitably humble reply, dreading that the gods will punish me for even hearing such extravagant praise.

At the reception I am introduced to a bewilderingly large number of people. I find it hard to accept that this huge party is being held in my honour. It feels unreal and I keep expecting something to go wrong. On cue, it does. A woman comes up to me and suddenly accuses me of ignoring her. Furthermore, she says, 'The sound in your film is terrible and you will never be a good film-maker unless you improve it.' 'Thank you for your comments', I reply with as much politeness as I can muster, and turn to reach for a drink of water as my lips are parched from talking and my face stiff with smiling.

Then she begins in earnest, grabbing me towards her and spitting into my face – 'Who do you think you are? You're so pretentious, so precious. I hate you, and I hate your film.' She is shaking with rage. I realize I have a serious situation on my hands and suddenly feel very alone and very unprotected. My friends and allies are all happily chatting to each other in the distance.

Suddenly I realize why 'celebrities' ask for bodyguards. My chest tightens with fear as the attack continues. I decide to try to calm her down by apologizing profusely for not having talked with her for longer, for having hurt her feelings. She gradually withdraws, her mouth drooping, her eyes confused by my response.

But afterwards *I* am shaking and a little tearful. It is the second verbal attack in the midst of a long stream of warm and sometimes frighteningly positive responses – 'you have saved my life', 'I admire you so much' and the like. I am dealing with projections both positive and negative. I have become a symbolic figure.

Later in the evening I turn to find Terence Davies beaming at me and we fall into each other's arms. He then proceeds to give me a one-man perform- ance of such comic intensity that we end up clutching each other, tears of laughter streaming down our faces, screeching and hooting with joy. One day he will make a film as funny as he is.

Sunday 9 May

For the next two days I am incarcerated in the hotel doing interviews, with the exception of an excursion to participate in a panel discussion on 'screen alchemy'. It is an interesting opportunity to listen to Dana Rotberg, John

Maybury, James MacKay and Michael Almereyda, as we rarely talk to each other in this way at home. I welcome the opportunity to talk about *national identity* rather than gender identity as it manifests itself in *Orlando*, and my response to a question about technological advances in cinema is to discuss the relative merits of various kinds of pencil in script-writing.

But panels seem such a dinosaur of a form. A row of individuals in the spotlight with their glasses of water and opinions and a sea of faces with their hidden stories, agendas and questions loaded with subtext.

At the end of the first day of interviews, I have dinner with writer and film critic Ruby Rich and we discuss the notion of 'success' and the inevitability of attack. We laugh a lot. Half-way through the dinner a man bursts into the restaurant, and in a loud, desperate voice begs for money to pay for a prescription for anti-depressant drugs. Other diners scurry for safety at the sight of this ragged black intruder, but Ruby gives him a twenty-dollar bill.

Monday 10 May

In today's interviews, several of the female journalists intelligently address the question of the 'post-feminist' climate in which we are talking. It seems we are all looking for or creating a new vocabulary to express the necessary ideas about ourselves as women without resorting to the old jargon. The attempt occasionally feels like skirting the issues, but more often like part of the process of transformation from naming ourselves as victims of oppression to gradually, slowly taking real power.

At the end of the day a friend I haven't seen for seventeen or eighteen years, and who was in my year at The Place in the early seventies, comes for a late-night cup of herb tea. We talk for hours about the intervening years, about our dance training, about relationships, and lessons learnt over the years. In particular her quest to integrate her political, personal and creative life and her life as an immigrant in San Francisco. She looks older, unsurprisingly, and I realize I must too.

Late at night I watch the first part of a tape fed-exed to me by Sony Pictures Classics of the video transfer of *Orlando*. I am wearied to find that, of course, it needs correction. Will this process *ever* end?

Tuesday 11 May

After an 8.45 a.m. telephone interview from Seattle, I meet Ruby for a couple of hours before setting out for the airport. She takes me to her house, where the film-maker Isaac Julien has been staying. He is as cuddly, ebullient and intelligent as ever, and we all laugh and eat together and they question me about the 'phenomenon' that *Orlando* is becoming. 'You should *enjoy* it', Isaac says. Both he and Ruby know of the years of struggle and pain and I gradually let down my guard, explaining that it doesn't really *feel* like success. In fact, in many ways the sensation is more akin to psychic attack. Ruby's friend Lourdes validates this, as does Isaac, talking about the Caribbean and Mexican understanding of the power of envy to destroy.

I feel warmed, accepted and understood. Their generosity allows me to be honest without fear of appearing ungrateful for all that is now coming my way.

Later, as we drive back into the city, Ruby and I agree that Isaac is, in fact, perfect.

Laura Thielen drives me to the airport and shares her experience of organizing such a large, successful festival whilst being a new mother. She has an eighteen-month-old daughter and says the end sequence of *Orlando* has a special significance for her as a consequence. We hug warmly at the airport. Another connection made. Another city. Another life. We joke about maybe meeting again in twenty years' time.

I am reminded of the intense nature of all these encounters, which are worth investing with the energy and clarity of attention of something which may never be repeated. Dearly beloved fellow travellers, our paths crossing in a sweetly melancholic moment of mutual recognition.

Diary Postscript

Seven weeks later I am lying happily on a small single bed in a grubby room in an enormous Moscow hotel, with a view of the granite, cliff-like face of the other wing opposite. Somehow it feels like home. The discomforts are familiar, even the dust and the strange smell. Nothing is cosmeticized. It is how it appears to be. Set against the grim background are the people I love. But the lives of many dear friends have changed.

I spend happily intense hours striding round the streets of the city with Alexei Rodionov, discussing our work together on *Orlando*; mutually appreciative and warm, looking forward to working together again. He has been approached by an LA agency and things are looking promising for him. He takes me to see a statue of Gogol, hidden amongst some trees.

Tilda is in Moscow on the Jury of the Film Festival. We pass each other hurrying down the long corridors of the hotel on our way to different events and commitments. But, eventually, we manage to find an early morning slot where we can meet. We sit wordlessly in my room gazing into each other's faces. I know her face so well – every curve of it, every nuance of expression.

There seems to be nothing to say, because so much has been said over the years, and yet never enough to begin to describe the complexity of our relationship and the extraordinary endeavour we have shared. So an hour passes in silence as we sit, open-faced, opposite each other, occasionally embracing. By the time we part the room is warm with acceptance.

Our Associate Producer, Anna Vronskaya, has been stricken with MS, but is facing it bravely with great good humour. We spend hours in her little flat, embracing and – with the daughter Arisha – plotting cures and holidays and valuing what we have.

Sian Thomas (who led my first trip to Russia in 1984 and has lived and worked there for a decade) has died, tragically, on a bicycle trip from Beijing to Paris. The accident happened in Siberia. Naum Kleiman, the generous, intelligent, scholarly director of the Eisenstein Museum, and now of the Kinocenter, and whom I first met through Sian, is at the funeral. We weep silently together and he tells me Sian's motivation for the trip was to see the real Russia before it disappears for ever. He describes Sian as a free spirit.

At the screenings of *Orlando* the audiences respond in much the same way as audiences everywhere, except they do not laugh. Not surprisingly, as the enormously loud simultaneous translation virtually obliterates the sound track and destroys the comic timing completely.

But it does not seem to matter. *Orlando* collects all the major prizes at St Petersburg, and despite the chaotic difficulties of the Moscow Festival – which led to a complete absence of written publicity – the word-of-mouth process is so efficient that people turn up in large numbers to fight their way into the cinema.

The response is a relief, because it feels as if on some level the film is returning to its point of origin. The Russian collaboration, above all, made it possible for me to make the film, and I realize I have been anxious about the reaction. But all is well, and my heart swells with relief. Now at last I can relax, and let *Orlando* go.

July 1993

The Hollywood Way

An excerpt from a novel in
progress by Gus Van Sant

Having arrived in Hollywood, I finally got together a deal with a movie star attached, and all the prerequisite bells and whistles for my next film project, which was *Looking for Lonnie*. This project had been passed on by as many small studios as had praised it. This concerned the drug-taking in the movie. Some people in Hollywood were still taking drugs, so there was added guilt when some of them considered producing such a movie in the middle of the anti-drug atmosphere of the late eighties.

Come to think of it, we were a little nervous ourselves, but this was just what we needed to work hard, so as not to blow it. This was going to be a no-bullshit movie. We hoped.

'That was a no-bullshit movie, Jim', one of the inmates at Walla-Walla State penitentiary said to the author of the original book. Jim had thought that the VHS tape copy of his movie was too much like reality. He was waiting for all the Hollywood gloss that should accompany such a story. Where were Warren Beatty and Faye Dunaway when he needed them?

But after a while, Jim conceded that to have one of his fellow-inmates say that it was a no-bullshit movie was about the highest compliment he could expect.

One more project later, which was *In a Blue Funk*, I found myself pitching *Lovers and Devils* to a producer in Hollywood, only to receive a 'Cease and Desist' letter from Julius Post, who was acting as Jim's agent while he was languishing in jail. Julius wanted to write the script himself, and he also wanted to produce the movie, having felt ripped off from his involvement in *Looking for Lonnie*. Since I wanted to write and produce myself, he had called it off.

During this time, looking for another project to pitch, I had mentioned my interest in the production of *The Sutter Proxy*. This was a high-profile project about the exploits of an early 'out' gay politician named Keith Sutter. Set in Memphis, Tennessee, it had drawn the scrutiny of many modern-day gay political groups, each having their opinion of how the project should be handled. It was set up at a major studio, and this upped the ante and the interest of the film community and political groups.

The workings of this particular project had an enthusiastic production group spearheaded by Melvin Time, who had a reputation of being a

65 Gus Van Sant (photo by Eric Alan Edwards)

hard-core deal-maker and mover in the power circles in Hollywood, having just come off his own political epic which was doing very good business around the world and ignited a political fury over still-existing government cover-ups and scandals.

The day that I mentioned my interest, Melvin put my name into the pot and the political ante was upped again. One of the problems that the project had was that it was so far not helmed by a gay film-maker. Now that they had me, they could move smoothly to the next step and try to get the project flying.

The decision was made, in face of my own scheduled shooting of *Blue Madonna Redux*, to hire a writer who would pump out a script in time to accommodate the equally hectic schedule of an as yet unattached but interested superstar that the studio wanted, and who could make the whole project sing like a canary.

The first meeting that I had with the production group and the studio had a pervasive question hanging in the air . . . 'Could I handle such a large story, and budget, and star?' I supposed that I could. At least I didn't feel intimidated by it.

My previous film, *In a Blue Funk*, although well received, indicated that I was a film-maker interested in 'small' stories and 'small' budgets, always a red light in the eyes of high-rolling film-makers and studios. They think 'BIG' and they don't want to do anything 'small'. Small was for the other guy.

After the success of *Looking For Lonnie*, I had purposely pushed through *In a Blue Funk* because I was sure that this was one time in my career that I could push it through. I had chosen to do that, but now I was saddled with an image of being quirky, small and limited as a film-maker.

At the same time that I was insisting on producing *In a Blue Funk*, there was another film-maker at a similar point in his career who had opted to go to the big budget/big star/big producer/big studio route, and who had been raked over the coals after directing a film that was singled out as an example of how tasteless and over-budget a big studio film could be. I'm sure that it had sounded like a good idea at the time.

Anyway, the point of any film, big or small, is to make a good one, and then let the scope and subject dictate the expansiveness of the audience. But a lot of the decision-making depends on what a person has done before. Opinions about art are so subjective that the only objective orientation becomes your past product. It becomes the only bet in town, which is too bad. People have left their personal opinions behind in favor of corporate thinking, which lessens the blame on any one person, and thus helps people keep their jobs.

At the time that I came on board *The Sutter Proxy* the producers were fairly happy with the way of script was going. I was doubtful, but I was also unaware of how much work the script might need. Sometimes this means that you can fix it up, and other times it means that you have to rethink the whole thing.

Meanwhile, you have to watch that you aren't eaten alive by the various animals that are roaming round the jungle. There are many famous stories of how a project can bite the dust and how a person's livelihood can go with it. Not being a major studio player as yet, I could only play it by ear and try to make as much sense of it as I could.

The dynamics of the studio system are, largely, the dynamics of power. Money is one of the most tangible and rational gauges of one's power within this system. Therefore nothing is strictly logical, because the flow of money itself is not. Money flows similarly to the way it flows in Las Vegas, so you have many people playing sure-bet numbers. But they are still just numbers. And it is the decade of numbers . . .

I, for one, do not have impressive numbers behind my films – not that they are embarrassing – but they're just not nine digits. Eight digits perhaps, world-wide. Not impressive. Also, the awards, which do have an effect, are not of the Oscar variety. Oscars and Oscar nominations can bring one power points.

The *Proxy* production team, of which there were four, had suggested a young writer who had worked with them before. His name was Ben Shills. Ben and I had a number of meetings about the story and agreed that it was not hard-hitting enough. Right away, he set about interviewing all the characters involved in the original events in Memphis, amassing much material. But how to digest it?

Ben's and my first draft was a little discombobulated, flashing forward and backward in an attempt to instil some life into the expansive but boring details of a man's life and death. All the events, all the reasons for the events.

My initial interest in the story was the gay neighborhood itself, which I thought should be a central character. After all, our lead character was an extension of that neighborhood, and a gay neighborhood had yet to be depicted in a large-budgeted epic. I thought that this was one thing that shouldn't get away from me. I needed to explain who our character was as a gay man, and what he stood for as a gay politician who represented his gay neighborhood. Seems like it could be very colorful. I moved to Memphis to immerse myself in the neighborhood itself, bringing with me my editing and production crew on *Blue Madonna Redux*.

At a crucial time during the evolution of the script we had a meeting wherein Melvin signed off on our new draft. And although this would normally make a film-maker happy, I was sceptical about the content of the screenplay. There was no orientation. There were only characters doing things. The orientation was yet to emerge. As I mentioned one time to one of the producers across the table at a meeting, this kind of thing doesn't necessarily happen overnight, it could take two years to develop.

The producer looked at me curtly and said, 'No, it won't.'

I kind of laughed and said, 'Well, why won't it?,' wondering if the producer felt immune to the inspirational clock imposed on all creative endeavors. Should I have smelled something funny? He might as well have said, 'We're doing it whether it is ready or not.'

The other thing that was troubling me was that this same producer had said that, after we were finished with this draft of the screenplay, the star was going to need the writer so that they could make changes to the screenplay.

'Why do they need to make changes?' I wondered.

'Because they always do,' he said.

'Why don't we just tell him that he can't?' I said – which prompted a very curious look from the guy, like I didn't know my place at the table, as if I had leaned over his plate to grab the salt and pepper.

'Oh,' I understood his look. 'It just isn't done that way, huh?' Uh-oh, here it comes. Everyone is going to jump into the creative pie. It seems that some sort of guidelines should be set up here. How loud can you yell?

Everyone having signed off on the script, but me . . . left me the odd man out.

'But I just don't see where these people are coming from,' I said to Melvin later. 'I want this project to be perfect.'

'Perfection is for Greek scholars,' he said.

'Well, not that kind of perfect. I mean, just manageable. It just doesn't seem to have any kind of life to it . . . I mean,' I said.

'Well, we have to submit this to the studio, then you can tell them what you want to do, and I'm sure that they'll listen to you,' Melvin said.

I had the meeting, and there were some who were listening, but then the unseen hands of the studio heads made their move. And it was communicated in the proverbial 'we'.

'We feel that the script is something that we can go with, and to work further on it wouldn't make sense,' two junior executives said to me over the phone. But where were the senior executives? Where were the producers? Where was Melvin? Oh, well, they're bummed out, I guess. Who is running this show anyway? I was certain it wasn't me. I was being fired.

'Okay. Good luck with it,' I said. And that is the last time I talked to anyone connected with the project. I got the trap door. I wasn't playing the game. What was the game? Where are your Oscars? Melvin has them. Ben has been nominated recently. Where are yours? Why are we listening to you anyway?

I had only been a gay pawn to calm the fury of the gay politicos so the studio or the procedures wouldn't have any trouble. They didn't care about the story or anything. For some reason, they just wanted it to start shooting. Was it really that they had the money this year, but could not count on the money next year – which is how long it would take to get the script right. Was there so little faith? Or were they really afraid that I was going to try to make *In a Blue Funk* all over again, a 'small' movie. Is a 'Big' movie really one with no point of view? Perhaps that's it.

There is also the Hollywood notion that someone in the group will try and stop the picture from getting made. Was that my role? Did they sense that I was just trying to hold things up?

This was a Hollywood way that I had not been prepared for, had never read or heard about. Maybe I won't fall into the fire the next time.

And for all who tread there, hold out and don't let them read your script before you want them to, even if it is a year after you started it. Perhaps that was the only power that I had. And I fucked up. I trusted them and let them read the early drafts, hoping to establish some sort of communication. To let them in on it. To bond.

(Extract from *How to Make Good Movies: A Novel*, which is published in the UK by Faber and Faber; and in the US by The Overlook Press.)

Dreams

Each year we pose a question to film-makers. This one went like this:

This year we want to explore the relationship between film and dream. The experience of dreaming and watching a film are clearly related. I (JB) have a recurring dream when I'm shooting a picture. The camera is stuck and won't follow the action. I know several directors who dream whole sequences. Do you dream in relation to film? Do dream-images find their way into your work? What are your dreams?

We were disappointed that so few responded. I believe the power of the movies is that they connect us to the dream world. Why we go on watching them when so many are disappointing is that they induce a kind of trance-state, they take us half-way to that elusive territory of sleep, that land that we can only fitfully recall, that other life that we lead each night.

In The Lost Girl, *D. H. Lawrence describes Nottingham coal miners watching the early silent films. The sly, shy looks they wore when watching the live acts were gone. They stared with a fixed stare at those shadows. Since then, these shadows have taken on colour and the appearance of corporeality. They speak, they are less dream-like, they resemble the waking world more than they did, yet they are still illusions, fanciful ghosts with the substantiality of dreams.*

So here are Monte Hellman, Richard Lowenstein, Paul Schrader, Steven Soderbergh, Alex van Warmerdam and Jaco van Dormael dreaming. And they are followed by Richard Stanley's nightmare. He set out to wrest a dream movie – Dust Devil *– from both a mythic African landscape and from his own unconscious. It went horribly wrong, but he kept a diary for us.*

13   The Burning Question:
Is there a relation between
Dream and Film?

Paul Schrader

I rarely dream *about* movies or making movies. I dream movies. Literally. I often have dreams of sustained narrative over a period of hours. I know this because I'll wake up, look at the clock, return to the dream (I also have sleep apnea). These dreams have characters, dialogue, plot development. I am also aware of the dreaming process; that is, I'll critique the 'dream story' as it occurs. I'll think, 'This is not a good scene,' 'I should drop this character,' 'I need some action' – back up and 're-dream' the scene. As a dream story develops, I'll sometimes think, 'This is not really a movie, but I want to keep dreaming it anyway,' or 'This is really a great idea, I'll have to pursue it when I wake up.' I'll then fix in mind some hallmark of the dream that I can use as a key to remember the rest when I wake up. Most often, I only remember parts of the narrative when I wake; I remember the 'critique'. To the extent that I can reconstruct the dream stories, I discover that they are, on a commercial or practical level, wildly implausible or, at the other extreme, mundane.

Alex van Warmerdam

Do I dream in relation to film?

Not yet. Actually, I've only made two films. Because I've written and directed seven-odd theatre performances to date, and always act in them myself as well, theatre often dominates my dreams. These are usually night-mares, not those of the writer or director, but those of the actor. I'm late. The performance has already begun. Very far away, I can hear the voices of my fellow-actors. The moment that I have to come on stage approaches. But where is the stage? In panic I race down dark corridors, run up against locked doors. The voices come closer, float away again. I get tangled up in the curtains.

When I finally come on stage and speak my lines, my fellow-actors look at me in amazement. The reason for their amazement varies with each dream: the lines I speak come from another play, or I speak the right lines in the wrong language. But most often I'm stark naked and have an ejaculation in front of the packed and deadly silent stalls. When I was still Catholic, I often dreamed that I was in a church and half-way through the High Mass I would notice I was naked, apart from a white shirt which came down to my navel. Naked in church, naked in theatre; there is a method in it. It won't be long before I'm standing naked in a dream behind or in front of the camera.

Do dream images find their way into my work?
   They find their way into the scenario. I film them, but up until now none has survived the editing. Dramatically speaking, dreams are dangerous stuff. The spectator quickly loses interest; after all, it's only a dream. What's more, the true essence of a dream is intangible. A film image exists by the grace of a frame, a cutout. Dreams have no frames. A dream is all around you – there are no cuts – and is out of focus in random places. Naturally, you employ these characteristics in film, but it remains imitation. In spite of this, my films as a whole are an attempt to give form to a dream. A day-dream. The images that I film are ones I have once seen. When I'm filming I try to capture the atmosphere of what I once saw as precisely as possible. A large part of that atmosphere is contained in the light. Because of this, most of my discussions are carried out with the cameraman. For me, dreams are obscure in their logic but brightly lit.

What are my dreams?
   Well, to make a Western one day. A Dutchman in the Wild West: a bicycle repair-man, or a seventeenth-century master-painter, or a canal-digger.

Steven Soderbergh
Strangely enough, I'm rather obsessed with dreams, and for years I've been trying to write something that expresses what they mean to me, with no success. The standard-bearers for me in this arena are Resnais and Polanski: Resnais because of his disjointed and yet highly organized repetition, in which associations come gradually (often after the fact), and Polanski because of his incredible ability to walk the line between waking and dream states (specifically in *Repulsion* and *The Tenant*), a technique which I actually refer to with some considerable pretension as the 'Polanski "non-dream" dream state'. I have abandoned many ideas dealing with this subject because I felt they weren't as good as the Polanski films or *Last Year at Marienbad*, etc.
   Personally, my dreams are invariably tense, and usually revolve around these subjects: being pursued by someone who intends to hurt me; my wife and/or daughter in danger, with me powerless to help; sex with someone I would be embarrassed to have sex with. Of course, when I'm filming I dream I am filming, but with actors that I didn't cast and who are completely wrong for their roles (example: Paul Hogan as Kafka). Now that I think about it, I don't think I've ever been unhappy to be awakened from a dream.

Richard Lowenstein

Film-making is a conscious dreaming that may or may not connect, as the case may be, with both the collective conscious and unconscious. The correlation between this and an audience's response to a film may well be the difference between a good and bad film. And if dreams are the flushing toilet-bowl of unnecessary concepts, frustrations, emotions and feelings, is cinema just the waste-paper basket where we try to place the same things? Or maybe they are how we deal with the necessary ones . . .

These questions and more may well be answered within the next millennium. One thing is for sure, though; most dreams I've experienced could do with a bloody good script editor. Then again, so could most films (including the ones I make) . . .

Sally Potter

Without doubt, my dream life is a personal archive that I visit at night to reorganize memories and experience into images which seem to have their own impenetrable logic, but are then delivered into daylight consciousness ready to be decoded. In this way, the creation and function of dreams are a perfect parallel to the making of films.

When writing an original screenplay, one is calling on an organizing principle that draws – as dreams do – on a chaotic infinity of experience and observation. If the ideas and images have their own precise logic then previously invisible connections can be made and a profound sense of meaning is generated.

As a member of the audience, you enter into a web of intelligence that stimulates your sense of self and creates a sometimes melancholy feeling of – at last – coming home.

I find that the discipline of frequently writing down my dreams has several effects.

One, I become a participant in my dream life rather than a passive observer. I can start to change the direction of my dreams. Or they start to communicate to me with more startling clarity.

Two, I trust the power of precise imagery, saturated with meaning, to illuminate vast and vague areas of experience.

Three, though the act of remembering and replaying the inner projection of the dream story or fragment, I have a feeling of the mind itself as a form of cinema.

Sometimes images from my dreams have found their way into my films. But mainly it's a principle at work: to respect and observe the hidden worlds – my own and others – and bring them into the light.

Monte Hellman

I have always had a difficult time differentiating between movies, fantasies and dreams. As a teenager I began drifting away from the narrative while watching a film, and creating my own drama parallel or perpendicular to the one I was watching. In remembering a film, I am never quite sure what was on the screen and what was only in my mind.

Today, when writing a script, I rely heavily on my subconscious. I frequently dream whole dialogues, then write them down quickly upon arising.

There are frequently certain scenes in my own films, usually not more than one or two, that affect me deeply, even after many viewings. When I watch these scenes I become lost in them, and forget that I have shot them. I am sure that they have originated in some dark recess of my psyche.

Likewise, when watching and re-watching my favourite films, I will be consistently moved by the same moments, usually actions rather than words, and sometimes as simple and brief as a single gesture or shot or juxtaposition of images. Several years ago I was on the jury at the Sundance Film Festival, and had the occasion to see Nancy Savoca's *True Love* several times within a few days. At each viewing I was moved to tears at the same moment, as I remember it, a dissolve from a moment of doubt and despair on the part of the bride-to-be to a shot of her putting on her wedding gown. I cannot explain why I was so deeply affected by this moment.

Jaco Van Dormael

I don't remember my dreams. I'm sure I do dream, but when I wake up, it's like a blackout. Over the past ten years, there's been one to two dreams that I remember, but they're pretty banal – like cooking potatoes and worrying about how long they've been boiling.

Maybe that's why I dream during the day. Being a film-maker is making dreams. I dream during the day, I sleep during the night.

Denys Arcand

I don't like this year's question. It's embarrassing to me. I don't remember my dreams very often, and when I do, they are as boring as my everyday life. So I guess it's just another proof, as if I needed one more, of my utter lack of talent. Once every two years though, I have a really strange almost Bunuelesque dream. So I go to my desk at four in the morning and write it down. I have five or six of those in a file somewhere. I was never able to use any of them in a film. One has to do with people fishing a white alligator out of a frozen lake. Nice image, no? Must mean something.

14   'I wake up, screaming'*
A Diary by Richard Stanley

Prologue

The dreams came first.

The dark man, his face hidden, his hat pulled low, his coat gathered around him, standing alone in the wasteland, staring towards the lights of the town, a storm brewing somewhere not far behind him.

His image found its way into my early student films and followed me in my sleep as I grew away from my homeland, riding with me as I deserted the army and fled South Africa and its politics of oppression, hitch-hiking across the Namibian border on my way to Windhoek and a plane to Frankfurt and the imagined freedom of Europe.

The dark man's shadow followed close behind me all the way up the Skeleton Coast, hinting in my dreams at some terrible conflagration to come, next to which all the suffering that had ever been would be the merest taper.

In Bethany district it was the seventh year of a seven-year drought and a shadow was on the land. Everywhere people were dying, their mutilated remains turning up in the boots of burned-out cars and strewn out across the remote farmsteads.

The local police hunted in vain for the killer, finding no clues, their enquiries met by silence. In the towns people whispered about a conspiracy to drive the black farmers off their land, in the bush the sangomas muttered about a black magician allied to the desert wind, a 'Nagtloper' come out of the wasteland to claim the souls of the damned, and in the local church the dominie ranted about the devil and his cohorts Azazel, Buzrael, Beelzebub and Belial, heralds of the baneful pestilence whose breath is the drought that withers the crops in the springtime and whose kin is the famine that slays the cattle in their fields and blights the land.

Behind all of it, I sensed the dark man's hand, the murders following so close behind me that at times I feared for my sanity.

Sleeping in a dry river bed near Keetmanshoop one evening, I was caught in

*(with apologies to Bertrand Tavernier)

66 Richard Stanley (photo by Liam Longman)

a sand-storm. The column of dust against the setting sun seemed transformed into a writhing pillar of living fire.

I hitched a ride with an armoured column to Bethany, where I hopped a steam train that wouldn't have been out of place in a Leone western. A day later I heard that the body of a prostitute had been found near the platform, and when I reached Luderitz I was beaten senseless by railway policemen driven mad with paranoia.

Even after I left the country the shadow stayed with me, and when a few months later I heard that a man suspected of the murders had been killed in a gun-battle near the canyons, I resolved that I would have to return to the Skeleton Coast once more to exorcise this demon from my dreams.

Although the murders apparently ceased after the shoot-out, the suspect involved was crucially disfigured by a shotgun blast and never formally identified, leaving the case open to this very day.

In 1984 I returned to Namibia with a 16mm clockwork Bolex, a home-made crane, five friends I had fired up with the idea, a forty-five-page script and a title, *Dust Devil*, derived from the name the locals give to those small, violent desert winds that blow from nowhere.

After two months on the Skeleton Coast, shooting was abandoned when our funds ran out and two of our party had to be hospitalized following a car smash on the freeway near Keetmanshoop.

For seven years the dreams continued to haunt me, and in 1991 I dusted off the script, fleshed it out to feature length and took it to Jo-Anne Sellar at

Palace Films, who had produced my first feature, *Hardware*, in the winter of 1989.

Shooting in Namibia had finally become feasible following the elections in March 1990, when a socialist government, the South West African People's Organization (SWAPO) came to power and I was able to return to the Skeleton Coast without fear of arrest. *Hardware's* healthy performance at the box office enabled Palace to pre-sell the film and secure a promised £2 million budget from Miramax and British Screen Finance. A surprising additional investor turned up in the shape of David Aukin, the head of drama for Channel Four Television, who acquired *Dust Devil's* rights for British television. Jo-Anne was able to secure the use of South African personnel and equipment with the aid of the ANC-affiliated Allied Workers Organization, while flying in the cast and heads of department from Britain and the United States, thus making the film financially viable without selling out to South African money and the politics of moral compromise.

In July 1991 I flew back to Namibia to finish what I had begun so many years before, praying that, with the support of an international co-production and the resources made available to me by the highest budget I had ever been entrusted with, I would finally have a chance to beat the jinx and capture the demon that was the soul of that bleak country on film.

From the outset it was apparent that shooting would be a nightmare. I had experienced the worst Namibia could hurl at me before, but the rest of the crew still awaited their baptism of fire. The film's backers seemed to be dangerously out of touch with my true intentions for the project, refusing to agree on a female lead and suggesting, even at a late stage, that we reset the script in Santa Fé and use American Indians in the lead roles instead of black South Africans.

My insistence on shooting the film in precise locations, following the trail of the original murders, meant that we would have to cover over one and a half thousand kilometres of road during the eight-week shoot and for the sake of an easier accommodation deal, Jo-Anne and Daniel Lupi, the production manager, based the production in the mist-shrouded, Bavarian-style resort town of Swakopmünd, hundreds of miles up the coast from Bethany and our main locations. All our stock would have to be flown back to Britain for processing, resulting in a turn-around of almost two weeks on the rushes that meant, in effect, that our sets would be struck without admitting the possibility of our ever having to reshoot a single frame.

Weather insurance was beyond the limits of our budget and the convoluted pre-production period had pushed our shoot right up against the start of the windy season. At their height, the gale-force winds that lash the Skeleton Coast make it impossible to stand up straight, and cars have to be weighted down with sandbags to avoid being blown off the roads.

Even then, at the very beginning, I must have been a little insane, confidently leading a celluloid safari into hell to search for a demon that I suspected was both very real and hungrily awaiting us.

On Thursday 8 August, I was precisely one week away from the first day of shooting and still had not reached an agreement over the casting of two of the most important roles: Wendy, the beleaguered South African housewife; and Joe Niemand, the enigmatic projectionist, witch-doctor and story-teller who would lead the film's nominal hero, South African police detective Ben Mukurob (played by Zakes Mokae), on his quest for the dust devil.

Thursday 8 August 1991

I come awake in my narrow bunk, still trying to scream.

The sheets are sticking to my body.

I half-remember my dream. Something about fire and flying and falling. Burning ships or oil platforms, black clouds hanging beneath me in greasy columns. Then the sound of a fog-horn comes to me and I remember where I am. Although Jo-Anne and Daniel wanted me to stay with the cast in the Café Anton, a decrepit resort hotel on the beach-front, I have elected instead to lodge with the rest of the crew in the grim tract of military-style concrete bunkers that passes as the local trailer park. At least here I have privacy and space, including a double garage that will come in useful as an impromptu studio for the second unit. Jo-Anne and Daniel have never been too keen on the idea of running a second unit, and when the chips are down, I know I will have to give their crew all the help I can. Steve Chivers, our director of photography, is garrisoned in the neighbouring bunker and Mad Mike Jay, a science-fiction writer and science programme researcher who will be acting as my personal assistant on the shoot, is billeted in the room next to mine. The sky as usual this morning is grey and listless, a thick sea-fog shrouding the town. There is a taste of salt and corroding metal in my mouth.

My bathroom window faces on to the freeway that runs behind the bunkers, and as I brush my teeth, I look out over the sandbagged barriers that mark the border of the South African enclave of Walvis Bay. A row of soldiers are stopping cars, lazily waving their AK47s, their outlines softened by the mist. The road beyond them is hazy and indistinct, as if they are guarding the perimeter of Tarkovsky's Zone.

Later, I drive inland with mad Mike.

The sea-mist comes to an end in an almost solid curtain some twenty kilometres inland, and beyond that, the day is hot and airless.

I inspect the progress of the work on our main set, the farmstead belonging to the killer's first victim, Saartjie Haarhoff, which is being lovingly reconstructed from a gutted ruin in the bottom of a dry river-bed near the Kaiser's ostrich farm, the very farm that provided so many of the plumes in the helmits of World War One era Germany. The work is being cheerfully supervised by our production designer Joseph Bennet, Jo-Anne's boyfriend since *Hardware*, whose work on that previous film contributed immeasurably to its success. Today he's looking relaxed, wearing the crumpled white suit and confident swagger of a classic colonial.

After a reassuring guided tour of the works we return to town, didgeridoo music playing on the car stereo, my spirits falling as we re-enter the dank wall of mist that surrounds Swakopmünd. I am on my way to my first meeting with Chelsea Fields, the only available actress whom all the financiers would approve, after my efforts to cast first Kerry Fox (the New Zealand actress from *Angel At My Table*) and then Stacey Travis (the star of *Hardware*) had failed to win their favour. The backers are less than happy with my emphasis on black South African actors and feel that Robert Burke, who will play the killer, is not enough of a name to carry the film.

Chelsea is deemed to be 'hot' on the basis of the three unreleased films she has completed the year before: *The Last Boy Scout, Harley Davidson and the Marlborough Man* and George Romero's *The Dark Half* – although the only videotape Palace has made available to me that features her is the Renny Harlin film *Prison*, which I detest. Being left with no choice in the casting of such a crucial part is a compromise that I am loath to accept, although I faced a similar situation before over the casting of the male lead in *Hardware*.

I smoke my first cigarette in six months on my way to her bunker, and hate myself for it. Chelsea is plainly as nervous as I am, besieged by Lisa Boni, our make-up girl and unofficial unit psychologist, who is testing burn make-up on her, and Michelle Clapton, our wardrobe mistress, who is taking her measurements and trying out costume ideas. We make small talk about her flight and her feelings about the script, but we both know from each other's eyes that we have more questions to ask than either of us can easily answer right now.

There is too much on my mind for me to be able to give her my undivided attention. The completion bond guarantor came in on the same flight as Chelsea, and even as we speak I know he is combing through the budget and schedule with Jo-Anne and Daniel back at the production office.

The fate of the film is still hanging by a thread.

At sunset I go down to the sea-front with Mad Mike and drop in for coffee and cigarettes at the only homely house in Swakopmünd, a beach cabin surrounded by whale bones rented by Ina and Amelia Roux, the production buyer and dresser, known affectionately by the art department as the 'Vixen Sisters'.

Tonight Ina, the practical one of the pair, gets in the beers while Amelia,

who affects a cape, and smokes too much, goes wandering off down the
moon-drenched tideline in what approaches an altered state of consciousness,
a joint smouldering in her hand.

Friday 9 August

As Woody Allen said, 'The truck arrives with fresh compromises every morning.' This morning is cold and misty as usual, and I spend the first part of the
day scouting locations around town. At three p.m. I return to the production
office to learn that the competition bond guarantor is demanding that I lose ten
pages from the script before he signs off on the bond.

I stagger back to my bunker to discover that hundreds of pelicans have taken
over the bungalow complex, sitting everywhere on lamp-posts and every
available inch of roof space.

I draw the curtains and lock the door, going into a huddle with Mad Mike to
do the necessary rewrite.

Tonight there is no time to sleep and the dreams will have to wait.

Saturday 10 August

I emerge red-eyed from an unbroken, twenty-seven hour rewrite that has
stretched to over one hundred handwritten pages consuming three full A4
pads.

Overnight I have simplified Chelsea's character, cutting the memory of her
rape as a child and the paranoid core of her relationship with her husband
Mark. Also gone is the character of Aaron the ticket-collector, who witnesses
the killer passing on the station platform.

I feel sad at letting go of them, but right now I'm too tired for it to hurt. Mad
Mike, who has hardly slept himself, takes the mound of scrawled pages in to
the production office to type up and I try to get some sleep.

Sunday 11 August

I hear that my old associate, the inimitable Immo Horn, has blown into town in
a battered pick-up truck and I go to meet him at the local pizza joint. Standing
nearly seven feet tall in his habitual black coat, sporting a profile reminiscent of
the Mervyn Peake character Steerpike, Mr Horn (who has worked with me on
a number of past ventures) is a talented underground film-maker in his own
right whose work I first encountered in Berlin almost ten years ago. In 1989 we
shot a documentary together in Afghanistan covering the events leading up to,
and immediately following, the Soviet withdrawal. Mr Horn was severely
wounded by shrapnel, losing the use of both legs in the battle for Jalalabad, the

capital of Ningrahar province, and in the weeks that followed it had been down to me to save his life and get him to a Red Crescent hospital in a frontier province and thence back to Europe for surgery.

Mr Horn has always felt he owed me a favour for this, and now I'm calling it in. I'm putting him in charge of the second unit, and supply him with copies of the storyboard and shooting schedule. If we are to have any chance at all, then the second unit must be able to function autonomously and often at a great distance from the main unit. Mr Horn is my insurance policy that, in my absence, the unit's work will meet a desirable standard. For a second-unit operator I have brought on Mr Horn's old schoolfriend Greg Copeland, a London-based lighting cameraman who shot all my music videos and came to Namibia with me before on the original *Dust Devil* 16mm shoot in 1984. I have to trust that their close working relationship and commitment to the material will help bring their rushes to life.

Robert Burke, our lead actor, a veteran of Hal Hartley's quirky *oeuvre* and the lead in the as yet unseen *Robocop 3*, has arrived in town and I go to see him at the Café Anton, where we sit in an enclosed back garden surrounded by a menagerie of tame animals. Robert has travelled well and is in good form. We talk long and hard about his character, whom we now perceive as a purely mythological figure, a synthesis of Leone's Man with No Name, the bushman 'Nagtloper' and the devil himself, portrayed in the script as an incubus, a demon lover from the id who exists only to lead Ben and Wendy to their deaths.

It will be a hard ride for Robert, for, in opening himself to this role, he will become a receptacle for the demon that stalks us, the dark man of my nightmares. In exorcising myself, he will become possessed.

As we talk, the mist clears long enough for the Southern Cross to be visible overhead, and a tame ground-squirrel climbs on to Robert's shoulder.

Tuesday 13 August

We drive out on reconnaissance for the cave scene to where the granite ramparts of Spitzkop oppose the sky, their cliffs rising sheer from the flat plain, brooding silently beneath the dead weight of the afternoon heat. I scale Spitzkop's bony flanks, accompanied by Robert, Greg Copeland and Mad Mike, coming at last to the lip of the hidden plateau that has served as a sacred place for the Khoisan people since time immemorial.

The plateau is ringed by overhangs and huge mushroom-like rock formations, their stone surfaces alive everywhere with ancient life. The faded, ithyphallic figures of the first men pursue zebra, ostrich and eland through the morning twilight of primeval time, their shapes all but hidden beneath the quiet dust of that still, hot plateau where the only movement is the imperceptible dance of the shadows around the prehistoric quiver trees, moving to the ceaseless music of the sun and moon. We linger here and, as the sun sets, Robert sits atop a huge volcanic boulder and plays the flute, while a swallow comes out of the brazen sky and circles him quite deliberately.

Wednesday 14 August

In my dreams I am back at Spitzkop.

The dark man is there. The man who has no face or name.

He takes me to a high place and shows me the world spread out before my boots.

Robert has begun to have the dreams as well now. We spend the morning in the school hall reading through the script with Chelsea and when we break for lunch he tells me he dreamed he saw me at Spitzkop. I stood on the edge of the cliff and, motioning for him to follow, I smiled and stepped out into the air.

Later, I go over to the props department to approve the faceless one's knife. Dirk, the props master, has engraved its blade with the design of the Midgard serpent. Amelia Roux flirts with me as she shows me the old photographs and their frames that she has amassed for the night-stand of the dark man's first victim, the lonely schoolteacher Saartjie Haarhoff.

I have grown very fond of the vixen sisters and am glad of their company now.

Thursday 15 August

Jo-Anne summons me urgently to the production office first thing in the morning. She presents me with an amendment to my contract that has been faxed over from Palace's legal department, claiming that unless I put my mark on it at once the completion bond guarantor will refuse to sign off and production will be closed down on the movie. The amendment waives my legal right to injunct the film's release or remove my name from the project. I find this very ominous, and refuse to sign unless I can first consult my agent or an entertainment lawyer. Jo-Anne takes this as a personal betrayal and is furious at me, telling me that Palace have already spent three hundred thousand pounds of uninsured production money on the project and that she'll call the whole thing off today unless I sign at once. Furthermore, Daniel refuses to let me use the production telephones unless I pay for my calls out of my own pocket.

At lunch-time I go on a reconnaissance of the mortuary set and call my agent from a payphone out back. It is very hard to get through to her, and when I do she is maddeningly vague, merely recommending that I sign everything I'm told to. When I get back to the production office I tell Jo-Anne I am willing to sign the contract only if I can sign it in blood as a symbol of protest, and to this effect I cut my hand with a razor.

Friday 16 August

The first day of 35mm shooting.

We start with a photo shoot of the schoolteacher and the young boy who will play Zake Mokae's lost wife and child in the film.

Second unit officially expose the first frames of 35mm stock.

Slate zero. Take one.

Sunday 18 August

A hideous first day of full main-unit shooting.

We are shooting on the freeway in a freezing fog that refuses to lift.

Everyone is cold and miserable, including Robert and Chelsea.

We wheel on the turbines and put a brave face on it by filming the scenes where Wendy's car is forced into the Bethany turn-off by a sandstorm.

After a grim lunch, we move further inland to find the sun and start work on the crucial sequence where Wendy first picks up the hitch-hiker. It becomes rapidly apparent that our car mounts and process trailer are woefully inadequate, and the Volkswagen quickly disappears beneath a tangle of scaffolding and G-clamps that seems to keep shaking itself apart as soon as we try to get it on to the road, strewing clanging debris across the asphalt and slowing shooting down to a painful crawl. By the evening I have already lost a set-up and gone four pages behind schedule.

I return to my bunker a gibbering, frozen wreck and am cheered only by Lisa and Amanda, the make-up girls, who surprise me with a hot meal before I crawl into bed.

Monday 19 August

At sunset we burn the Haarhoff house.

The scene calls for Robert to walk away from the blazing building, climb into the car and drive off, circling the sundial in the middle of the driveway before heading out into the open desert. Like all scenes of this nature, it can be staged only once and while I intend to cover the action from the dolly in an elaborate tracking shot, I hedge my bets by using two other cameras. A second emplacement in the bottom of a shallow pit behind the sundial will provide us with a static master, while Creg Copeland mans the roving second-unit camera to pick up telephoto detail shots as the action happens.

Jo-Anne, Daniel and poor Steve Earnhardt (Miramax's executive in charge

67 *Dust Devil*: the car rig with Robert Burke and Chelsea Fields inside

of production) watch from the flanks of the hill, tension mounting as the afternoon slips by. We rehearse the scene again and again until everything is running like clockwork, waiting until the shadow of the sundial signals the onset of the magic hour and the mountains behind the house glow like ruddy gold.

The set falls silent and everyone takes their positions.

I signal my first assistant and he calls action on the bull-horn, setting the mechanics of the shot into action.

Rick, our stunt co-ordinator, presses the detonator but nothing happens. Something has gone wrong with the wiring of their pyrotechnics.

Robert stands, looking puzzled, at the head of the steps, the cameras rolling.

I call 'Cut' and our other stunt co-ordinator Roly goes running over to the house to trace the fault. The shadow of the sundial lengthens.

There is a sudden crack inside the house and black smoke begins to pour from the window frames.

I can't see Roly, and no one seems sure whether he's clear of the blaze or not. Jo-Anne is running towards me, cursing and shouting for us to roll cameras. There is still no sign of Roly.

There is a flicker of orange fire inside the downstairs windows.

I call for turn-over and the cameras are already rolling by the time the first assistant relays the command on the bull-horn.

I cue Robert and he starts down the steps without looking back, flames climbing higher in the windows behind him. Then the glass explodes outwards and the fire begins to take hold of the veranda.

Robert reaches the car and climbs inside, but now seems to be having trouble getting it started. He takes off the brake and for a heart-stopping instant the car begins to roll backwards, before the engine grumbles into life and he heads away down the driveway, circling the sundial as the house disappears into a column of flame and greasy black smoke behind him.

In the midst of the conflagration a flock of geese fly slowly out of the east, forming a huge V-formation as they soar directly over the burning house. This additional, unplanned detail is captured only by Mad Mike on his Super 8 camera. It will not appear in the film, but at least I can prove it really happened and isn't just some weird, stress-induced hallucination.

When I finally call for the cameras to cut and a phalanx of stunt assistants descend on the inferno with fire extinguishers, I learn that Roly has managed to escape out of the back of the house and a tragedy has been averted.

Thursday 22 August

Today is our first day of interior shooting in a roadhouse-cum-service station outside Swakopmünd that has been restored from a gutted shell by Joseph and his art sluts with such loving care that several motorists pull off the freeway during the course of the day to try and tank up there.

During the shoot I bump into a gaunt, raven-haired girl who is hanging about the set watching the proceedings. I introduce myself, and she seems surprised that I am the director. She rather sweetly tells me that I look more like some kind of acid casualty or burned-out bag-person, and for the first time I notice that my military fatigues are covered in a thick layer of grime and glistening mica. Her name is Deborah Deats and she is to be Chelsea's stunt double. Wasting no time, I turn her over to Lisa and Amanda, who dye her hair red and start to transform her into Chelsea's doppelgänger. I note with interest that her first appearance on set coincides with the passing of Roll 13, Slate 66, Take 6, which of course is a complete screw-up.

It is full moon tonight, a time traditionally associated with the mixing of the pigments used in the elaborate rock paintings central to Khoisan magic, and Mad Mike and I plan to head out to Spitzkop and spend the night under the stars at the ancient ceremonial site. We have arranged to rendezvous at the plateau with Greg and Mr Horn, who have been out at Spitzkop today doing time-lapse work. The gore boys, Chris Halls and Little John, who are responsible for the shoot's quota of latex, gelatine and karo syrup, tag along, riding in the back seat on the long journey across the moonlit plains, as we thread the back roads out to Spitzkop with Mad Mike at the wheel and a selection of Golden Oldies on the stereo. At one point, a great white owl looms up in the headlights, narrowly missing the windscreen as it swoops over us. At another, a strange hopping animal like a rabbit bouncing on its hind legs crosses the track in front of us, its eyes glowing like embers.

We plunge deeper into the heart of the wasteland – Spitzkop's crags coming into view on the horizon, a deeper patch of darkness against the night – passing every now and then solitary figures wandering on the verge of the road, dressed in suits or what seem to be shrouds, looking like they're on their way to a casting call for a George Romero movie.

Just before we hit Spitzkop itself, another set of headlights comes up hard behind us, bearing down on our tail and then swerving around us to cut us off.

Our car skids to a halt, dust rising in the headlights.

The doors of the battered, maroon-coloured touring car blocking our way burst open, disgorging a posse of unlikely-looking individuals, so many of them that it's hard to imagine how they all fitted into a single vehicle. At first Mad Mike thinks they must be connected with the shoot and rolls down his window, but as they come shambling into the circle of our headlights he realizes that this is not the case. Their dark faces are unfamiliar, even though they are grinning at us to a man, their movements strange and erratic, their limbs trembling as if they are either very drunk or in the last stages of some degenerative nerve disease.

There is something oddly animalistic about them, and as one slaps his hand against our bonnet I see his eyes glint in the headlights like a dog's.

He leans forward, his face twitching spastically, his lips parting in a horrid mockery of a smile, his eyes wide and moon-crazy, brimming over with monstrous mirth and a stupid, bestial rage.

He reaches for the handle of my door and I bring my fist down on the lock, my other hand going to the hilt of my knife.

Then 'Suzie Q' comes on the stereo and Mad Mike floors the accelerator, skidding around the touring car and leaving our assailants behind us in a cloud of dust. I watch in the rear-view mirror as they pile back into their car and gun its engine into life, following hot on our heels.

The dirt track comes to a dead end at the base of Spitzkop's granite cliffs and Mad Mike has to effect a three-point turn, narrowly avoiding a head-on collision with the touring car that is now determined to try and run us off the road. Mad Mike is pushing the car to its limits, the vehicle slaloming from side to side, its wheels barely holding the switchback surface of the track, its suspension jarring as it leaps depressions and wash-outs.

As we come back up fast from Spitzkop, the touring car still on our tail, a pair of figures suddenly appear in our headlights.

A woman seems to be lying in the middle of the road with a man standing over her who appears, in that insane split-second that we see them for, to be beating her. Mad Mike swerves to avoid them, narrowly missing mowing them down, the car trembling as it skids across the sandy verge, threatening to go into a roll at any time. By the time he regains control of the car, the figures are lost from view behind us and we can only guess at what we have seen.

We screech to a halt when we hit the dirt track to Hentie's Bay, flagging down a passing car that turns out to be a local farmer on his way home.

The touring car has turned off its lights and disappeared from sight behind us as if it never existed.

The farmer, a doughty, middle-aged German, readily believes our story and casually explains that he is carrying several guns in his pick-up truck, including a couple of lightweight pump-action shotguns designed for riot control. He coolly suggests that if the occupants of the touring car show up we should simply shoot it out with them, confident that his fire-power is vastly superior to anything our assailants might be packing.

As we wait in ambush, the farmer explains that one has to expect this kind of thing when one visits Spitzkop, and come prepared. The local psychos are apparently a well-known hazard of the area. Apparently Spitzkop has attracted a considerable squatter population who scratch a living scouring the mountain's flanks for rock crystals that they sell to those tourists foolhardy enough to venture this far from the beaten track. The lazy ones spend their time grinding down the bottoms of Coca-cola bottles that they try to pass off to the tourists as the real thing.

The crystal gleaners have come to form a tribe in themselves, defined by the physical stigmata of inbreeding, their behaviour further deformed by the malignant influence of the local well-water. The former describes the water as *brak*, salt or poisoned, claiming that it drives anyone who drinks from it homicidally insane. The district's history reeks of overt viciousness and half-hidden murders. Even the farmer seems unsure of exactly what is the matter with Spitzkop, referring obliquely to 'something to do with magnetic fields', loud crackings and rumblings that are heard frequently from within the rocks, and the old legends of conclaves of bushmen who once called shadowy shapes out of the hills and celebrated blood-drenched rites here to the gods of pre-Christian Africa.

By now the moon is past its zenith and a further confrontation with our pursuers is starting to seem increasingly unlikely. Finally, wishing us luck and warning us to stay away from Spitzkop in future during the full moon, the farmer clambers back into his pick-up truck and goes on his way, leaving us alone with the sibilant African night. Mad Mike, whose nerves are worked to shreds, refuses to drive any further and Little John volunteers to take the wheel.

We head slowly and cautiously back down the dirt track, determined to reach our destination while the moon is still in the sky, driving with our headlights and stereo turned off now.

This time around we make it to the foot of the mountain and, gathering our gear, we begin our ascent of its eastern ridge, coming at last past the mushroom rock formation and into the sacred valley, while the moon blazes down and the stars gleam above us like innumerable camp-fires or, as the Khoisan liked to believe, tiny burn-holes in the blanket of the night.

We lower our packs and sit in silence on the topmost ridge. Then, without a word, but as if by some prearranged signal, we slip one by one into a deep sleep.

Saturday 24 August

The rising sun wakes me, the rock growing warm against my face.

My mind is awash with fragmentary yet vivid dream images.

A dark man, his naked body covered in mud, sitting in the middle of a dry salt-pan beating a drum.

Myself running naked through the desert at night, my body bristling with an animal's fur, the knife-blade glinting in my hand, graven with the design of the Midgard serpent. I open my eyes and see Greg and Mr Horn, a tripod over one shoulder, hiking up the slope towards us, the rising sun at their backs.

I turn over, pressing my face against the rock and close my eyes once more. When I wake again, it is full day.

Mad Mike, Little John and Chris Halls are standing some way off down the ridge smoking a joint. I amble over and ask about the whereabouts of Greg and Mr Horn, but no one besides myself has seen them.

We wait at the plateau until the early part of the afternoon, during which time I sit and meditate for a while in the cave of the rock-paintings, but still there is no sign of the second unit.

Finally, we go back down the rock and turn the car towards Swakopmünd, Mad Mike at the wheel once more. Driving away from Spitzkop, we pass a man standing watching the road. I am convinced he is one of the individuals who attacked our car last night, but no one feels like stopping to ask him any questions.

On the freeway back into town we overtake a government delegation travelling in convoy, flanked by police cars, heading for the local sports centre where another bizarre ceremony is under way.

The production is holding a reception in the striped catering tent. Daniel, our beloved production manager, gives a short speech and Robert Burke, in the guise of the dark man, presents a hefty cheque made out by Palace Devil Limited to the visiting party members as a 'goodwill donation' to the South West African People's Organization. Nobody asks me to say anything, nor do I volunteer to.

Afterwards, the crew play a rather one-sided match with the local team. Needless to say, the locals win.

The latest batch of rushes are in and I return to the production office, where once again I am thoroughly entertained, the footage proving to be of a consistently satisfying quality.

Derek Trigg, the editor, has set up a Steenbeck in the suite next door and is attempting to move towards an assembly of the scenes already shot, but is having trouble getting his edge-numbering machine to work. The machine has jammed on 666, stubbornly refusing to print any other numbers. Derek's team are feeling a little spooked by this. They have only been here forty-eight hours and already they're getting the creeps.

Later, while I am at the office, the vixen sisters turn up to announce that the props department has been broken into and that a key prop, the dark man's knife carved with the design of the Midgard serpent, has disappeared. Now I start to get the creeps as well.

Monday 26 August

Guy Travis, my first assistant, tells me that I've been riding the crew too hard lately. He urges me to use a more hands-off approach and to stand back after giving my brief, to allow the art department and lighting crew to get along with setting up the shot at their own pace.

I try out an experiment and give Steve Chivers and Carrie Fisher, our operator, their heads for the first set-up, waiting on a bench on the station platform and reading from Andrei Tarkovsky's *Sculpting in Time* until Guy comes to tell me that the crew is ready.

As a result of this new policy, we go some three hours behind schedule and I have to tell Guy that, regrettably, a return to my old ways is in order until he proves that he can make the crew hold their pace without me.

After wrap I have dinner with Marianne Sägebrecht,* whom I have not seen since a film festival in Sitges, Spain, the year before. Marianne is a big fan of *Hardware* and having told me that it was her ambition to cameo in a horror film one day, I made a point of offering her a part when it came to casting *Dust Devil*. She has brought a gift that she now presents to me, a carved wand startlingly similar to the kierie that the witchdoctor, Joe Niemand, gives to Zakes' character in the film.

In Khoisan mythology, the vampire Nagtlöper (literally 'night walker') can only be trapped by being tricked into stepping over the magic kierie traditionally laid across the threshold of the hut to guard against nocturnal visitations. There is an obvious parallel here with the stake hammered through the heart to exterminate the undead in the European vampire myth, and although the kierie used as a prop in our film is a genuine magical artefact carved for these very purposes, it in fact hails from Borneo, where there is a parallel tradition.

Marianne's kierie is of local origin, carved with the figure of a naked fertility goddess and decorated with lucky beans, designed to ward off evil and ensure a good harvest. I thank her for the gift, and promise to carry it with me on the shoot from now on as a way of symbolically protecting the crew.

Tuesday 27 August

We are in Joseph's vast, sepulchral mortuary set today, shooting the scene where Zakes' character goes to consult the local pathologist, played by Marianne, who points out the connection between the murders and ritual magic. We spend all morning lighting and rehearsing the scene, but when we come to the first master take, things go hellishly awry.

In the scene, Zakes and Marianne are standing in the fluorescent glow of a slide bench, poring over transparencies of the mysterious blood mural from the scene of the first murder, when a morgue attendant bursts into the room to announce that there is an urgent telephone call from Bethany police station.

The room is lined with two rows of motionless extras, made up by Chris Halls and Little John as partially dissected corpses, their faces and stomachs

---

* Best known for her performance in Percy Adlon's *Baghdad Café*.

68 *Dust Devil*: the mortuary (Marianne Sägebrecht and Zakes Mokae)

pinned back by surgical clamps. The morgue attendant is played by a weird-looking local who in real life pedals around the town on a rickety bicycle selling Bibles, and who is now waiting excitedly in the wings to storm in and say his one line.

Zakes and Marianne have just crossed to the slide bench on the first take when something inexplicable happens.

Although it is still early in the day, the atmosphere in the railway shed where the set has been constructed is hot and airless, and as the flickering fluorescent tubes come on inside the slide bench I start to feel strangely giddy.

It is almost as if the walls of the room, of reality itself, have suddenly become very thin, warping in and out of focus and seething like hot Silly Putty.

I stagger, putting one hand against the door-frame to steady myself, my other hand clutching Marianne's kierie.

Then the morgue attendant begins to scream and comes running into the shot uncued, his arms pinwheeling. Zakes and Marianne are plainly confused, vainly trying to continue their dialogue as I struggle to call the shot to a halt, only to find the command sticking in my throat.

The morgue attendant is doing some kind of weird dance now in the aisle between the slabs, stamping his feet and chanting something almost unintelligible.

For a moment it is as if he is speaking in tongues, but then I manage to make out some of his words.

'Hallelujah! Hallelujah! He is come! The Lord is come!'

His words disintegrate into an agonized gurgle, his eyes rolling up into their sockets so that only their whites remain visible. His legs fold under him and he drops to the floor, his body convulsing in a full-blown epileptic seizure, his lips flecked with foam, his teeth gnashing, Zakes and Marianne breaking off their dialogue and turning in shock.

For a split second everyone seems paralysed.

Then Daniel and Guy come running into the shot and start trying to force a metal ruler into the morgue attendant's mouth to stop him from swallowing his tongue, and I find my voice at last, calling for the cameras to cut, the kierie waving in my hand. Even after the cameras have stopped rolling, the corpses refuse to rise from their slabs, the extras having apparently fallen into such a deep sleep that they remain blissfully unaware of Daniel and Guy struggling to hold down the screaming morgue attendant in the aisle, his legs thrashing against the concrete floor.

'Hallelujah! Hallelujah! He is come!'

I turn away, gasping for fresh air, as Zakes and Marianne flee the set, joining me in the doorway. Zakes complains that he can feel a weird pressure at the base of his brain, and Marianne tells me bluntly that 'there are too many psychics in the room.' We clear the set and break for lunch without a single usable take in the can.

It is Marianne's birthday today, and we have laid on a seafood lunch with a platter of Lüderitz oysters shipped in specially for her.

I try to make light of the morning's events, rationalizing the morgue attendant's behaviour as an epileptic seizure brought on by the flickering of the fluorescent tubes.

By mid-afternoon we have resumed shooting, with a new extra cast as the morgue attendant. On the first take of the afternoon, when Marianne and Zakes reach the slide bench once more and the same line of dialogue that triggered the first morgue attendant's seizure, there is an electrical malfunction and the fluorescent tubes begin to flicker maddeningly, sputtering on and off for no apparent rhyme or reason.

We try to continue with the take, but eventually have to call another halt to repair the fuses and restore everyone's calm.

Marianne insists that there is a presence in the room.

Something unborn trying to break through into our reality.

I no longer try to deny that something weird is going on, but instead try to assume a quasi-shamanic role, insisting that we can only exorcise the demon by pressing on with our work. This strategy proves to be an effective one, and we are able to complete the sequence without further interference from the ether, although we have to rush the scene and simplify the coverage considerably to make up for lost time. Just when our spirits are starting to lift, an urgent fax arrives for Marianne. Her mother has had a serious stroke that afternoon and she is asked to return at once to Munich.

Later, sitting outside Marianne's trailer, my head in my hands, I am approached by Dirk and the vixen sisters from the art department.

They tell me there has been a street fight in the local township, Mondessa, and that a vigilante group hired by the production has succeeded in recovering the stolen knife after a pitched battle with one of the neighbourhood gangs.

Ina puts the knife in my hand and I hold it up in the glare of the floodlights. Its gleaming edge is notched and the etched design of the Midgard serpent is clotted with blood and bits of hair.

Later still, after a series of frantic telephone calls from the production office, we learn that Marianne's mother is out of danger, and Marianne volunteers to stay another three days to complete her scenes before returning to Germany.

Friday 30 August

Today we begin work on Marianne's final scene in the mortuary set, which has now been re-dressed with glowing murals and lit by hundreds of church candles, the floor dampened down to reflect their glow.

The set is intensely humid and Marianne is more than a little nervous.

During the morning there has been another odd incident. While the second unit were shooting pick-up shots with Marianne, the slide bench malfunctioned again on the same line of dialogue as before, the fluorescents beginning to flicker once more as if on cue. I try to reassure Marianne that our work today will be a kind of exorcism, laying the demons raised by the previous shoot, and have cause to reflect on how the film-maker seems to have taken on the same cultural role in this century as the shaman in times of old. The West has displaced its unconscious mind into the media and now we are called upon to act as dream doctors for the masses.

Kierie in hand, I glide through the afternoon, the shoot presenting few problems.

Saturday 31 August

Today is the first official rest day I have allowed myself for all too long. I take the chance to drive up the coast into the uninhabited wasteland beyond Hentie's Bay to visit the seal colony at Cape Cross.

With a thousand miles of trackless volcanic desert on one side and the fathomless depths of the South Atlantic on the other, Cape Cross feels like the very edge of man's universe. Beyond where I stand, there is nothing save wind and water sweeping away to the ends of the earth and the barren shores of Antarctica and the Falklands. The air here is thick with the stench of excrement and decaying flesh, and raucous with the roaring and bellowing of the huge sea lions whose writhing bodies undulate across the jagged rocks, fighting, fucking and foraging for food, as vast glacial waves burst over the top of them.

Everywhere around me there are creatures being born and dying, the living copulating on the bodies of the dead, the young going in constant threat of either being crushed by the adults or eaten by the jackals who boldly weave in and out of even the thickest parts of the press, their eyes glistening with a constant, seemingly insatiable hunger. I am reminded somewhat uncomfortably of Gustav Doré's engravings for Dante's *Divine Comedy*, the souls of the damned languishing on the jagged reefs of the sunless seas of hell.

On the beach at the world's end lies scattered the decay of the centuries. Mussel shell, seagull's feather, tiger's eye, the shattered spars of man lie entangled with the bones of dead leviathans, for all that is lost must one day fetch up on that flat expanse.

The beach-comber of this desolate shore walks alone with his wicker basket and, waiting and watching with infinite care, he plucks one by one unto himself the derelict dreams of Earth.

Sunday 1 September

Today is one of the single most expensive days of our shoot.

On a windswept railway siding at Usakos, Joseph has reconstructed Bethany railway station and a steam train has been brought in from Windhoek in order for us to film the dark man's arrival in the town.

In the afternoon and evening we board the train to shoot a dialogue scene in one of the cattle-trucks between Robert and two South African soldiers, played by Phillip Hen and Luke Cornell, the animal handler; in real life, both are veterans of the Angolan bush war. Before the light goes, we have to complete a helicopter shot of the steam train approaching Bethany, our rushed schedule requiring the scene to be shot simultaneously with our work in the train's interior. Daniel sees this as being the sequence's 'money shot' and insists on personally taking charge of the helicopter rather than leaving it up to the second unit. Once he is airborne, he discovers that in order for the shot to cut with the rest of the sequence he has to use the same filter as the main unit camera; however, his own budget cuts have allowed for the provision of only one filter pack, which is already on the train. This leads to the insane scenario of Daniel chasing the train in the helicopter, yelling over the two-way radio for us to pass him the filter pack.

We have to complete the rather leisurely on-board dialogue scene while Daniel hovers impatiently overhead, cursing at us through the static. When I finally call cut on the last take, he brings the helicopter alongside the cattle-truck so fast that we are still busy checking the gate. The crew has to rush to reseal the camera before the cloud of dust kicked up by the rotors clogs the works and ruins the afternoon's footage.

Passing the filter to the helicopter is a crazy business that seems far more dangerous than anything on-screen, and I end up on the roof of the moving train, jumping from carriage to carriage as the desert flatlands stream past us, bathed in the golden glow of the magic hour. I am so preoccupied with staying on the train that I narrowly miss being struck on the back of the head by a power-line that goes flashing past. I duck under it with only a split second to spare, and afterwards exude a false confidence in order to mask my own awareness that I have come within a hair's breadth of a very nasty death. I would almost certainly have been decapitated or swept beneath the train's wheels, had I not glanced around in the nick of time, and this serves as a sobering warning to me.

As in my memories of combat, being under shell-fire, saturation bombing or in a particularly bad car accident, reality has a habit of flattening out and slowing down, becoming dreamy and distant at times like this, so that the fact of one's own death seems suddenly of frighteningly little consequence. I am determined not to let this film put me in my grave prematurely and resolve to take more care from now on, knowing as I do that the shoot will collapse if anything happens to me. Daniel completes the helicopter shot and I call a wrap, riding back to camp on the roof of the train, the sky turning from beaten bronze to a sullen red behind us.

That night there is an inexplicable orange glow in the northern sky that I first notice just after midnight.

Several of the crew, including Mad Mike, Little John and Michelle Clapton, the costume designer, see the glow as well and we stand dumbstruck outside our bunkers watching the light for more than an hour.

The eerie nimbus comes from the direction of the deep desert, where all of us know there is no human habitation or artificial light source, although the intensity of the glow seems almost to betoken the presence of a large city – such as the glare of Los Angeles' lights reflected against the smog as seen from the back of Topanga canyon. We stand for a long while, gaping like yokels who behold a marvel beyond their comprehension, filled with a sort of half-mystic wonder and dreamy curiosity. The light is no aurora or human beacon, and whether it comes from just beyond the craggy, volcanic horizon or a billion miles away in intergalactic space, none of us can say. Just after one in the morning it grows dim and starts to fade, leaving my sense of wonder acutely sharpened. My knowledge of natural science, although far from extensive, can afford no plausible clue to the light's origin and I feel with a wild, half-fearful, half-exultant thrilling that the thing we witnessed is not to be found in the annals of human observers.

The phenomenon leaves me in a state of profound excitement and sleep, when it comes, is intermittent.

Tomorrow marks our biggest company move, over a thousand miles to the south to Bethany district proper, to shoot the climactic ghost-town scenes and the canyon sequence that can be shot in no other part of the world but those regions where the original events took place back in 1984.

The winds are already picking up down south and if we leave it any longer it will make shooting impossible, although a company move now is a logistical nightmare that will cost us at least two days of precious shooting time.

Jo-Anne and Daniel try to insist on me taking a charter flight south with the cast and heads of department on Sunday, but as I have a morbid fear of flying ever since a narrow escape in Zambia many years ago, I stubbornly refuse, insisting instead that I travel overland, driving down tomorrow with the rest of the crew.

Jo-Anne is frightened that for some reason I might go AWOL, but I swear to her that I will reach the airstrip in Lüderitz before her.

Despite my willingness to take a substantial wager on the matter, Jo-Anne for some reason remains curiously sceptical, as if already convinced in her heart that I am plotting to abandon her and disappear back into the desert.

Her lack of faith saddens me and encourages me to go hell for leather to prove her wrong.

Saturday 7 September

I set off on the road south just before dawn, travelling in a hired car with the taciturn Mr Horn, Deborah Deats (Chelsea's stand-in) and Mad Mike, who as usual takes the first spell at the wheel.

We call a halt for the evening at the point where the tar road gives out, on the banks of the Fish River, which winds through the second-largest natural canyon on Earth, a place that the Khoisan people knew as the home of the great snake-father Kouteign Kouroo. Back in the first times, in the time of the red light, Kouteign Kouroo, the great serpent and father of the rainbow, made this place from the lashing of his coils. We climb down the side of the canyon, the river glistening below us in the darkness, and pitch camp beneath the stars on a dry sandbank, the sound of the running water whispering to us in our sleep, our fire sending up its sparks to greet the backbone of the night that arches above us. In some strange way I feel, as I slip into deeper slumber, that I am coming home, returning at last to the source of my dreams.

Sunday 8 September

I sit naked on a flat rock beside the river, breathing in the breathless tranquillity of the prehistoric landscape that surrounds me, allowing the sun's first rays to warm me just as they warm the rock, feeling my strength returning to me as if I too am made of stone. Then rising, I dive into the sluggish orange waters of the Fish River that runs wide and tumid across the sandbanks, holding my breath and swimming along the bottom until I reach the far shore.

When I break surface once more, I feel cleansed and somehow rejuvenated by the river's embrace, as if the dust of all that has gone before has been washed away from me. Later, refreshed and revitalized, we climb back up from the river and turn the car on to the dirt track to Lüderitz, Mad Mike at the wheel once more.

Just before Aus we pass the Bethany turn-off and, leaving behind the canyon and mesa country, emerge on to a seemingly limitless primordial plain, dotted with ant hills, that sweeps away to meet the steely sky at a point infinitely remote from us. On the westernmost rim of the horizon we can see the huge igneous rocks that surround the blighted hamlet of Aus and which once served as back-projection plates for part of the opening sequence of Stanley Kubrick's *2001: A Space Odyssey*.

We arrive at the airstrip on the outskirts of Lüderitz just as the charter flight from Swakopmünd is getting in, winning our wager by a hair's breadth. I amble out on to the runway to greet Jo-Anne and the principal cast members as they disembark, welcoming them to the town and assuming a relaxed air as if I've been waiting here for days already. After freshening up in the seaside cabin that has been allocated to me, I head back into town to rendezvous with Jo-Anne and organize a scout of tomorrow's location.

When I reach the steps of the production office I hear the sounds of screams and breaking glass coming from within and Sheila Frazer Milne, the starchy production secretary who once worked with the sainted Andrei Tarkovsky on the production of *The Sacrifice*, comes running out of the building.

She bumps into me on the steps and seeing me, starts to scream: 'Don't go in there! Don't go in there!'

I try to get some sense out of her, and she explains that Joseph has found out that Jo-Anne is having an affair with Daniel and has stormed into the production office and tried to attack them, beating them with his fishing rod. Glancing over her shoulder, I see at once that Daniel has got the better of Joseph and is busy slamming him around the room, while Jo-Anne stands in one corner screaming abuse and Deborah Deats, who was apparently trying to make a long-distance call to her boyfriend, cowers under the table, still clutching the receiver.

Sheila cuts and runs, telling me to guard the steps and make sure that no one comes or goes. A moment later Robert appears, also in a blind rage, and insists on trying to push past me to see Jo-Anne. He claims that his hotel room has no running water and threatens to walk off the shoot unless it is seen to immediately.

I try to make light conversation with him, leaning from side to side to block his view of the commotion in the office, while he cranes his neck to try and see past me. Insanely, neither of us comments on the violent tableau unfolding behind us, and eventually, seeing that it is an inopportune moment, Robert goes on his way, promising to return later with a vengeance.

A split second after Robert has gone around the corner, Daniel throws Joseph out of the office, both of them swearing loudly that they'll kill each other. Joseph is a mess, his face streaming with blood, his fishing rod still clutched in one hand, his white suit streaked with gore. I walk him as far as the local bar and try to comfort him a little, hoping at least to convince him not to do anything rash. Over the grim, Bavarian-style bar counter shamelessly hangs a cherished portrait of Adolf Hitler, who is obviously still a hero to the unrehabilitated locals.

Thursday 12 September

Today we begin work on the climactic showdown in the ghost town's main street. The sequence is deliberately designed to evoke echoes of a classic Western shoot-out, although in *Dust Devil* it is a shoot-out in which the man with no name's pocket watch turns backwards, none of the guns are loaded and the antagonists are a white man, a black man and a woman. I drew my initial inspiration from the climax of *The Good, the Bad and the Ugly*, which I analysed for long hours as a teenager, but only now do I begin to realize the full extent of Leone's genius.

In *The Good, the Bad and the Ugly*, the three gunslingers, Lee Van Cleef, Eli Wallach and Clint Eastwood, fan out around a circular arena in the centre of an enormous graveyard. (See photo #63.) The strength of the scene derives in part from the extraordinary rhythm of Leone's editing, building up a complex montage of images and angles that plainly demand a vast number of set-ups to achieve.

I realize my cardinal error before we are even half-way through the day. By locating my shoot-out in the horizontal perspective of the main street, I have inadvertently locked us into a rigid continuity of light and shadow, with too many identifying landmarks for us to be able to cheat. Leone's sequence is set at the hub of a vast wheel, with the characters surrounded by a uniform background of anonymous graves, thus allowing him to cheat the action to follow the sun, rotating the actors as if on a vast sundial and enabling himself to continue shooting throughout the day. In a single, almighty error of

69 *Dust Devil*: the showdown (Robert Burke and Chelsea Fields)

judgement, I have trapped us into shooting this sequence only in the morning, before the angle of the light begins to differ too dramatically from the master take. With the sand-storms closing in on us, I have pinned the main unit and principal cast down in this one exterior location for what may turn out to be weeks. I have no choice but to chalk it up to experience and put a damage-limitation scheme into action, splitting our days between the showdown sequence and the interior scenes.

At least tomorrow will be a rest day, and I resolve to travel back out to canyon country to help collect my thoughts and get a fresh perspective on all this.

Sunday 14 September

I have to delay my departure for a scheduling meeting at the production office, and decide to ride out to canyon country with Deborah Deats, who is also making for the river.

We finally get under way around noon with Deborah at the wheel, driving a little too fast, perhaps to make up for lost time.

We have just hit the dirt road beyond Aus, roughly at the same point where we had the blow-out last Sunday when, predictably, we have another blow-out. The front left tyre goes soft and the car begins to waver, skidding from side to side on the dry, dirt surface as Deborah struggles to bring it back under control.

I brace my boots against the dashboard, seeing the road running out beneath us. Then with a thud and a rush of gravel we hit the soft shoulder and begin to roll. The horizon spins around us, the ground coming up to slap the side of the car, the door crumpling beside me and the windows imploding in a luminous spray.

I close my eyes too late, feeling the flying glass rake my face in a cloud of stinging, insect pain, the car rolling and rolling, threatening to tear itself apart, the roof caving in above me. Then, its momentum spent, the mangled chassis comes to rest on its wheels once more, rocking and shivering, the sounds of twisted metal ticking and cooling all round us, Verdi's *Requiem* still playing on the stereo.

My face is wet with blood and I try to open my eyes, only to feel a jab of pain and something like broken glass grating against the inside of my closed lid. I manage to get the buckled door open and pull myself from the wreck, my wet shirt chafing against raw nerve endings as I paw at my face, trying to wipe away the splinters still embedded there.

I turn my eyes towards the sun, feeling its heat on my upturned face and sensing the silent immensity of the landscape that surrounds me, yet I see no light.

I stagger a few paces down the road and then sit down in the dust, Verdi's music lending the scene a farcically operatic quality.

I dab at my eyes with part of my shirt, feeling pain once more.

Then I feel Deborah beside me and I ask her if she's all right.

She reminds me that she crashes cars for a living and then tries to apologize, obviously spooked at the idea of being held responsible for putting me out of action.

She brushes some of the glass off my face and tells me to try not to move or open my eyes. I sit waiting in darkness on the soft shoulder while she fetches water from the wreck, a giddy sense of calm enveloping me.

I keep seeing the same thing over and over.

The last split second before it all went dark.

The glowing halo of flying glass fanning out in the air before me so slowly that I can see every individual fragment in sharp focus as they rush up to meet my face.

My thoughts turn towards the shoot and the still uncompleted film.

I begin to feel afraid.

Then I feel water on my face and Deborah's touch once more. I try to tell her that it's all right but she tells me to be quiet and relax as she tries to remove a particularly dangerous splinter from the corner of my left eyeball. As I blink, there comes a spark of light. The spark irises up and the world comes mercifully back into focus.

The first thing I see is Deborah's face as she leans over me, the sky behind her over-exposed, burned out to a white glare, an almost comical expression of concern on her face. I find this absurdly touching, a massive sense of relief flooding through me as I realize that I haven't lost an eye after all. My head hurts and friction burns have flayed the skin from part of my left arm and shoulder, but otherwise I have been afforded a remarkable escape.

Deborah has come off even better than me, and after taking a breather we clamber back into the wreck and manage to restart the engine. To our mutual surprise, the car still runs despite its battered shape. We get the clattering wreck turned around and limp back towards the nearest town, Aus, where we stop for a drink to steady our nerves at the local hotel.

Sitting on the hotel veranda, I realize that my temporary blindness could not have been down to the glass splinter alone, and finding a raised lump on the back of my skull, deduce that I must have struck my head against the roof and am probably suffering from a mild form of concussion.

The ageing German matron who runs the hotel joins us on the veranda and we strike up a conversation with her.

Aus, whose name literally means 'out' or 'exit' in German, was originally a concentration camp, one of the earliest, set up by the South Africans for German prisoners in World War One.

The South Africans got the idea from the British, who came up with the prototypes of the modern death-camps during the Boer War. The unsettling idea that Aus might have in turn inspired the Germans comes over me.

The matron who runs the hotel in what was formerly the hub of the camp tells me that three years ago Aus froze over, in an unprecedented bout of freak weather that produced an isolated blizzard in the middle of the Namib desert, the only one in recorded history. She disappears back into the hotel to dig out some photographs of Aus under snow, and while she is gone an elderly bushman clutching a guitar comes wandering up on to the veranda and sits down beside us. He is the first and only bushman I have come across on the shoot and I try to speak to him, although his English is non-existent and my Afrikaans and German are equally poor.

The bushman tells us that we look very beautiful together, apparently failing to notice that we are covered in blood. He begins to serenade us on his guitar, singing an inane romantic ballad.

The German matron returns and without warning or provocation starts to yell at the bushman, driving him off the veranda and making as if to strike him. Then she cheerfully sits down beside us once more and continues the conversation. I remark on how few bushmen are left and she tells me how, back before World War One, the German settlers massacred most of the locals, burying them in mass graves beneath what is now the local golf course.

Every time she turns her back the bushman creeps back on to the veranda, grinning mischievously and attempts to continue his song, prompting further outbursts of abuse from the hotelier.

All this talk of death-camps seems to make Deborah uncomfortable, and eventually she urges me to move on, driving back to Lüderitz as the day shelves off into night, the car's shattered headlights casting amusingly psychedelic patterns on the road ahead. Even when I reach my cabin back at the beach-front, Deborah seems loath to leave me, still apprehensive at my condition and perhaps wanting some reassurance herself. She waits while I take a shower, washing my hair to make sure all the fine debris has been removed from my scalp.

The hot water stings against the raw flesh of my back and I close my eyes once more, turning my face towards the cleansing spray.

Then there is a soft draught as someone draws the curtain, and I feel Deborah suddenly beside me, her hand brushing against my cheek.

I turn and her voice comes to me in darkness once more before her lips touch mine: 'Don't be frightened. Don't spoil it. It's just love.'

Thursday 19 September

The company relocates some three hundred kilometres inland to resume shooting on the edge of the Fish River Canyon, for a swooning romantic interlude between Chelsea and the dark man, shot from the crane and semi-circular tracks.

The grandeur of the landscape stuns everyone into something like religious awe and the shoot runs like clockwork, with the crew talking in whispers as if working in a cathedral. After getting the big kiss in the can, I sit with Deborah and Mad Mike on the lip of the canyon and watch a half-mystical sunset, the clouds turning into twisting tongues of fire in the brazen furnace of the west, the heated heavens reflecting in the coils of the river far below us, where the first patches of night are already lurking, climbing up every gully and cleft as the desert sky slowly lapses into night and the Southern Cross appears with an almost hallucinatory vividness overhead.

Driving back from the canyon we strike and kill a rabbit, which I take as a bad omen and my mood remains sombre for the rest of the evening, which I spend with Deborah beside a campfire at the river's edge, watching as an endless armada of night creatures fling themselves hissing and spluttering into the flames.

A huge moth sears its wings and goes fluttering around my feet in a frenzied death rictus that only ends when a hunting spider scurries quickly out of the shadows and latches on to it, prompting the dying moth to get itself airborne once more and disappear back into the night, the spider still clinging tenaciously to its underbelly. Even here, then, there is no peace.

Only the silent slaughter-house of the desert night.

The quiet holocaust of nature.

70 *Dust Devil*: shooting

71 *Dust Devil*: figures in a landscape (Robert Burke and Chelsea Fields)

Sunday 29 September

I join the crew on the set of the Star of Bethany Drive-In Theatre that Joseph has constructed in the shadow of Spitkop's crags.

The drive-in is a re-creation of a real theatre in the Keetmanshoop area, its purpose in the film being in part to illustrate the contamination of the witch-doctor's cosmology by western B-movie imagery. By putting an equal weight on mythology and pop culture, I hope to draw attention to the complex iconographic roots of the man-with-no-name figure and the magical possibilities of film itself. The witch-doctor's role as drive-in projectionist helps illustrate the complicated idea behind the dark man's murders, the gnostic belief that life only exists as a result of a war between light and dark, between spirit and matter. The dark man, like us, is trapped in material incarnation and yearns to escape the linear continuity of time like a character in a film who plots to escape from the scene itself.

As night comes on and we move into Spitzkop's caves and deeper into the cosmology of *Dust Devil*, a posse of confused British journalists arrive with the film's publicist to watch as John Matshikiza, the witch-doctor, squats on a rock beside a fake campfire and expounds on how the black magician knows that there is a spark of light trapped within all of us, a splinter of the true God. Through the ritual of murder the magician can control the release of the spark and ride the light-beam beyond time, beyond matter, into infinity. Our world has no more substance to him than a projected image caught for an instant on the palm of an upraised hand.

Friday 11 October

We spend all night on the eerie, sand-filled set of the abandoned Empire Cinema, the dead heart of the ghost town where Zakes' character confronts the dark man and the ghostly presence of his wife and child.

The sanded-in cinema is somehow an astonishingly apt place to end the last day of our official main unit shoot, and for the first time in weeks the quality of tonight's sequence matches the visionary power of its description in the script. Today is Day Forty-Six of our forty-six day shoot.

From now on we will be working on borrowed time, our continued presence here sustained only by Jo-Anne's successful insurance claim on the damaged mortuary footage.

Thursday 17 October

We spend the morning shooting insert work before relocating to the local shooting-range to complete a sequence torn from the script a fortnight ago.

The shooting-range sequence involves me taking charge of a class of local schoolchildren armed with .22 rifles and live ammunition and working with a vestigial crew without assistant directors, production support or insurance cover.

The personal and ambiguous nature of the scene has always called it into doubt from the point of view of the film's backers, who are ceaselessly engaged in trying to pare my work back to the bare, exploitative bone and I realize that, even if I manage to get it into the can on the sly, it will probably still be cut from the final release prints.

Coming at the end of the dark man's walk through Bethany, the scene depicts a group of children dressed in cadet uniforms reminiscent of the Hitler Youth being tutored in the finer points of marksmanship by a Marist monk.

The scene is intended as another omen of the coming holocaust and an evocation of Christianity's moral and spiritual bankruptcy, as well as serving as one of the film's only hints at the dark man's past, a moment of strange recognition flickering between him and one of the pupils.

The scene is a direct re-creation of a precise moment from a vanished hour of a vanished day from my own childhood. Incarcerated in a Catholic military academy for two years, I learned swiftly that if I could shoot straight I would be exempt from the tiresome and degrading ritual of square-bashing and formation-marching. Lying on my belly in the dust, squinting down the barrel of my rifle, I felt strangely superior to the other boys, who were forced to march in endless circles in the midday sun. If my aim was good, the monks smiled on me and I was treated to time off and away trips for competitive shooting competitions.

I really believed then, even at that early age, that all the difference between our squad and the rest of the boys lay in our possessing the will and the specialized skills necessary for killing. We were an élite amongst the other cadets, privileged to spend our time goofing off, lying on our bellies like lizards in the African sun, concentrating on our targets until the only thing we could still feel were the tips of our fingers against the triggers. In this way I first learned, in the very bosom of the church, the art and privilege of killing, a lesson that for my sins I have never forgotten, even after I tore off my uniform and broke with the programme.

It was on a bright day like this that I first glimpsed the dark man strolling past our school fence, his face strangely shadowed beneath the brim of his hat, the air around him seething like quicksilver. I remember feeling afraid but fascinated at the same time. His coat, old even then and thick with dust, seemed redolent of adventure and intrigue. Even then I felt a strange allure, a lethal glamour that told me that one day I would be just like him. I have felt him just behind me at every turn since then, threatening and cajoling me, my dark half, my murderous *alter ego*, my very shadow, the man that poor Deborah has mistaken me for.

In Afghanistan when my marksmanship and talent for killing became central to my survival, once again the line between us became all but invisible.

Now at last, here in Namibia where it all began, I pray I have finally drained that residue of darkness from my soul, dragged the dark man kicking from my wounded psyche and trapped him safely on film, caught forever behind the rolling frame bars of a cinematic prison specially constructed for him.

Maybe now at last I will be free from his shadow.

Only time will tell.

I spend the evening burning cows' skulls and dressing up in coat, hat and dog mask to take over briefly from Robert and become the dark man for an insert shot of his partially transformed figure caught in the headlights of an incoming car. After the shoot when I discard the costume, I really feel that I am discarding that part of my life for ever and when sleep finds me, it is deep and dreamless.

Saturday 19 October

Jo-Anne and Daniel slip out of town today, heading for home without saying goodbye and I am left to fight on alone until the bitter end.

I still have the helicopter for another forty-eight hours and there is just about enough stock left to keep us busy, although we are desperately short on fuel.

I quit my bunker just before dawn and report to the airstrip, where I solemnly say farewell to Mad Mike and strap myself into the chopper for the ride south. All day we fly across a lifeless world of red dust, naked lava ridges and broken quartz, the ceaseless thrum and flicker of the rotor blades lulling all of us in the cockpit into something close to a trance.

Gliding like a solitary vulture on the high thermals, we cross a land that no longer seems to be part of man's universe, an untenanted, unfinished world, the terrain of Gods and Spirits. Several times I have to splash water on the pilot's face to keep him alert, and near Keetmanshoop we have to cut across the freeway and land at a service station to refuel. Then we are flying over the flat-topped mesas of Bethany district, mustangs running on the plain below us. We find the railway line and trace its gleaming tracks until they cross the curve of the Fish River and we follow the dark man's trail back along its shining coils into canyon country and the timeless gorge that in Khoisan mythology is home to the Great Snake Father.

There on the canyon's wall the last of the production's red Volkswagens has been pushed into place, A pick-up truck is parked a little way off, with the shoot's last two survivors standing by.

Deborah and our runner, Desperate Dan Zeff (who always wanted to be more involved in the movie), have been driving all night to make this rendezvous. She is dressed in Chelsea's wardrobe and during the night she has crudely peroxided Dan's hair in a convenient service-station basin and dressed him to resemble Robert.

Now, as we circle them in the fading light of our final magic hour, she takes Desperate Dan in her arms and standing on the very edge of the cliff, draws him into a last embrace, planting a lingering kiss on his lips.

The moment seems eternal, as if somehow abstracted from time, and I roll the camera until I am out of stock, the chopper lurching perilously beneath me, buffeted by the canyon's curious air currents, the river spinning far below us.

I cut the camera and we bring the chopper in to land on the edge of the abyss. I unstrap myself and bundle Desperate Dan into the seat in my place, shaking him by the hand before signalling all clear to the pilot to lift off.

The chopper circles us one last time before banking and heading away north, anxious to reach civilization before the light fades, the throb of its rotors ebbing slowly like a fading pulse, leaving me and Deborah marooned in the silent, golden glory of the Great Namib.

By nightfall we have arrived at our final port of call, the decaying spa town of Warmbad, on the bank of the Orage river, that was in ancient times known to the Khoisan people as Too-Gah, the navel of the universe, the ancestral point of emergence and portal to the spirit world.

Deborah and I pitch camp beside the volcanic spring, a storm brewing in the distance, a vaporous column of living steam rising to the stars behind us, its writhing contours suggesting an ethereal bestiary drawn from some forgotten mythology.

Alone now with Deborah, I finally have to confront the truth about her identity and mine. I ask about her surname and she admits that it has been anglicized from Dietz, and when I probe further, she admits that her grandfather fled from Germany at the end of World War Two. He had been involved in a chemical factory that had manufactured Zyklon B for the gas chambers of Belsen and Auschwitz. Her father, Michael Julius Dietz, had followed in his footsteps by becoming an important mover in ESCOM, South Africa's state-owned power suppliers, and is in personal charge of the nation's fledgeling nuclear power programme. Deborah herself plans to follow suit and dreams of a career in the state-owned broadcasting network.

Her dreams get out of hand and she tells me of her vision of a new South Africa, arguing that I can never be happy living amongst the 'white worms' of the West, that my duty is to remain here and become one of the leaders of this brave new world, a midwife attending to the birth-pains of a strange new order.

She tells me how some of the right-wingers are planning to reclaim this part of Namibia and build a huge wall out into the ocean to divert the Benguela current and cause a temperature inversion to bring rain to the wasteland and make the desert fertile so that the new, pure-white nation of Orandia can be founded.

I shake my head and tell her that she is insane.

I tell her that the white man will never be able to bend the desert to his will. The sleeping giants of the wasteland will awaken and break their bones if they try. She tells me that I am just like her beneath the skin, that no matter what, I will always be one of 'them'.

I laugh and tell her that the only thing I know for sure now is that I'm nothing like her. I never have been and never will be one of 'them'.

She rages at me and threatens me with a soda-water bottle.

She calls me a traitor.

I pull a knife on her and tell her to drop the bottle.

Now she accuses me of the murders, of having killed all those people when I first hitch-hiked up here after deserting from the army.

She claims she has heard me talking in my sleep.

I start to laugh again and sit down, sheathing my knife.

Eventually she gets tired of threatening me and sits down as well.

I patiently explain to her that I am not the dark man, nor am I a black magician or a mass murderer, nor am I a worm or a traitor.

I'm just a film-maker and a pretty mediocre one at that.

She curses me and I leave her the car keys.

I shoulder my pack and she yells after me that I'm damned, that I'm condemning myself to a life of obscurity as a hack horror-film director, a life of wasted dreams and worthless prophecies.

I tell her that this is true and she spits at me.

Not wanting to hear any more, I start down the road, heading north once more, determined to try and hitch a ride.

A little while later it starts to rain.

Epilogue

In December 1991 I delivered a 120-minute cut of *Dust Devil* to Palace Pictures. The film was cut to 95 minutes and test-screened at Wimbledon, to a confused audience response. In April 1992 Palace Pictures went into liquidation and post-production on *Dust Devil* was closed down. After Palace went under, *Dust Devil*'s British distribution rights were taken over by Polygram who subsequently shelved it. In the intervening time, Miramax produced an ungraded 86-minute cut of their own, eliminating the dream imagery and supernatural subtext, redubbing and wildly restructuring the remaining scenes into a new order that bore little resemblance either to the original script or a cohesive narrative. In January 1993 I learned that one of Palace's creditors had grabbed the 86-minute cutting copy and that another held the negative. I persuaded them to hand over the material and tracked down the rushes and the remaining excised footage to a storage locker in Rickmansworth, Hertfordshire.

In the next few months I spent forty thousand pounds of my own money recutting and redubbing the film as effectively as I could with the aid of its new editor, Paul Carlin. Eighteen months after wrapping in Namibia, I delivered a final cut to Polygram running at 105 minutes. The film was subsequently given a token theatrical release, using the one print that I had already paid for, garnering some glowing reviews and somehow actually managing to show a profit on its UK release, grossing more money than the Palme d'Or winner *Barton Fink* before being dumped unceremoniously on to video, hidden from view behind a tasteless and misleading box cover.

The only cut that has ever been seen outside Britain is the garbled, ungraded Miramax cut that crept out on to video release in Europe and the United States. Channel Four plans to televise the complete *Dust Devil* this autumn, and plans are in the works to try to re-release the film theatrically in several territories including the United States.

My contract with Palace Pictures has never been honoured. I have yet to receive my final pay cheque, and will never be compensated for my subsidy of the post-production period. Partially as a result of the contract I signed in blood back in August 1991, I have no legal claim to the film's box-office earnings or right to screen the completed film without the prior consent of the distributors.

I no longer have dreams of the dark man, but suffer from nightmares of a different kind. Jo-Anne and Daniel are currently in Utah producing a George Sluizer film described by its publicist as a 'desertbound psychological thriller'.

Poor Steve Earnhardt is still working for Miramax.

Deborah Dietz drove the pick-up truck down to Cape Town where she was reunited with her Argentinian boyfriend Jorge.

On the way back to Johannesburg they were both injured in a serious car smash after the windscreen of their pick-up truck was struck by a white owl.

The vixen sisters, Ina and Amelia Roux, were less fortunate. Coming back from another shoot a few months after *Dust Devil*'s wrap, Ina fell asleep at the wheel while driving through the desert night, and steered their car directly into the path of an oncoming truck.

Ina was killed on impact and Amelia survived with serious injuries.

It is to them that the film and this report on its making are dedicated.

Richard Stanley (director)
Malibu, Southern California
Summer 1993

The Script

In each Projections *so far we have included a screenplay.
The more cinematic a script, the more unreadable it
becomes. Hal Hartley's* Flirt *is an easy read. It is a short
film that is told in dialogue characterized by verbal
dexterity and mordant humour; it is very witty and
entertaining. Does this mean that it is uncinematic? Well,
all film theories fall down. Film is mostly rule of thumb.*
Projections *has taken a continuing interest in Hal
Hartley's work because he has a unique voice. Like
Quentin Tarantino, his films are driven by dialogue, yet
they are not plays or TV films – they are distinctly movies.*

72 Hal Hartley (photo by Richard Sylvarnes)

15   Flirt
Hal Hartley

Introduction

In the spring of 1992 I was asked by an American Pay TV network to contribute a half-hour segment to a series they wanted to do on prostitution. I was excited to do something on this topic. But before long the theme of the series had changed to something like 'Women In The City'. A bit later on, it became 'Women In The City At Night' and then, simply, 'The City At Night'. Eventually, the whole thing was shelved.

This version of *Flirt* originates, I guess, from the 'City At Night' period. I wrote it quickly, pulling its parts together from some older, obsolete screenplays, and in August 1992 I produced a version of what is now the bathroom scene as a ten-minute skit for the Cucaracha Cabaret in New York City. In that version, two young men (Dave Simmonds and Hugh Palmer) consult three mysteriously articulate young women (Elina Lowensohn, Adrienne Shelly, and Parker Posey).

I finally shot the film over four days in February 1993. It has become, apart from anything else, the test film for the new computer I've begun cutting my films with. I have to admit that, perhaps as a result, I've maintained a sort of scientific detachment from this film which suits me and, I believe, the subject matter just fine. *Flirt* isn't concerned with being necessarily dramatic. Although it trades in plot and characterization as much as any of my films, it nevertheless says the obvious without too much emotional pitch: people (in this case men) often want more than they should reasonably want, and kick and scream when they're forced to choose between one thing and another.

This is nothing new. And, I guess, it was this attitude of timeless, mundane inevitability that I embraced right from the start. The film, for me, is like reciting a particularly apt passage of a traditional text. I remember writing the action and saying to myself, 'Go through the motions'; state the facts about the obvious and the mysterious will make itself apparent on its own terms.

I don't really know what I've ended up with. I hadn't seen the film in weeks since I was busy with pre-production on a new feature. But we mixed it yesterday morning and I found myself sitting back, startled. I was anxious, intrigued, and even a little embarrassed. So what else is new? I've learned a lot from this brash little bastard.

73 *Flirt*: Emily (Parker Posey)

74 *Flirt*: Bill (Bill Sage)

75 *Flirt*: Walter (Martin Donovan)

76 *Flirt*: Man #3 (Robert Burke)

SCENE I INT. EMILY'S APT. EARLY EVENING

BILL *and* EMILY *have been making love all afternoon. They discuss their future.*

EMILY: I feel disgusting.

BILL: Why?

EMILY: I'm a liar.

BILL: No, you're not.

EMILY: He writes to me and says he misses me. He calls and says he loves me.
> And I reply, 'I miss you too.'
> (*Turns to* BILL . . .)
> But I don't.

BILL: Maybe you don't know what you feel.

EMILY: But I do know what I feel. I love you. Maybe I love him too. But I love
> you more.

BILL: And I love you.
> (*She sighs and gets off the bed, wrapping the sheet around her as she stands at the*
> *open window. She lights a cigarette and gazes down into the city streets.*)

EMILY: (*Finally*) We're using the same language I use when I lie to him. It
> poisons everything.
> (BILL *gets out of bed and puts on his trousers. He moves to the fridge and takes a*
> *swig of Evian. Then . . .*)

BILL: What time's your flight?

EMILY: Seven o'clock.

BILL: Is he going to meet you at the airport in Paris?

EMILY: Yes.
> (BILL *comes over and looks down into the street, leaning out over the balcony*
> *railing.*)

BILL: What will you tell him?

EMILY: (*Watching him, then . . .*) What do you want me to tell him?

BILL: I don't want to tell you what to do.

EMILY: Then tell me what you want.

BILL: That would be the same thing.

EMILY: (*Smokes, then . . .*) It would help me decide.
> (*He turns and looks in at her. After a thoughtful pause, he sighs and looks at his*
> *feet.*)

BILL: He wants you to stay with him in Paris, huh?

EMILY: Yes.
> (*She goes back inside and begins dressing.*)

BILL: He wants to marry you?

EMILY: I guess, eventually.
> (EMILY *sits on the edge of the bed.* BILL *sits down beside her.*)

BILL: What do you want me to say?

EMILY: I want you to tell me if there is a future for me and you.

BILL: A future, huh?

EMILY: Yes.

(*She gets up, throws her suitcase on the bed, and starts tossing clothes into it.*)

BILL: How can I answer that?

EMILY: (*Packing*) Yes or no.

BILL: I can't see the future.

(*She pauses, leans up from her suitcase, and regards him calmly.*)

EMILY: You don't need to see it if you know it's there.

(*He takes a deep breath and stands up. Troubled and preoccupied, he glances at his watch.*)

BILL: What time's your flight?

EMILY: (*Packing*) Seven.

BILL: (*Pacing*) Seven, huh. OK. It's four now . . .

(*She keeps packing while watching him pace. He's thinking. He lights a cigarette and stops.*)

BILL: Look, let me go get Michael's truck. I'll drive you out to JFK.

EMILY: I can take a taxi.

(*He comes over and takes her by the arms.*)

BILL: No, I want to. Can you wait here?

EMILY: How long?

BILL: (*Considers*) An hour and a half.

EMILY: Then what?

BILL: Then I'll tell you the future.

EMILY: (*Looks at her watch*) Five-thirty?

BILL: Without fail.

(*She looks at him and considers. He seems earnest. She smiles.*)

EMILY: Five-thirty.

(*They kiss.*)

SCENE 2 EXT. STREET/PHONE BOOTH. 4.10

BILL *comes out on to the street, throwing on his coat, and heads for a telephone booth.*

He has to wait for the phone because there is a cute young woman deep in conversation. We can't hear what the person on the other side is saying, but the GIRL *just answers* . . .

GIRL: No.

No.

No.

No?

No.

No.

(*She and* BILL *make eye contact. She smiles briefly, then is called back to the receiver.*)

GIRL: (*Urgent*) No!

No.

No?

My time is up. I'll call you right back.

(*She hangs up and searches for a quarter. She can't find one and looks to* BILL.)

GIRL: Excuse me, have you gotta quarter?

(BILL *comes closer, obliging.*)

BILL: Sure.

(*He gives her a quarter. Their hands touch and linger. She smiles coquettishly as she drifts back to the receiver.*

BILL *leans on the side of the booth, close.*

She dials and flashes an apologetic glance at him.)

GIRL: It won't be long.

BILL: (*Flirting*) It's OK.

(*The phone is answered and she continues her conversation, all the while watching* BILL.)

GIRL: It's me again.

No . . .

No?

No.

No.

No.

No.

(BILL *furtively looks at his watch. He seems to be growing a little impatient. He gestures good-naturedly to the* GIRL *that he's going to go up the street to another phone booth. But she reaches out and touches his hand, urging him not to.*

He stops in his tracks at her touch. He waits and she brings the conversation to a close.)

GIRL: No!

No.

No.

No.

OK.

No.

Bye.

(*And she hangs up. She stays in the booth and smiles at* BILL.)

GIRL: Sorry.

BILL: Excuse me, have you gotta quarter?

GIRL: Thank you.

(*Finally, she leaves the booth and starts away.* BILL *steps into the booth, watching her go.*)

BILL: See you around.

(*She glances back at him, flirting.*)

GIRL: Maybe.

(BILL *grins and dials. He waits. Then . . .*)

BILL: Margaret?

It's me, Bill.

It's important.

I have to ask you one question.

I want you to tell me if there's a future for me and you?

Yes or no.

You don't need to see it if you know it's there.

Meet me at the bar in ten minutes.

SCENE 3 INT. PUFFY'S TAVERN. 4.20

BILL *strides into the bar and shakes hands with the bartender,* MAC.

MAC: You owe me money.

BILL: That's true.

MAC: Michael's back there .

BILL: Margaret here?

MAC: No.

BILL: Gimme a beer, will ya?

(MAC *gets him a beer and slides it towards him.* BILL *gives him two bucks.*)

MAC: You *do* owe me money.

BILL: (*Moves away . . .*) I owe lots of people money.

(*Towards the back of the bar,* BILL *finds his friend* MICHAEL.)

BILL: Michael, let me borrow your truck. I gotta drive Emily to the airport.

MICHAEL: She's finally leaving you, huh?

BILL: (*Irritated*) Look, she's just going to France because she's got a job there for three months. OK?

MICHAEL: You hear the news?

BILL: What news?

MICHAEL: Margaret left her husband.

(BILL *comes closer, intense.*)

BILL: Do you know that for a fact?

MICHAEL: Well, I guess so. I got it from Trish.

(BILL *comes closer, intense.*)

BILL: Listen, Michael, something happened between me and Margaret.

MICHAEL: Yeah? like what?

BILL: We got romantic.

MICHAEL: Excuse me?

BILL: Romantic.

MICHAEL: (*Considers*) Romantic.

BILL: We kissed. Once.

MICHAEL: (*Realizes*) Ah, romantic.

BILL: Yeah.

MICHAEL: When?

BILL: A few weeks ago.

MICHAEL: How?

> (BILL *drinks his beer, then sets it down on the bar. He paces back and forth, thinking.*)

BILL: We were at a party.

> She and Walter had had a fight.
>
> She was upset.
>
> I got her a drink.
>
> She cried on my shoulder.
>
> I told her a joke.
>
> We kissed.

> (*He stops and looks at* MICHAEL. MICHAEL *considers it all, then scratches his head.*)

MICHAEL: That's it?

BILL: Well, it means a lot to me.

MICHAEL: What about Emily?

> (BILL *nods, sits back down, and reaches for his beer.*)

BILL: Emily all of a sudden wants me to tell her the future.

MICHAEL: Emily is a pretty remarkable girl.

BILL: Yeah, I know, but Margaret's always fascinated me too.

MICHAEL: I'd go for the sure thing.

BILL: You would, huh?

MICHAEL: Emily loves you and you love her.

BILL: Yeah, but she's going away to France for three months.

MICHAEL: Don't you trust her?

BILL: Yeah, but she's going away to France for three months.

MICHAEL: Ah, that's complicated. But then Margaret is married to Walter.

BILL: But she just left him.

MICHAEL: That's true.

BILL: They could get back together again, though.

MICHAEL: Happens all the time.

BILL: Unless, of course, I get in there now and make my play.

MICHAEL: Might be your only chance to know for sure.

> (*They drink.* BILL *is anxious and preoccupied. He looks around. Finally . . .*)

BILL: Where's Trish?

SCENE 4 INT. KITCHEN. MOMENTS LATER

TRISH *is one of the waitresses. She's impatient, but* BILL *demands a moment of her time.*

TRISH: Look, Bill, Margaret is in a very mixed-up place in her life right now. She doesn't need to get mixed up with someone like you.

BILL: (*Insulted*) Someone like me. What's that supposed to mean?

TRISH: You know what I mean.

BILL: No, I don't.

TRISH: You're not *serious*.

BILL: Serious like Walter, you mean.

TRISH: Hey! Walter's a pretty successful and well-thought-of guy most of the time!

BILL: He's smothering her.

TRISH: Well, that's no reason for her to take up with an aimless flirt like you.

BILL: Hey!

TRISH: You are with a different girl every time I see you!

BILL: So, I'm lucky!

TRISH: You're not lucky, Bill. You're loose.

BILL: Loose?

TRISH: You just can't careen from one cute little behind to the next – never investing anything in any one of them.
(*This stuns him a little, but he collects himself and comes right back at her.*)

BILL: What about Emily?

TRISH: What about Emily?

BILL: I've been with Emily for six months and I haven't strayed once!

TRISH: So what do you want – a medal?

BILL: Listen, Trish, if there were any woman who could come between me and Emily, it's Margaret.
(*This gives her pause. They are both quiet. Then . . .*)

TRISH: Oh really?

BILL: (*Not so certain any more*) Well . . . yeah, I guess.

TRISH: What happened with you and Margaret anyway?

BILL: (*Waits, then . . .*) *Nothing* happened!
(*He paces, thinking, and finally sighs . . .*)
But it might.
(*He comes to a stop and leans on the sink. There's a young guy washing dishes looking at him.* BILL *gives him his cigarettes.*)

BILL: (*To dishwasher*) Here. Go smoke my cigarettes.
(*The* DISHWASHER *takes them and leaves.*
BILL *comes over to* TRISH.)

BILL: Are you upset?
(*She looks at him, pauses, then . . .*)

TRISH: Your problems are trivial.
(*They kiss. Hold, then cut to . . .*)

SCENE 5 INT. MEN'S BATHROOM. MOMENTS LATER
BILL *collapses in through the door and finds himself kneeling on the floor. He sighs, then looks up to . . .*

A group of men: MAN # 1 *is washing his hands.* MAN # 2 *is at the urinal taking a leak. And* MAN # 3 *pauses as he steps out from one of the toilet stalls.*

BILL *looks down from them and gathers his wits. He speaks, still kneeling.*
BILL: Gentlemen . . .

Excuse me.

(*They wait. He stands.*)

My girlfriend of *six* months is going away to Paris, France, for *three* months.
(*A discouraging collective sigh as they relax and settle.* BILL *moves to the urinals and takes a piss.*)

BILL: (con't) She's beautiful, young, intelligent and very conscientious. She says she loves me and that she'll miss me terribly.

Before she leaves, she wants me to tell her if there's a future for us.
(*He steps away from the urinal and washes his hands.*)

My question is: Am I wrong in wanting more time? More proof? Is it wrong of me to be so scared?
(*He steps away from the sink and waits for a reply.*)

INT. MEN'S ROOM. SAME TIME
Angle on MAN # 1; *like interview footage.*

MAN # 1: It's important to keep the girl constantly within your sphere of influence. Of course, this is difficult to do if she is in another country. I would not feel guilty about this fear of losing her. People are people and things happen. But perhaps the things that do happen are not serious. I would write many letters. Daily, if possible. And I do not think it inadvisable to let her know, frankly and before she leaves, that you have these fears of losing her. She's young. Perhaps she's impressionable. This sounds harsh and manipulating, I know, but remember, she's not just going anywhere; she's going to Paris, France. The city of lights. They *claim*, at least, to have invented love.

INT. MEN'S ROOM. SAME TIME
Angle on MAN # 2.

MAN # 2: I would be careful of exhibiting a too fearful nature to a woman, myself. Lack of confidence is not a very attractive trait in anyone. She's young. Well, an ever-widening horizon of experience is what youth was invented for.

The best of all possible approaches to this dilemma is for the two of you to firmly embrace reality for what it is: cruel, brutal, cold, and entirely unconcerned with the individual.

INT. MEN'S ROOM. SAME TIME

Angle on MAN #3.

MAN #3: Relinquishing our hold on someone is an act of love. The giving of
affection and the determination to provide comfort are the two practicable
elements of love.

Love requires no proof. Seen in this light, love is a sort of faith, since a
faith that required proof would not be a faith at all.

But I will make this distinction; love is an act and faith is an ability. You
can make the act of love by letting her go and sincerely wishing her the
best of times while she's gone. You can only attempt to develop the faith
needed to keep yourself from going insane with jealousy and the fear of
approaching loneliness.

I don't want to sound despairing or at a loss for ideas, but the fact is you
can do nothing to retain the girl's love but be the best man you know how
to be.

SCENE 6 INT. PUFFY'S TAVERN. MOMENTS LATER

WALTER *comes into the bar with a chip on his shoulder. He stands there looking
around the place.*

   MAC *and* MICHAEL *and some other* GUYS *hush themselves and watch him.*

MAC: Hey, Walter.

WALTER: Bill been in here tonight?

   (MAC *hesitates and looks at* MICHAEL.)

WALTER: He's in the men's room.

   (WALTER *throws a tortured and confused glance over at the men's room, then
   steps over and hangs on the bar.*)

WALTER: Gimme a bottle of Jack Daniels and two glasses, Mac.

   (MAC *does as he's told.* WALTER *tosses two twenties on the bar and heads back
   to the tables.*

   MICHAEL, MAC *and the other* GUYS *watch him go.*)

MAC: (*Explains*) His wife left him.

GUY: For Bill?

MAC: Most likely.

GUY: Bill's a flirt, huh?

MICHAEL: Gets more ass than a toilet-seat.

   (BILL *comes out of the men's room and finds* WALTER *sitting at a table, loading
   a gun.*

   BILL *flashes a look over to* . . .

   MAC, MICHAEL, *and the* GUYS. *They just sit there, watching nervously.* MAC
   starts to go for the phone, but . . .

   BILL *gestures for him to relax. He looks back over at* WALTER, *pulls himself up,
   and approaches.*)

BILL: Evening, Walter.

(WALTER *looks up, distraught, and finishes putting a single bullet in the gun. He lays the gun on the table and reaches for his drink.*)

WALTER: How are you, Bill?

BILL: Mind if I sit down?

WALTER: (*Self-pitying*) No. Why would *I* mind?

(BILL *sits down.*)

BILL: (*Of gun*) What are you gunna do with that?

WALTER: I'm gunna shoot myself.

BILL: (*Unloading gun*) That's pretty stupid, Walter.

WALTER: Yeah, I guess I oughta shoot Margaret, huh?

(BILL *pockets the bullet and lays the gun back down.*)

BILL: (*Pours a drink*) No, you're not gunna shoot anybody.

WALTER: Maybe I oughta shoot you.

BILL: Why me?

WALTER: Because you're a single guy with no responsibilities.

BILL: You make it sound so easy.

WALTER: Why is she doing this to me?

BILL: I don't know, Walter.

(WALTER *takes up the gun and reloads it from a supply of bullets in his coat pocket. He puts just one in and lays the gun back down.*)

WALTER: She loved me once. Why can't she love me now?

BILL: People change.

WALTER: I won't change.

(BILL *takes the gun and empties it again. He puts it in his coat pocket.*)

BILL: Well, maybe you will.

WALTER: I don't want to change.

BILL: Sometimes you have no choice.

WALTER: Have you changed?

(WALTER *reaches over and calmly removes the gun from* BILL's *pocket. He starts putting another bullet in.*)

BILL: I'm changing all the time.

WALTER: That's why the girls like you so much.

BILL: The girls don't all like me that much.

WALTER: Margaret likes you.

BILL: (*Intrigued*) Did she say that?

WALTER: She didn't have to.

(*Knocks back a drink, then . . .*)

I could tell.

BILL: Look, Walter, nothing happened with me and Margaret.

WALTER: But it might.

BILL: Impossible.

WALTER: Why, don't you think she's attractive?

BILL: She's very attractive.

WALTER: She's my wife, goddam it!

BILL: And a wonderful woman besides.

WALTER: Why is it impossible? Why's nothing gunna happen between you and Margaret?

BILL: Because I'm in love with Emily.

WALTER: Liar.

BILL: What?

WALTER: You've never loved anyone in your life. You go through women like pairs of dirty underwear. You wouldn't know what commitment was if it came up and bit you in the leg!

BILL: (*Getting up*) I don't have to sit here and listen to this.

WALTER: Sit down.

BILL: I gotta take Emily to the airport.

WALTER: Look, come on, I'm sorry. Have one more drink with me.

(BILL *acquiesces and sits back down.*
They drink. Silence. Finally . . .)

WALTER: You ever think of settling down, Bill?

BILL: Occasionally.

WALTER: Lately?

BILL: A little.

WALTER: With Emily?

BILL: Probably.

WALTER: She's a good woman.

(BILL *considers this and slowly becomes convinced. He nods and sighs, resigned.*)

BILL: Yes, she is.

WALTER: You oughta propose to her.

BILL: You think so?

WALTER: Yes.

(BILL *thinks about this, tosses the idea around, then . . .*)

BILL: I guess you're right.

WALTER: You oughta do it now.

BILL: Excuse me?

(WALTER *points the newly loaded gun at him.*)

WALTER: Call her on the phone.

BILL: What?

WALTER: (*Gets up*) Come on.

(*He nudges* BILL *along with the gun.*
PEOPLE *at the bar throw themselves aside.*
WALTER *leads him to the phone booth and hands him a quarter.*
BILL *stares at it, then up at* WALTER.

WALTER *shoves him into the booth*.)
WALTER: Dial.
>   (BILL *just looks at him in shock.*
>   WALTER *is blankly determined.*
>   BILL *swallows, scared, and looks out at . . .*
>   MICHAEL, MAC, *and others. They all just look on, frightened but intrigued.*)

BILL: Will somebody do something? He's gotta gun, for crying out loud!
WALTER: Don't anyone move! I'll shoot 'em. I swear to God I'll shoot 'em.
MICHAEL: Come on, Walter. Lighten up!
>   (WALTER *jabs the gun up into* BILL*'s back, but pauses and glares back over his shoulder at the bar.*
>   *No one moves.*
>   WALTER *looks back at* BILL.)

WALTER: Dial.
>   (BILL *hesitates, looks at the phone, hesitates some more, then sighs and dials.*
>   WALTER *watches as . . .*
>   BILL *waits. But . . .*)

BILL: It's busy.
>   (WALTER, *suspicious, grabs the receiver and listens.*)

WALTER: (*Hanging up*) Damn!
>   (*They're just about to step from the booth, when . . .*
>   RING!!!!!!!
>   *They stop dead.* BILL *looks at* WALTER.
>   WALTER *looks from* BILL *to the phone.*)

WALTER: Answer it.
>   (BILL *reaches out slowly and lifts the receiver.*)

BILL: Hello?
>   (*His face goes blank. Carefully, he looks out at* WALTER.)
>   It's Margaret.
>   (WALTER *steps back, confused and uncertain.*
>   BILL *returns to the phone, anxious to get her talking to* WALTER.)

BILL: What? No. Don't worry about that. No. Really. Walter's here. You wanna talk to him?
>   (WALTER *stands there anxiously, hopefully, pathetically . . .*
>   BILL*'s face drops and he glances out at* WALTER.)

BILL: No?
>   (WALTER*'s shoulders fall forward and he begins to dissolve.*
>   BILL *hangs up the phone, sadly. He looks out at* WALTER *commiserating.*
>   WALTER *lowers the gun and holds it flat against his chest, staring at the floor.*
>   BILL *comes out to him and lays a hand on his shoulder.* WALTER, *surprisingly, comes forward and presses himself against* BILL, *crying.*
>   BILL *tenses up at first and looks over at . . .*

The GUYS *at the bar, who all look away in embarrassment.*
But BILL *returns his attention to* WALTER *and hugs him. He holds him for a moment, then* . . .
POW!!!!!! *The gun goes off and* BILL *falls back, holding his face.)*
BILL: OWWW!!!!!!
(He falls back through some tables as . . .
WALTER *drops the gun, stunned.*
MAC, MICHAEL, *and the* OTHERS *rush over from the bar and help* BILL.
BILL *rolls around on the floor, holding his face, bleeding a lot.*
WALTER *collapses in a chair.*
MICHAEL *leans down over him and looks. Going white, he gets back up and turns to* MAC.)
MICHAEL: He shot him in the face.
MAC: Get your truck! Quick! We gotta get him to a hospital!
MICHAEL: *(Running out)* Get an ice-pack or something!
*(*WALTER *stands and tries to say something meaningful* . . .)*
WALTER: Sorry, Bill.
(And MAC *shoves him back down in his seat, before returning to* BILL.
The other GUYS *help* MAC *carry* BILL *out of the bar as* MICHAEL *screeches to a halt out front in his truck.*
WALTER *sits there, shaking his head. He kicks a chair across the room.)*

SCENE 7 INT. OPERATING ROOM. NIGHT
DOCTOR CLINT *is over* BILL, *who lies on the table. The* NURSE *is holding his head still as* CLINT *inspects the wounds.*
CLINT: Hm-mm. This is bad.
(To NURSE . . .) Can you wipe away all this?
(The NURSE *cleans up a portion of* BILL's *face as* CLINT *steps aside to check her instruments. She moves back to* BILL, *down to business.)*
CLINT: Now, I'm going to have to give you something for the pain, but this is going to be painful in any event.
*(*BILL *nods* . . .) Are you allergic to novocaine?
BILL: No.
(She approaches with the needle, trying to decide how to proceed.)
CLINT: OK. Your entire upper lip is in three pieces. Can you feel that?
BILL: *(Uncertain)* I think so.
CLINT: There are two tears. One goes right up the side of your nose. You can feel that, can't you?
BILL: Yes.
CLINT: Are you having any trouble breathing?
BILL: No.
CLINT: Good. Now I'm going to have to inject the novocaine almost directly

into the wounds, OK?

BILL: OK.

CLINT: I'm telling you this because it won't help to ignore what's going on here. I'm going to need you to co-operate.

BILL: Right.

(BILL *is scared. He stares straight up into the lights.* CLINT *begins.*)

CLINT: This is going to pinch. There'll be a number of injections.

(*She makes the first injection and* BILL *stiffens and moans.* CLINT *nods as she continues . . .*)

CLINT: I know. Uh-huh, I know.

(*And she makes the next . . .*)

NURSE: (*In his ear*) Breathe.

CLINT: OK. One more on this side.

(*And he stiffens again.*)

NURSE: Just remember to breathe.

CLINT: This isn't going to last too long. It's running right out of you. There's no place for the novocaine to stay. That's what's in your mouth right now. Novocaine. It's not blood. Do you need to spit?

(*The* NURSE *presses a wad of gauze up to the side of his face. He turns and drools into it.*)

NURSE: Keep thinking about something. Something specific.

BILL: I'm trying.

NURSE: What are you thinking about?

BILL: Girls.

NURSE: That's good. Tell me about the girls.

BILL: Soft skin. My hand cupping her breast. Caressing her bottom. Her thighs squeezing my leg. Kissing. Her tongue in my mouth. My mouth on her breast. Spooning.

NURSE: (*Busy*) Spooning?

BILL: We lie side by side. Your back to me. I put my arm around your waist. We draw up our knees.

NURSE: Keep still.

SCENE 8 INT. HOSPITAL LOBBY. NIGHT
BILL *comes down the hall with a bandage over his upper lip and cheek. He stops and stares at the floor.* DISSOLVE . . .

SCENE 9 EXT. PHONE BOOTH. NIGHT
BILL *listens as Emily's phone rings. No answer. He hangs up.*

DISSOLVE TO . . .

SCENE 10 EXT. STREETS. NIGHT
BILL *runs across the street and hails a cab.*
 The cab stops and BILL *leans down to talk to the* DRIVER.
BILL: Good evening.
DRIVER: What happened to you?
BILL: I was shot by the husband of a woman I thought I might be in love with.
DRIVER: I hate when that happens.
BILL: Look, can you drive me to a bank machine and then out to the airport?
DRIVER: You gunna travel looking like that?
BILL: What's wrong with the way I look?
DRIVER: You got blood on your shirt.
 (*But* BILL's *already getting in the car . . .*)
BILL: Come on, let's go.
DRIVER: (*Takes off*) Where are you going?
BILL: Paris.
 Cut to black . . .

BILL	Bill Sage
EMILY	Parker Posey
GIRL ON TELEPHONE	Liana Pai
MAC	Holt McCallany
MICHAEL	Michael Imperioli
TRISH	Hannah Sullivan
MAN #1	Harold Perrineau
MAN #2	Robert Burke
MAN #3	Paul Austin
WALTER	Martin Donovan
DOCTOR CLINT	Karen Sillas
NURSE	Erica Cimple
DRIVER	Jose Zunica
Cinematographer	Mike Spiller
Production Designer	Steve Rosenzweig
Editor	Steve Hamilton
Music	Jeff Taylor and Ned Rifle
Associate Producer	Carleen Hsu
Executive Producer	Jerome Brownstein
Producer	Ted Hope
Written and Directed by	Hal Hartley

Coda: Cry from Croatia

When Zrinko Ogresta's piece landed on my desk, it threw all our problems with the movie industry into sharp relief. This testament by a young film-maker is as sad and heart-rending as anything that has come out of that tortured land.

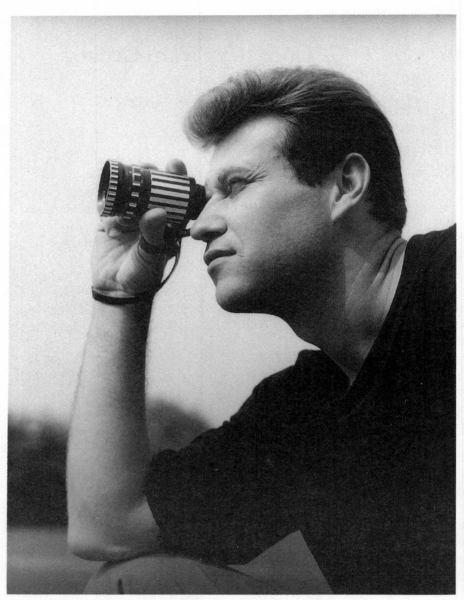

77 Zrinko Ogresta (photo by Mio Vesović)

In Front of the Cracked Mirror
Zrinko Ogresta

. . . And now what?

Almost two years have passed since I finished *Shatters* (*Krhotine*), my first full-length feature film. With it, I succeeded in experiencing any young director's dream: the joy of creative work, the sweet smell of national as well as international success . . .

And then suddenly, by force, standing in the way of a child's dream coming true – a barricade! Unanticipated, bitter, painful. War! Everything stopped that autumn. Film projectors in the cinemas were turned off, paintings and sculptures were hidden under protective layers of boards, the lights in the theatres were turned off. Soccer fields turned into deserted meadows. In the breaks between air-raids we simply vegetated; the only thing that mattered was to make sure you had enough food, medicine, torches. We were being attacked by The Neighbours from the East; we used to attend the same film festivals, they acted in our theatres, we played basketball together. They destroyed the pearls of our country: Dubrovnik, Vukovar, Osijek, Zadar, Sibenik, Karlovac, Gospic . . . They obliterated hundreds of our villages and injured more than fifty towns. Croatian engineers, lawyers, waiters, actors, directors, carpenters . . . almost overnight left their offices, pencils, cameras, tools, and took up things they had never thought about. The time of weapons had started . . .

. . . I am on the front line in Slavonia. With my cameraman. The camera is the deadliest of weapons. The Weapon of The Truth. We are filming burnt-out Croatian houses, the bodies of Croatian women and old men disfigured in a massacre, a baby's buggy thrown in the mud, starved hens pecking at the fingers of a dead woman. Then came the news: on a job just the same as ours, Gordan Leder, a young cameraman, was killed by a Serbian sniper. We studied together at the Academy. His camera registered the last moment of his life. How absurd: he spent his whole short life recording other people's destinies – and to pass away with his camera recording his own death . . .

. . . Days have passed. Again I am with my cameraman shooting a war documentary, this time in the vicinity of Dubrovnik, the area where my ancestors were born. I am passing through the recently liberated village of Doli, my father's birthplace. It was here that I – a ten-year-old boy who ran around with a 8mm camera in his hand filming Grandma and Grandpa and the

78 *Shatters*: the protagonist (Filip Šovagović) obsessed . . .

79 *Shatters*: . . . with the past (Nada Subotić and Matja Prskalo)

sea and the Assumption procession – fell in love with film. The village is deserted and completely burnt down. I can feel the smell of decaying cattle. I am afraid to enter my ancestral home. Mines are everywhere. Uneasily, I peep through the badly damaged front door. The furniture in the sitting room is completely wrecked. On the wall there is the Serbian coat-of-arms drawn in black paint, along with the graffiti DIE, USTASHE! 'Ustashe' – the stigma they so treacherously glued to all the Croats was the motive behind shooting my début film. What an irony! For them, the war never really ended; since 1945 it has been living on in their cold hearts ... And again, exactly the same as a few weeks ago, came the news: near Karlovac a Serbian grenade killed Zivko Krstičević, another cameraman doing his job. He was one of my best friends. Last summer he stayed with me here, in this now-demolished house, enjoying his holiday. I am staring at the burnt surf-board he left behind. Again, a man carrying a camera was shot at. The Truth was shot at. Luckily, the Truth cannot be shot down. Even when it seems everyone has abandoned it, a Friend stays that can never betray it: Time.

Zivko was also killed with his camera rolling. He also recorded his own death. That last motionless frame is ghastly; after seeing the motion that shows every muscle and every step of the man carrying the camera, all of a sudden all you see is a short, uncontrolled straying of the camera and then the fall. What you see looks like a frozen frame; everything is still – stopped – in the extreme low camera angle, and the lifeless composition shows the contours of a hardly recognizable place ...

It's all over! I am infected. Tainted by the worst of illnesses – Hatred. It has sneaked into my every pore. And what's even worse, it has become the driving force behind all my activities. If it weren't for this hatred, I do not think I would even be able to write these lines! Although the flames of war seem to have remained diminished – or hidden – in the past year, the Hatred hasn't disappeared from my soul. What do I do, how do I get rid of it? I feel it suffocating me. What concerns me most, I feel it eating away at everything I do. It has crept into the lives of my scripts. They have become gnarled, rough, lacking refinement. They disseminate like weeds. But I thank God for not denying me the ability to realize it. Could this be the serum that will save me?

In the last couple of months, after more than a year of utter stagnation in film production in Croatia, there have been rumours about restoring – on a modest scale, at least – feature-film production to life. But what to write about, what to film without tainting it with this hatred? Can I, and may I, speak about something else apart from from this hell we're vegetating in? I am turning over in my mind all the Croatian artists who worked after World War II. Many years had to pass before we could obtain works of art which showed those times for what they were. In the period between 1945 and 1960 there were hardly any. Was Hatred smouldering in those artists as well, or is it true that Time needs to pass? Maybe both. Again, I am thinking about *Shatters*. How is it that I, who did not live through the times the film is about, was lucky enough to be given a chance to bring some *soul* into those times? Maybe it's just because *I did not* live in those times, because I don't have their real, living scars but have them only in my genes. Yes, that is correct. The first film about the Croatian Glory and Tragedy of the Nineties will see the light of day in ten, fifteen, or maybe even more years from now. I wish I were wrong. But it seems to me that such a film will be created by a being who came into this world in the past months, or maybe isn't even born yet, who is in its mother's womb feeling her throbbing pulse, eternally marked by these turbulent, restless times . . .

. . . And what do I do? What film do I make?

. . . Please help me eliminate this Hatred.

'If I hate, I take something from myself; if I love, I become richer because of what I love. To forgive is to rediscover something of oneself which has been stolen.' Schiller.

(*Editor's note:* On the day this piece was faxed to London, a Serbian bomb fell on Zagreb 800 yards from Ogresta's apartment.)

80 Vukovar, Croatia

81 Sunja, Croatia (photo by R. Ibrišević)

Filmography

1 Journals 1989–1993
FRANCIS FORD COPPOLA is the director of, among others, *Apocalypse Now*, *The Godfather* and *Dracula*.

2 The Narrow Path
CHEN KAIGE is the director of, among others, *Yellow Earth*, *Life on a String*, and *Farewell to my Concubine*.
TONY RAYNS is a film-maker and critic with a special interest in the cinemas of East Asia. His TV documentaries include *New Chinese Cinema*.

3 Acting is Doing
SYDNEY POLLACK is the director of, among others, *The Way We Were*, *Out of Africa* and *The Firm*.
JOHN BOORMAN is the editor of *Projections*, and the director of *Point Blank*, *Excalibur* and *Beyond Rangoon*.

4 Art Direction: From Wajda to Spielberg
ALLAN STARSKI is the art director of, among others, *Man of Marble*, *Europa, Europa* and *Schindler's List*.

5 Making Music for *Short Cuts*
HALL WILLNER has composed music for, among others, *Night of the Living Duck*, *Candy Mountain* and *Saturday Night Live*.

6 My Stunning Future: The Luxuries of Pixelvision
MICHAEL ALMEREYDA is the director of, among others, *Twister*, *A Hero of our Time* and *Another Girl Another Planet*.

7 Kasdan on Kasdan
LAWRENCE KASDAN is the writer/director of, among others, *Body Heat*, *The Big Chill* and *Wyatt Earp*.

8 The Struggles of a Screenwriter
MICHAEL TOLKIN is the writer of *The Player* and the writer/director of *The Rapture* and *The New Age*.

9 The Perils of Producing
ART LINSON is the producer of, among others, *Car Wash*, *Melvin and Howard* and *The Untouchables*.

10 Answers First, Questions Later

QUENTIN TARANTINO is the writer/director of *Reservoir Dogs* and the writer of *True Romance* and *Natural Born Killers*.

GRAHAM FULLER is the Executive Editor of *Interview* magazine. He has contributed interviews for both *Projections 1* and *2*; he has interviewed Hal Hartley for the edition of the *Simple Men* and *Trust* screenplays, and Gus Van Sant for the *Even Cowgirls Get the Blues* and *My Own Private Idaho* screenplays; he also edited *Potter on Potter*.

11 On Tour with *Orlando*

SALLY POTTER is the director of, among others, *Golddiggers*, *Thriller* and *Orlando*.

12 The Hollywood Way

GUS VAN SANT is the director of, among others, *Drugstore Cowboy*, *My Own Private Idaho* and *Even Cowgirls Get the Blues*.

13 The Burning Question

PAUL SCHRADER is the writer/director of, among others, *Blue Collar*, *Mishima* and *Light Sleeper*.

ALEX VAN WARMERDAM is the director of *The Northerners*.

STEVEN SODERBERGH is the director of *sex, lies and videotape*, *Kafka* and *King of the Hill*.

RICHARD LOWENSTEIN is the director of *Strikebound*, *Dogs in Space* and *Say a Little Prayer*.

MONTE HELLMAN is the director of, among others, *The Shooting* and *Two Lane Blacktop*, and was an Executive Producer on *Reservoir Dogs*.

JACO VAN DORMAEL is the director of, among others, *Maedli-la-Brache*, *De Boot* and *Toto le Heros*.

DENYS ARCAND is the director of, among others, *La Maudite Galette*, *Jesus of Montreal* and *Unidentified Human Remains*.

14 'I Wake Up Screaming'

RICHARD STANLEY is the director of *Hardware* and *Dust Devil*.

15 Flirt

HAL HARTLEY is the director of, among others, *The Unbelievable Truth*, *Simple Men* and *Amateur*.

16 In Front of the Cracked Mirror

ZRINKO OGRESTA is the director of *Emergency Exit* and *Shatters*. He lectures on Film and TV direction at the Academy of Dramatic Arts in Zagreb.

Faber Film List

New and Forthcoming

Directors series

Woody Allen on Woody Allen

Biographies

Fragments: Portraits from the Inside
Andre de Toth

Turnaround
Milos Forman

Screenplays

The Hudsucker Proxy
Joel Coen and Ethan Coen and Sam Raimi

Amateur
Hal Hartley

Orlando
Sally Potter

Barcelona and Metropolitan
Whit Stillman

If you would like a complete Faber Film
Books stocklist, please write to the
Promotions Department
Faber and Faber
3 Queen Square
London WCIN 3AU

Projections 1

Winner
British Film Institute
Michael Powell Award
Best Film Book of 1992

Projections is a forum for practitioners of the cinema to reflect on the year in cinema and to speculate on the future. The first issue contains:

Bright Dreams, Hard Knocks
a journal for 1991 by John Boorman

Film Fiction
an essay by Sam Fuller

The Early Life of a Screenwriter
from the Berlin diaries of Emeric Pressburger

Demme on Demme
a comprehensive survey of the career of 1991's Oscar-winning director

Matters of Photogenics
an essay on photographing the human face by Oscar-winning cameraman Nestor Almendros

My Director and I
a conversation between River Phoenix and Gus Van Sant during the shooting of River Phoenix's most memorable film, *My Own Private Idaho*.

Surviving Desire
a screenplay by Hal Hartley

Making Some Light
Michael Mann discusses the making of *The Last of the Mohicans*.

There are also contributions from: Denys Arcand, David Byrne, Jane Campion, Costa-Gavras, Terry Gilliam, Mike Figgis, Tony Harrison, Kzysztof Kieślowski, Richard Lowenstein, Louis Malle, Claude Miller, Arthur Penn, Sydney Pollack, Kevin Reynolds, Francesco Rosi, Ken Russell, Ettore Scola, Istvan Szabo, Paolo and Vittorio Taviani, Michael Verhoeven, Paul Verhoeven, Vincent Ward and Zhang Yimou

Projections 2

The second issue contains:

Shadow and Substance
George Miller charts the journey he has made
from the *Mad Max* trilogy to *Lorenzo's Oil*.

Movie Lessons
Jaco van Dormael discusses the creative
process that led to *Toto the Hero*.

Searching for the Serpent
New Zealand director Alison Maclean
discusses her work.

Freewheelin'
a free-ranging phonecall between Derek
Jarman and Gus Van Sant.

Acting on Impulse
Willem Dafoe describes his approach to
acting.

The Early Life of a Screenwriter
Veteran writer/director Sydney Gilliat relives
the early days of British cinema.

Altman on Altman
From *M★A★S★H* to *Short Cuts*, Robert
Altman discusses his career.

Bob Roberts
Tim Robbins's stunning, incisive political
satire

I Wake Up, Dreaming: A Journal for 1992
Bertrand Tavernier's diary records the
evolution of his controversial film *L627* against
the shifting European cultural landscape.

There are also contributions from:
Denys Arcand, David Byrne, Monte Hellman,
Richard Lowenstein, Jocelyn Moorhouse,
Arthur Penn, Nicholas Roeg, Philippe
Rousselet, Paul Shrader, Ron Shelton, Roger
Spottiswoode, István Szabó, Michael
Verhoeven, Vincent Ward and
Fred Zinneman.

ff

'The publisher with the strongest film list is Faber.' *Guardian*

Whether you are an avid film buff or an occasional cinema-goer, Faber's books on film studies, biographies and screen-plays are sure to be of interest.

If you would like further information about Faber's film list, please complete the details below – either tear out this page or take a photocopy and send it to our freepost address below.

Please send details of Faber and Faber film books to:

Name _____

Address _____

_____

Postcode _____

Send to: Film Promotions, Faber and Faber Ltd, Freepost WC5082, 3 Queen Square, London WC1N 3BR

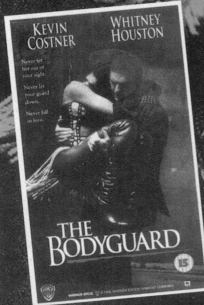

The finest in independent and world cinema
1994

Friends

Starring Kerry Fox, a powerful and moving story of three women from distinctly different cultures who live together in the fast and furious urban chaos of Johannesburg. They think they know each other, but dramatic and unforeseen events are about to blow their worlds apart. Winner of 2 awards at the 1993 Dinard Festival of British Film. Kerry Fox of "Angel At My Table" and "Last Days of Chez Nous", stars as Sophie.

Jack Be Nimble

By first time writer-director New Zealander Garth Maxwell, "Jack Be Nimble" is a serious, supernatural, horror movie, a brooding, dark, fairytale fantasy and a chilling revenge thriller. It's a tale of a brother and sister who are adopted by very different families, Dora has a relatively normal, though lonely, childhood but Jack is brutalized by his adoptive father and menaced by his strange hill-billy sisters. They are reunited as adults in an uneasy and ultimately violent, revengeful relationship.

Prince of Shadows

Starring Patsy Kensit and Terence Stamp, a crisp and taut political thriller set in a world where abuse of power, betrayal and perversion reign, the story of a reluctant hitman and a showgirl, set in 1960's Madrid. Winner of the Silver Bear at Berlin Film Festival 1992.

La Scorta (The Escort)

Italy's "Reservoir Dogs" and a box office smash, this is an entertaining, tense action film about Mafia infiltration, law enforcement and protection, set in a world where trust and honesty are constantly tested. The big hit of Cannes 1993.

Who's The Man

A riotous rap movie with an outstanding soundtrack, starring Dr Dre and Ed Lover as two failed barbers forced to sell out, go against all their hip-hop principles and join the New York Police Department. Directed by Ted Demme, nephew of Jonathan, it has vitality and humour, with cameos by Queen Latifah, Kriss Kross and Flavour Flav.

Welcome To The Terradome

A fast-paced and vibrant action thriller set in a city of the near future - terradome. A story of gangs, race, violence and betrayal, strongly reminiscent of "Bladerunner".

Les Edades De Lulu

The story of a girl's intense path to adulthood, marked by a haunting sexual experience, repeated years later with the same man. Together they create a private universe for themselves, plunging Lulu helplessly and feverishly into a hell of dangerous and forbidden desires.

Hercules Returns

A hilarious and inventive tale in the vein of "What's Up Tiger Lily?" and "The Rocky Horror Picture Show". Three friends are forced to revamp and revoice an old Italian peplum, "Hercules", which they plan to screen at a gala opening of their run-down picture palace. However, when the 'sword and sandal' epic transpires to be in its original unsubtitled Italian format, a frantic and wickedly funny voiceover improvisation ensues, and the film is a hit.

The Red Squirrel

Directed by Julio Medem, "The Red Squirrel" is a complex love story that draws its characters, and the audience, into a game of lies and deceit. A 'mystery comedy', that was a major success at Cannes in 1993.

Golden Balls

Bigas Luna's follow up feature to "Jamon Jamon", this erotic comedy stars Javier Bardem, the naked bullfighting stud from Luna's previous outrageous hit, as a man with a passion for fried-eggs and a desire to erect a skyscraper in his own honour.

I Love A Man in Uniform

A story of an aspiring actor who lands the role of a policeman in a television series, and prepares for the part by wearing his uniform in public. Becoming addicted to the power and authority that wearing the uniform endows, his grip on reality begins to deteriorate and his identity is subsumed by his fictional alter-ego.

Metro Tartan Ltd.,
79 Wardour Street, London W1V 3TH.
Tel: 071 734 8508 Fax: 071 287 2112
TX: 262 433 REF. 3294

TARTAN VIDEO

Tartan Video offers you the finest in world cinema. Films of distinction and enduring excellence digitally remastered for superior quality and presented with extensive liner notes.

An outstanding collection of beautifully packaged classic films, including Patrice Leconte's dazzling **"The Hairdresser's Husband"**, Jean Luc Godard's groundbreaking **"A Bout de Souffle"**, Bigas Luna's outrageous sex farce **"Jamon Jamon"**, Almodovar's sleek and sensual **"Matador"**, the urban hip hop drama **"Just Another Girl on the IRT"** and the hit black comedy **"Man Bites Dog"** now available for a limited time only in a special collectors box set.

These and many others are now available on high quality VHS and Laserdisc* in their original widescreen format**.

Forthcoming titles for 1994 include Alan Rudolph's **"Trouble in Mind"**, **"Choose Me"** and **"Equinox"**, **"La Fille de L'Air"** with the stunning Beatrice Dalle, Kieslowski's acclaimed **"A Short Film About Killing"** and **"A Short Film About Love"**, Milos Forman's **"The Fireman's Ball"**, Andrew Birkin's powerful **"The Cement Garden"**, Bergman's classic **"Smiles of a Summer Night"** and **"Virgin Spring"** and the award-winning **"L'Accompagnatrice"**.

Cinema Paradiso

Jamon Jamon

Man Bites Dog

Tartan Video. Committed to excellence.

•Selected titles only For further information on how to order these titles **Where available
please write to Tartan Video,
79 Wardour Street, London W1V 3TH or call 071 437 5695

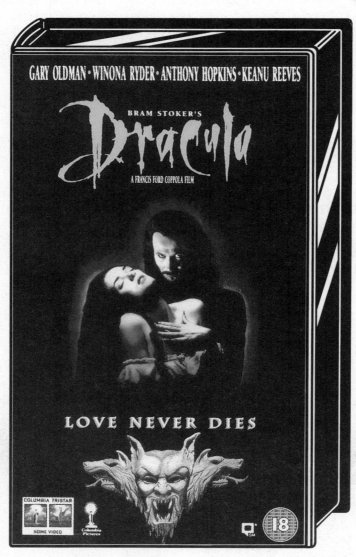

Available on video
Also in a special limited edition coffin box-set from all good video stockists.

霸
王
別
姫

WINNER
PALME D'OR
CANNES FILM
FESTIVAL 1993

BEST FILM

A FILM BY CHEN KAIGE

FAREWELL MY CONCUBINE 15

LESLIE CHEUNG   ZHANG FENGYI   GONG LI

ENGLISH SUBTITLES   **An Artificial Eye Release**

COMING SOON ON VIDEO

The Player
Michael Tolkin

Griffin Mill is senior vice president of production at a major Hollywood studio and he's in trouble. He has been getting postcards from a writer he rejected: 'You said you'd get back to me. You didn't. And now I'm going to kill you.'

'An entertaining novel brimming with intriguing and unsavoury characters. I enjoyed the scenes of the movie executives trying to out-manipulate one another.' Michael Douglas

The Player has also been made into an award-winning film, directed by Robert Altman.

Among the Dead
Michael Tolkin

Frank Gale plans to take his wife and daughter to Mexico, where he will come clean about an affair, and try to make it up to them. However, he discovers that the plane he missed has crashed, killing everyone on board including his family. And so begins a comedy of horrors wherein Gale discovers the many unpleasant truths about himself and the life that lies hidden *Among the Dead*.

'It is impossible not to respect the author's technical skill, his acumen in depicting the mind in crisis, and his boldness in setting himself, after *The Player*, such a joyless challenge.' *Literary Review*